In 1980, Terence Conran plucked **Stephen Bayley** from the obscurity of provincial academe to do his good works. One result was The Boilerhouse Project, promoting design in London's V&A, which became the most successful gallery of the eighties. Another result was the influential Design Museum. Stephen has since become one of the world's best-known commentators on design and popular culture. His is a Chevalier de l'Ordre des Arts et Lettres, an Honorary Fellow of The RIBA, Honorary Visiting Professor at University of Liverpool School of Architecture and Chairman of The Royal Fine Art Commission Trust.

Roger Mavity had been hired by Terence many times and fired nearly as often. First at the French Gold Abbott ad agency where Roger won the Habitat advertising account; then at two more agencies including Mavity Gilmore, his own business. In 2006 he became Chief Executive of Conran Holdings, Terence's business empire, where he stayed for seven years. Roger also ran his own ad agency for ten years and was Chief Executive of Granada Group's technology and leisure divisions for another ten years. He quit business to work as a writer and photographer.

Praise for *Terence*

'It's a masterpiece'
Dylan Jones

'Juicy . . . interesting'
Evening Standard

'A close reading of one of the most influential men in design
history by two of his closest allies and collaborators, Stephen Bayley
and Roger Mavity. There is a brutal honesty about the way in
which they have painted their late colleague and friend . . .'
Independent

'Bayley, the author of books on style, design and taste, tells
the Habitat story with his customary polycultural panache . . .
[Mavity is] good at conveying the experience of being in a
room with Conran'
John Walsh, *Sunday Times*

'Compelling . . . gossipy and entertaining'
Irish Independent

'[A] fascinating personality, captured here – both affectionately and
critically . . . A terrific read, bubbling with anecdotes and insight'
Daily Mail

'Irresistibly spiky . . . fun . . . rollicking'
Spectator

'A must-read'
Tablet

Terence

The Man Who Invented Design

Stephen Bayley
and Roger Mavity

CONSTABLE

CONSTABLE

First published in Great Britain in 2021 by Constable
This paperback edition published in 2022 by Constable

1 3 5 7 9 10 8 6 4 2

A CIP catalogue record for this book
is available from the British Library.

ISBN: 978-1-40871-521-5

Typeset in Electra LT Std by SX Composing DTP, Rayleigh, Essex
Printed and bound in Great Britain by Clays Ltd, Elocgraf, S.p.A.

Papers used by Constable are from well-managed forests
and other responsible sources.

Constable
An imprint of
Little, Brown Book Group
Carmelite House
50 Victoria Embankment
London EC4Y 0DZ

An Hachette UK Company

www.hachette.co.uk

www.littlebrown.co.uk

To: Lunch with friends in the sunshine . . . but with work to be done in the afternoon.

Contents

Monetising Taste

S.B.

I had just come back from a run and was still collecting my breath when I took a call from the *Sunday Times*. Did I know that Terence Conran had died? I did not. Could I write an appreciation? I could.

Now I had to collect my thoughts as well as my breath. And I had two hours to summarise an extraordinary man who had been a presence in my life for forty years and in the nation's for sixty.

There was quite a lot of collecting to do. So much to say. I wanted then – and still do now – to understand how Terence managed to achieve such extraordinary influence, almost all for the good, when his tangible achievements were actually quite modest, even if a lot greater than most.

I wanted also to understand how someone capable of great charm, inspired and inspiring, possessed of a singular personal vision, unusual energy and an astonishing ability just *to get things done*, to see opportunities where others did not, could also, from time to time, be a mean-spirited, selfish bastard.

How could someone who genuinely cared about people living better lives also be so shockingly callous in his dealings with those closest to him?

He might, in his own telling, improve the nation's sex life by selling duvets to romantically inclined couples, but would often not spare a moment to empathise with a friend, colleague or even relation. Still less, actively support them or anticipate their needs. I think the smell of failure or any sense of sadness distressed him. He sanctified hard work, but did not bother with onerous chores. (Hence the duvet proposition: doing away with tiresome sheets and blankets allowed passion to thrive uninhibited.)

But I guess a lot of great men have similar traits.

Towards the end of his life, Terence's businesses were either shuttered or in disarray. His last restaurant, a faux-French brasserie that opened when *jamón ibérico* was more *dans le vent* than *pâté de campagne*, had been an expensive calamity. And, bizarrely for someone with such perfect pitch in matters of taste, embarrassingly out of touch with contemporary ambitions in both food and décor.

He had been made a Companion of Honour for 'services to design', but struggled to explain what 'design' actually meant. At one stage he was saying it simply meant curling up with a good book. Daily, he still avidly pored over old-fashioned press cuttings, searching for approval. As he got older, the morning whisky got earlier and earlier.

But, immediately, more benign and amusing memories returned. Before I met the woman who has been my wife for four decades, I was having trouble with my girlfriend *du jour*. Terence called me on a Saturday afternoon and I explained that the night before, a plate of spaghetti had been emptied on my head. He chuckled and said: 'Ah. Well. You had better come straight to Barton Court, hadn't you?' Of course, I went.

Or what about this? Early on in the days before wheel-clamps became a real deterrent to adventurous parking, Terence stopping his petrol-blue Porsche outside the front door of Enzo Apicella's Meridiana restaurant in Chelsea and explaining: 'I'll buy lunch, but you pay the ticket.'

Or Terence saying of Roy Strong, the brilliant but occasionally precious director of the Victoria & Albert Museum, 'Let's give him the clap he so richly deserves.' Or in 2006, Terence giving an appreciation at the memorial service of Robert Carrier, the restaurateur and hotelier. This was in the Actors' Church in Covent Garden. A solemn pause came. And, looking around the magnificent Inigo Jones temple, he said, with a sense of wonder: 'This would make a very nice restaurant.' Whimsical and knowingly so, it changed the mood. As Terence had so often done in the past.

(But, in truth, he was a terrible public speaker. Instead, he was at his best one on one, and ideally with a supplicant. He spoke softly, which required the other party to lean forward, never a position of strength. I don't think there was much calculation in this: the dynamics of power-play seemed to come naturally to him.)

There was an inevitability about the news of his death. Terence had been unwell for some time. But, while not unexpected, the news still shocked: even crippled by ailments for at least his last ten years, the essential persona was youthful and irreverent; he was never a comfortable old man.

The residue was, for me, a complicated mix. Sadness and loss, of course, even if we had not been on speaking terms for several years, but also a peculiar sense of exhilaration at being freed at last from the influence of such a dominating individual. And an individual who, for all the various hurt, expense, anxiety and exasperation he had caused me, I liked and admired very much.

This is what I wrote.

Terence Orby Conran was born 4 October 1931 in Kingston-upon-Thames, Surrey. Ever since, he made it his life's work to escape suburban mediocrity. And to help the rest of us escape too.

Very few people made a better contribution to British material life in the past sixty years. If you see a gutsy butcher's block and think, 'How lovely!', that's his influence. If your local pub is serving *pâté* and not pickled eggs, that is his influence too.

Terence had two genius insights. The first was to realise that 'design' was no longer something people do, like throwing a pot, but something people can *buy*. No longer an activity, Terence made 'design' a commodity. And it was connected to social promotion. With this alchemy, he greatly enriched himself and the rest of us too.

The agent of this change was Habitat, which opened in Chelsea on 14 May 1964. This was the year the Beatles made it in America. Thwarted by the traditional department stores refusing to sell his own modernist furniture, Terence set up shop himself. His second genius insight was that there was a new generation who had to buy their own furniture: a constituency hitherto ignored.

Terence had a deluxe vision of the simple life. 'Any wine served *en magnum* becomes a luxury', he liked to say. But he was a complex character. In a process involving the keenest possible sense of style, unusual charisma, prodigal effort, no small amount of ego, a love affair with the media, a genuine passion for material things, a genius for opportunity and an absolute conviction of what life should be, 'Conran' became an eponym for 'design' itself.

Yet he was not, in the artistic sense, a great designer at all, rather an editor of merchandise, an organiser of things, a motivator, a man who monetised his own taste. And then sold it to us as 'design'. Terence's great achievement was to persuade himself, and then persuade others, that his personal preferences were absolutely correct, true and universal.

For example: liberation through modular shelving, bean bags and directors' chairs, a paradisiac world of perpetual lunch under spotlights in Fulham or bathed in French sunshine. The celebrated chicken brick. A fake 'Bauhaus' chair.

He was a hedonist and a puritan: a conflict defining him. Another defining conflict was how well his posh accent penetrated a world of artisans: this public school boy knew how to weld.

Another generation thinks of Terence as a serial restaurateur. His 1956 Soup Kitchen near Charing Cross was London's very first bistro:

here he made the furniture as well as the chicken stock. In 1987, Bibendum opened in Chelsea's newly restored Michelin Building, opposite the site of the original Habitat. The French connection allowed him to indulge his sometimes over-romanticised Francophilia. Terence's France was the bosky Dordogne, or the heat and dust, lavender and vines of Provence, not a dire Parisian *banlieue*.

Today, another generation thinks of Terence as patron of the Design Museum, perhaps his most enduring monument and the most baffling one. It opened in August 1989 when his business empire was very publicly collapsing. Hauntingly paradoxical, Terence funded a museum about creativity at just the time when the City banished him on account of his own restless creative personality being unsuited to organised wealth creation.

(Full disclosure: I was the Design Museum's founding director. I think it was my idea and got him to pay for it. He thought it was his idea and got me to do the legwork: this was a dispute typical of our close, but fractious, relationship.)

Terence lost an eye in a childhood workshop accident, but his one good eye was very sharp indeed. His critics maintain he was not too scrupulous in distinguishing between inspiration and plagiarism when sourcing his designs. Others say that he did not always encourage competition, enjoying centre-stage himself.

But Terence was a true hero to everyone who cares about the nature of ordinary things. He had democratic instincts, but did not possess the common touch. His beautiful Berkshire house was a demonstration of his beloved art-de-vivre, you entered this gentry pile through the kitchen-door . . . as if a servant.

We Are All Designers Now

R.M.

The subhead to this book, 'the man who invented design', is clearly ironic. Design has always been with us. Everything that is made, be it as mundane as a toothpick or a garage door or as complex as an orbiting space station or the Guggenheim Museum in Bilbao, has been designed. Someone had to specify how big, how long, what material, what shape. That is design.

Even a copy has been designed. The Russian camera industry used to make shamelessly cheap copies of the admired and expensive Leica 35mm rangefinder camera. But somewhere an unscrupulous Russian must have shown the factory a real Leica, and said, 'Make it like this.' That was the design: it may have been stolen, but it still existed.

But in life-before-Terence, people didn't talk about design. Architects and, no doubt, designers themselves must have discussed design, but you and I didn't. The weather, politics, the irritating habits of others in the office, football – these were all legitimate subjects for discourse. But not design. It existed, but it wasn't on the menu.

Terence changed all that.

He made us design aware. It began with Habitat. Before then, chairs were to sit on, desks to work at, glasses to drink from. Suddenly Habitat gave us permission to think about these objects as things of beauty as well as of use, things with the power to make our life joyful as well as functional.

It all became magnified by the *Sunday Times* magazine. For the first time, a black-and-white newspaper came with a colourful bible of middle-class good taste. It wasn't about politics, news and world affairs. No, it was about more important things, like whether Florence was better than Venice for a weekend break, or how to cook an aubergine. 'Lifestyle' crept into our dictionary and into our lives.

Lifestyle embraced everything: the clothes we wore, the food we ate, the car we drove, the holidays we took, the newspaper we read were all part of it. But nothing was more important than how we furnished our homes. And the people who designed objects for our homes became celebrities. We all wanted a Charles Eames chair and eventually a Philippe Starck lemon squeezer.

The word 'designer' changed its meaning. Some wit recently said he was old enough to remember when 'a Brazilian' meant a person living in Brazil – as opposed to the more modern meaning. Similarly, 'designer' ceased to mean someone who designed things: it became an adjective, applied to any object that was vaguely aspirational – as in 'designer handbag'. Which really means a handbag you can't buy in Marks & Spencer. The currency was becoming devalued. 'Designer' once implied superior conception and superior execution; by about 1986 it suggested meretricious excess and irrelevance.

Yet beneath this trivialisation, a revolution had taken place. We had all become sensitised to the notion that things don't just get made, they get designed first. And just as we had always cherished things that were made better, now we also cherished things that were designed better. Our lives would be that tiny bit richer if we chose things that were designed well.

But this begged a huge question: what is a 'better' design? Who decides?

Terence decided he should tell us what is good for us. But even if we may argue about what 'good design' is, it's vividly clear that the concept of design has entered our lives with a vengeance. We furnish our homes with a care and a respect for style not known in previous generations. Indeed, the politician Alan Clark's sneer about his more successful rival, Michael Heseltine – that he was 'the kind of person who bought his own furniture' – now seems not just snobbish, but quaint and out of touch. Much better to be buying a Barcelona chair from Terence than inheriting some brown ghastliness from Mother and Father.

That new-found respect for design extended well beyond the way we furnish our homes. Concorde became a symbol of a new kind of high-technology patriotic pride, not just because it went so fast, but also because it looked so beautiful. In spite of the English preoccupation with heritage and the past, dramatic new buildings – Norman Foster's gherkin at St Mary Axe in the City of London or his footbridge from Tate Modern to St Paul's – excite genuine admiration.

Design matters today. In large part, we have Terence to thank for that. Indeed, if we examine Terence's achievement as a designer, in the narrow sense of a designer of objects, while he has created some gracious pieces of furniture, no one, even Terence himself, thought he was up there with Charles Eames, Eileen Gray or Marcel Breuer. No, his contribution is much more fundamental; more to do with the way we live than the chair we sit on.

He has designed experiences rather than things.

Habitat was an experience twice over. Of course it made furnishing your home an exciting experience – young London had never before been able to buy furniture like that, at prices like that. But it wasn't only about what you could buy in the shop: simply being there was an experience.

With places like the Apple Stores all around us now, the idea of a shop having a sense of theatre is a commonplace. But it wasn't in 1964. That first Habitat was a revolution. The staff were young and sexy. So were the customers. And so were the products. Habitat had good vibrations . . . in the same year that the Beach Boys did too.

The restaurants were an experience. In life-before-Terence, good restaurants had largely been about good food. Terence added a completely new dimension. The food was still good, but now there was energy, excitement, style, people-watching. Terence reinvented dinner as entertainment.

Alan Fletcher, a brilliant designer and one of the founders of the highly influential Fletcher Forbes Gill design consultancy, studied art and design in London at much the same time as an extraordinarily talented cohort, which, as well as Conran, included Peter Blake, Richard Hamilton, R. B. Kitaj and David Hockney. When asked which of the group he admired most, Fletcher gave a withering look and said:

'Obviously, Terence. The others just did some nice pictures. Terence changed the way we live.'

That wouldn't be a bad epitaph.

This is the true measure of Terence's achievement as a designer: he didn't merely design the objects we use, he designed the way we live.

The Ultimate Design Object

R.M.

Terence designed many things – chairs, tables, cups and saucers, restaurants, shops, even hotels and a museum. But arguably his most remarkable design achievement was Terence himself.

There was something about the Terence persona that was as perfectly suited to its purpose as a chair by Thonet or a building by Mies van der Rohe. Consider how Terence has been photographed. Almost invariably the great man is relaxing in a huge chair – his favourite was the Karuselli design, which has the sumptuous comfort of the fabled Charles Eames lounge chair, but the extra merit of being that little bit more unusual. A plump Hoyo de Monterrey Epicure No. 2 (just about the fattest cigar you can buy) will be smouldering. And a glass of wine will not be far away. This was an image of a man who knew how to enjoy the good things life has to offer.

But while he may be at ease, he's certainly not at rest. The aura of relaxation is invariably punctured by more than a hint of alertness. Like a predator in the veldt, Terence is ready to pounce in a millisecond at the merest sniff of an opportunity. The oft-repeated image of Terence stretched out in splendid comfort is not a picture of a man of repose; it is a picture of a man of power.

Similarly, the way Terence moved was revealing. When he was an old man, the fact that he walked with a sense of slow deliberation might appear to be a function of age. But in truth Terence always walked slowly, purposefully, with the manner of a man who knows exactly where he is going but won't be hurried getting there. In much the same way, he talked slowly and economically. He could be witty, and at times he could be brusque, but he never said more than was necessary to make the point. In his speech as in his gait, there was a studied calm: he radiated control.

The success of Terence's businesses owed much to the success of Terence's reputation. The excitement of a new shop or a new restaurant is – or was – much the greater if one is inspired by the mythology of the man who created it.

It's hard to tell whether Terence's manipulation of himself-as-brand was a considered calculation, or simply an instinctive response. It could be deliberate. And why not? After all, Picasso (also no mean self-publicist) would only permit himself to be photographed by a small number of approved photographers. Picasso was a true master of brand management. Yet Terence's uncanny sense of how to project a potent personal charisma did not seem to be a plan; it had a natural quality, it seemed to come from within. It appeared to be just how he was as a person. But one couldn't be sure. It is frustratingly difficult to unravel the complexities of Terence's character. It's very easy to see how he was, but very hard to see why.

Looking at Terence was a bit like looking at a pointillist painting: you get a clear image at long range, but when you move up closer to see it better, it starts to become blurred. There is a wonderful scene in Antonioni's classic film, *Blow-Up*, in which the central figure, a professional photographer, thinks he has by chance taken a picture of a murder. But the image isn't clear enough for him to be sure, so he blows it up to see more clearly. The more he enlarges it, however, the more grainy and illegible the image becomes. He is never able to answer his own question.

The scene is a perfect metaphor for the difficulty of understanding a brilliant but complex character. On first meeting, Terence's charisma was vivid: there was an immediate aura of authority and power, underscored by an engaging dry wit. But over time, the enigma of what drove this extraordinary man refused to become clearer. The way Terence presented himself is fascinating for what it reveals about the man, but more fascinating for what it conceals.

The £54-million Question

S.B.

'What *is* Design?' This is a £54-million question. That's the amount Terence once reckoned he had spent on getting London's Design Museum from an exciting, fragile, elusive idea we discussed in a South Kensington drawing room in 1978 to a sensational, if muddled, relaunch in an ambitiously, perhaps over-ambitiously, repurposed Commonwealth Institute thirty-eight years later.

Over the years, the precise figure kept fluctuating, depending on the company being kept. When I met him in late summer 2015, at a party given in Deirdre Dyson's high-concept rug shop in Chelsea, a very Conran sort of venue if ever there was one, he told me, forgetting the dramatic emphasis that he had already given the earlier figure, that he was now in for £75 million. At the time, he was sitting rather miserably on a side chair, a flute of champagne to hand, while the party roared in the middle distance.

Maybe the close presence of the wife of billionaire bagless-suction designer-inventor James Dyson had an inflationary effect on his estimate. Terence did not explain the accounting methodology used to establish this designed-to-impress sum. Still, it has to be said that, however many millions it may have been, this was a magnificently generous investment in his belief system. He knew it was. This is why he kept repeating and inflating it. Every time he mentioned what the

Design Museum had cost him, it was with a theatrical mixture of martyred anguish, long-sufferance and pained modesty. Like many of Terence's ear-catching utterances, this was, whether £54 million or £75 million, at the same time memorable, impressive, self-serving and perhaps not entirely factual.

But like many of those other utterances, repeated often enough with signature conviction and plausibility, it acquires a mysterious truth of its own. What I tell you three times is true.

The new Design Museum is Terence's ultimate monument . . . no matter what it cost or what it means. The cost has been huge, but the meaning is still to be determined. Its home is in the old Commonwealth Institute in Kensington, a strange architectural spasm of late-imperial *modernismo* by Edinburgh architects Robert Matthew Johnson-Marshall. An already abandoned monument to benign colonialism, it was soon to be on a course that would remove it further still from relevance.

People of Terence's generation remember the Commonwealth Institute as a place where you might see an exhibition of groundnut cultivation in Ghana. That's to say worthy, but deadly dull. For those with minds prepared, there is plenty of enjoyable symbolism here. The Commonwealth Institute advertised fading grandeur, but with a bold nod to the future. Its architectural signature is a structurally complex hyperbolic paraboloid roof, as if to indicate a new age of optimism and complexity.

Terence could do his own hyperbole, sending mere facts on astonishingly imaginative trajectories. And his career followed a parabola of its own, a dizzying arc described by a fast-moving, stylish rocket that was fuelled by a very high-octane ego. From a difficult and solitary, craft-inclined public schoolboy, to an inspired synthesiser; to a taste-making retailer in the Age of Pop, lifestyle evangelist, social redeemer, professional Francophile, to retail tycoon, City darling and then City prodigal, restaurant revivalist and reformer, benefactor, to national treasure; to grand, if grumpy, old man, savouring his achievements, but also noticing the bitter aftertaste of a promise that was both unrealised yet realised most as a sense of loss. Terence was very well known, but not really known at all.

By measures which an oligarchic Caucasus gas entrepreneur would understand, Terence's fortune did not even make him very rich. The super-yacht he did not want, he could not afford. (Roman Abramovitch's latest cost £450 million.) He said he would refuse a peerage, but don't we all? He did not want the new Design Museum named after him, although he was not displeased that everyone knew how much he spent on it. Maybe money was a proxy of self.

He was also late to receive the proper acknowledgement of the design profession whose purposes he served so well: Terence was nearly eighty before he was made a Royal Designer for Industry. Much more modest talents – weavers and stamp designers, engineers of non-return valves, for example – won acceptance earlier. It irked. The profession disliked his commercialism. He resented its disapproval.

Maybe purists once thought Terence's true vocation was vulgar commerce rather than the sterner disciplines of design. And maybe that was true. In Terence's era, taste was determined by old print media. These he always appreciated supremely well, adroitly exploiting the synergy between magazines hungry for attractive material, and his own businesses hungry for customers who were avid for inspiration. He was a print-media influencer.

If much of Terence's life was lived like a feature in a Sunday newspaper supplement from the sixties or seventies, that is only to confirm how very well he understood and directed the appetites of his era and all who lived and loved in it.

Much of it was an illusion, although illusions are not bad things.

At the 2015 funeral of Ann Barr, the influential *Harpers & Queen* editor who created *The Official Sloane Ranger Handbook* and the gastropornographic successor, *The Foodie*, thus supplying the language with two denominational gifts, I bumped into Loyd Grossman, whose astonishing career Barr had incubated.

Years before, Grossman had been commissioned to write a book about Terence, but, for unexplained reasons, it never happened. I mentioned that I was writing this book. With language surprisingly robust in a church context, Grossman made it very clear that he felt Terence's inclinations towards shameless self-mythologising and rampant fantasy quite often got the better of his good sense as much as they got the better of the facts. Then, perhaps anxious not to commit blasphemy, cause further offence or visit contingent damage on his pasta-sauce business (Terence was an adroit litigator), Loyd refused any elaboration or any further comment.

Grossman is not alone in seeing Terence as an expletive fantasist. But if you can live a fantasy, perhaps it becomes real.

Wherever you go in artistic or literate London, there are people of a certain generation with spectacular Terence Conran stories, by no means all flattering. The novelist Celia Brayfield is an exception. She was assistant to Shirley Conran, Terence's second wife, on the 'Hers' desk at the *Observer* in 1969 and confessed, at least to me, that the Conran way of life was such that she was 'completely devastated by the glamour of it all'. This was exactly as intended: all Conrans have a genius for and an addiction to publicity. The Conran domestic example was designed as a seductive one: a demonstration to be consumed by hungry observers.

This iconography of cheerful lunches enjoyed in good company in surroundings of laid-back and unthreatening modernism became known as 'lifestyle'. It's a term Terence virulently disliked, even if it was exactly what his disciples admired and his customers spent money on. Ever the Francophile, he would prefer '*l'art de vivre*'. But lifestyle is exactly what it was, with all that term's associations of delight and fragility.

A familiar-sounding request to the young and impressionable Brayfield was: 'Would you gift-wrap this basket of fresh limes and send them to Mary Quant?' But soon Brayfield became disenchanted with this stylish existence. There was, she observed, a mind-the-gap between the life so often photographed at Regent's Park Terrace and the reality of existence there, which seemed to one visitor to be a 'permanent state of rage'.

The Conran family dream, she said, was a fragile one, better realised on public magazine pages than behind private closed doors. Terence disavowed money-making as an end in itself, but in a turbulent existence, making money was the way to escape the frustrations of domestic life. Making money was a core family value.

'Design' was the means to that end. It is one of the most mysterious properties of the modern age: it styles products and enhances experiences. It excites desire and makes money. It is not something anyone wants to be without. But what exactly is it? No one can really say with any precision, least of all Terence himself, but he very cleverly made his own name an eponym for it. And in so doing established a hugely influential creative persona, crafted a lasting legacy and argued into existence a briefly impressive, but unstable, business imperium . . . that became all but a handful of bitterly disputed dust.

What Terence achieved was a truly remarkable transformation. He turned design from an activity into a commodity. 'Design' was once something designers did: whittling a stick, building a cathedral, conceptualising a car. But after Terence, 'design' was something consumers bought, or bought into. It became something you could acquire. Something you could put in a museum. Terence commodi-fied an idea. He invented design.

And he invented a persona for himself. In some ways this was similar to the influential American food personality, James Beard. Because Beard was no great cook, but he was a great actor who took on the role of great cook. He acted the part so well, no one could distinguish between fact and fantasy. The similarities with Terence are striking. In the *New Yorker*, Adam Gopnik described Beard as 'someone impersonating a gourmet, more than actually knowing how to be one . . . all you have to do is swirl the wine around and sniff it to pass as an oenophile. But the role that Beard invented and played was vital in creating a new idea of what American cooking was.'

For a while, Terence, with his campaign for democratic pleasure, for aestheticising the ordinary, seemed to dominate Britain, or, more accurately England, or at least the agreeable parts of it that read magazines and bought furniture or knew, or who wanted, at one point, to find out, what *agneau à sept heures* was. These were people who wanted to buy an asparagus kettle and a Danish chair. That's not to mock. It's to admire.

Terence's old friend, Hockney's first dealer, (John) Kasmin, amusingly said without any irony whatsoever: 'The problem with Terence is that he wants the whole world to have a better salad bowl.' Or perhaps more accurately, he wanted the whole world to buy it. From him.

Nearly sixty years ago his Habitat stores changed the way we furnished our homes and simultaneously revolutionised for ever shopping in Britain. Before online, Habitat was the biggest revolution in British retail since Selfridges in 1908. Choices once only available to an educated cosmopolitan elite were suddenly for sale on provincial high streets. Bromley suddenly became a little bit more like Helsinki. The impact of this to a population brought up on brown furniture with memories of antimacassars was as forceful as blunt-trauma injury. After Habitat, shopping changed for ever. As did the consumers' expectations.

Very few people have had as much beneficial influence on British life in the past half-century. But Terence became bored with his best idea and was seduced into reckless expansion during the mergers-and-acquisitions madness of the eighties. His headstrong ways irritated the City and forced him into a rich man's version of early retirement. This led to his second great success: restaurants.

Quaglino's, Bibendum, the Pont de la Tour and Bluebird set new standards in both food and design, and raised expectations, dramatically energising popular taste and inspiring countless imitators. It is significant, of course, that the names of Terence's most famous restaurants were foreign, evoking Italian glamour or French sophistication. In the history of taste, the principle of exotic validation is an important one.

Rescue and revival were continuous themes in Terence's life and work. He would find neglected products or properties, reinvent and popularise them. Rescue and revival duly occurred at Quaglino's and, for a moment, in fact a rather short moment, it was a design and gastronomic sensation.

Not everyone approved. Fiona MacCarthy was the distinguished biographer and pioneer writer on design whose insights into hospitality were founded on being born in the Dorchester, which her family owned. She acidly described Quaglino's as a 'deprived child's dream of sophisticated living'. Dreams, of course, are notoriously insubstantial.

And Quaglino's was also a fine, if disturbing, case study of Terence's view of authorship, which was often arrogant and dismissive of others, while correspondingly generous to himself. Keith Hobbs, Terence's chief designer of that moment, was the man permanently on site in the Quaglino's project in Bury Street, St James's, and the man who made Terence's powerful but sketchy vision assume real life, marshalling junior designers and engineers and contractors to realise that dream.

That's a serious undertaking. Besides, design is often a collaborative activity. But Terence has always insisted on exclusive authorship, dismissing Hobbs, the man with the power of execution, as only a 'competent contract administrator'. In the same way, Terence was later to dismiss his third wife of thirty years and active force in the shaping of Habitat as mere domestic help. Hobbs's revenge was to call Terence 'one of the best copyists ever'.

Terence's reluctance to give credit also affected Joel Kissin, the managing director of the restaurants during their most successful period. It was Kissin who found the Quaglino's site and talked Terence into it. This you would never infer from any of Terence's discourse on the matter. Kissin also explained that Terence was not specially efficient in his oversight of his properties: 'Months would go by between [his] visits to some of the restaurants . . . After a year or two he also did not even appear at the monthly meetings with the managers and chef.'

In this peculiar fashion, Terence busily created more than thirty restaurants in London, New York, Copenhagen, Tokyo and Paris. That's an impressive figure, but it is also true that he exaggerated the number: if a single restaurant had a formal dining-room and separate bar menu, Terence would count it as two operations. Still, however many establishments there were, they created a platform for moralising about design that was at least as robust as Habitat. Talking to the *New York Times* about the opening of Quaglino's in 1993, he said: 'I always thought it was my sort of God-sent job to disprove the theory that the upper and middle classes have good taste and the working class doesn't. Working-class people have been offered bad things for so many generations in a cynical way that if they were offered better, their taste would automatically improve.'

For its mixture of well-meaning patrician arrogance, boggling grandiosity, mingled with a tin ear for nuance and an impressive disregard for subtleties of 'class' and 'taste', this cannot easily be surpassed as a summary of Terence's world-view. *De haut en bas*, you could call it.

Terence also established the first modern design consultancy, allowing clients to enjoy for themselves a sprinkling of his well-pub-licised stardust. Additionally he was a furniture manufacturer, an author, educator and patron. He married and separated from four women, fathered five children, made several enemies, antagonised countless shareholders, provided thousands, possibly millions, of column inches, and smoked over £1 million worth of cigars.

That impressive seven-figure estimate is, of course, his own. People who know him accept that this is, at least, a poetic truth. It might even have been an underestimation.

Before his late discovery of the iPad, this modern man did not use a computer or a mobile phone. He could see out of only a single eye, having injured the other one in a workshop accident. But that single eye was a very, very good one. Its vision enriched us all in many intangible ways. He had such a fine visual memory, cameras were of little interest or use.

And he fought harsh and cruel battles with intimates in and out of his family. His sister Priscilla once told Keith Hobbs: 'He does not have love in his heart.' Fiona MacCarthy, whose late husband, the distinguished cutler David Mellor, came off very much the worse in a property deal with Terence, accused him of 'façadism' and of being in thrall to '1960s here-and-nowism'. Terence was not dull, but neither was he altogether lovable.

Most astonishing, perhaps, of his personal characteristics were motivation and appetite for work. These were at levels that humble the merely committed and very busy. Just when you thought he had had enough, Terence wanted more. Imagine him one day in the early nineties, travelling home in the evening from a site meeting at his new restaurant Zinc. Here he would have been nagging the contractors and the designers, as any restaurant proprietor would. But Terence would not merely be nagging. He would tell them how to get it right. And he would have *been* right.

Restaurants are all-consuming affairs, and the successful ones demand total attention. For most people, even professional restaurant people, one at a time is quite enough. But Terence was restless. On the day of this site visit he would have been writing new menus, thinking about other projects, new formats, the P&L accounts of his old businesses, the two or three books he had simultaneously going through the press, meetings with the bankers and advisors, his investments, his commitment to the Design Museum, trusteeships, foreign ventures, licences, wives, children, wine cellars and where to go for dinner.

At one peak of his multi-tasking circa 1980, Terence would return late to the studio where I was industriously hammering away at a typewriter. He often came with delicious and irreverent stories to accompany the all-pervasive aroma of burning Havana tobacco. For example, Mrs Thatcher once put her hand on his knee and said: 'You know, Sir Terence, it can be very lonely being prime minister.' Or so he told me. It was a great story, at once self-deprecating, self-aggrandising and very funny. On another occasion, he returned from a meeting with Robert Maxwell, declaring him to be 'the rudest man I have ever met'. Here we are in pot-and-kettle territory.

Anecdotes are revealing, especially as they pile up so very impressively in Terence's story. But there are even more arresting truths to be found in the larger picture. The narrative of Terence's life included indomitable ambition, great achievements, mixed successes and, eventually, resonant disappointments. It was an astonishing life, but not always a contented one.

Terence described himself as ambitious, mean, kind, greedy, frustrated, emotional, tiresome, intolerant, shy and fat. It's an interesting list whose amusing self-deprecation hints at gigantic egotism. 'I dare you to agree,' he seemed to be saying.

There's a list of other characteristics to be debated: a visionary with myopia, the creator of 'lifestyle' who then repudiated it, a hedonistic puritan, arrogant, but diffident too, a Francophile who could not speak French, a socialist who was selfish, a misogynist, but a womaniser (perhaps these are often connected), an ideologue who did not read books, a sensitive man insensitive to others, a gourmand who only cooked roast chicken, a sentimentalist who was ruthless, a democrat lacking the common touch, a national figure who was an enigma, an obsessive who lost concentration and focus, a businessman who was not good with money, a man besotted by the visual who did not use a camera, a success and a failure.

Terence the hedonist enjoyed fine wines, good food, Cuban cigars, flowers, bespoke suits, beautiful women, fast cars, magnificent homes. And yet he was a puritan. His work ethic was extreme; he claimed (from the back of a superlatively incongruous old-school Bentley) that 'plain, simple, useful' was his design mantra, yet Chelsea's famous Conran Shop became full of trinkets and gewgaws and faddish knick-knacks.

To save money on notepads, he drew on the backs of scrunched-up memos filched from other people's waste-paper baskets; he instructed his chauffeur to take a wide detour to avoid the congestion charge. One of his biggest disappointments was leaving it so late in life to start using private jets. His frugality was a force-field. And then he would ask if you'd like a glass of nicely chilled Puligny-Montrachet (an excellent breakfast wine).

Chez Terence, interesting connections went up, down and side-ways. And this was the pay-off for many of those close to him who might otherwise have found the company of an exigent curmudgeon too demanding.

One of his secretaries, Christina Smith, whose clever property speculations later put her among the leading landlords of Covent Garden, was, in the early eighties, the first champion of Fergus Henderson, then a young architecture student intent on food-related projects. Fergus created the notion of nose-to-tail eating, and at his landmark St John restaurant in Smithfield you might sometimes find squirrel on the menu and always a deep-fried extremity of pig. It was routinely cited, by the American chef Anthony Bourdain and oth-ers, as one of the best restaurants in the world. Fergus Henderson is the son of the late architect Brian Henderson, designer, among other things, of Gatwick Airport, who had as good a claim as anyone in a small field to being a close friend of Terence's: his network of influence in architecture, art, commerce and food was as far-flung as it was astonishing.

Another example: many years later, one lazy afternoon at Brunelys, Terence's gorgeous Provençal house in the Alpilles, every house-guest was pleasantly surprised to find Evangeline Bruce (widow of the most famous US ambassador), Nico Henderson (the most famous British ambassador to Washington and no relation to the other Hendersons), John Wells (the most famous sixties satirist), Anthony Beevor (the most famous military historian) and his wife Artemis Cooper (the most famous biographer of Elizabeth David) all ambling up the drive. If Terence felt anything, it was only mild annoyance at being disturbed during an afternoon of idleness.

With big names he could cope. He could appear to have a nonchalant attitude to titles and positions, but this, perhaps, disguised several layers of calculation. Before Iraq, he spoke of 'Tony' and knew it would be understood to suggest an intimacy between him and the prime minister that never actually existed. But before that, he never spoke of 'Margaret'. This omission was equally self-conscious and just as telling. Terence had a rigid mind, but was nonetheless very good at denominational flexibility.

A function of this connectedness was that Terence was a compulsive networker, although that is certainly not a term he would have used or enjoyed. Kasmin, the influential art dealer, explained that the early Terence was 'a great one for catching on' and was keen to get to know David Hockney. Terence saw the advantage in a great shopkeeper being associated with a great painter. Meanwhile Hockney thought Terence 'a nice guy who had a good restaurant'.

He accepted every invitation he received, and there were many, even to parties in high-concept rug stores. His address book was endless. He was on close terms with the great and good, or some of them; the international freemasonry of the rich is part of every wealthy person's milieu. His own parties had a Gatsbyesque flamboyance. Yet Terence was isolated. He had few, if any, close friends, a solitary figure even at his own parties; he was more at ease with objects than with people.

And he could be spectacularly rude. Bored, at a party, he once asked a banker, well respected at the time: 'Why have you got tassels on your shoes?' When an accountant was sounding off at a meeting, Terence asked: 'If you're so fucking clever, why aren't you as rich as me?' It's a corny old line, but devastating when you hear it delivered with such authority and appropriateness. Joel Kissin, the eminence grise behind Terence's best restaurants, commiserated with him about a flood, only be told: 'Piss off, Joel.'

While Terence was an eloquent spokesman for creativity, he was also an adroit lifter, happy to take inspiration where he could. Many can recall Terence at meetings with junior designers tearing illustrated pages out of magazines saying (I paraphrase a bit): 'You do this. You do that.'

Keith Hobbs remembers a chair being wheeled into the studio for the same purpose. Pointing at the work of someone else: 'Design me one of these for Habitat,' Terence would say to young recruits in his studio.

One interpretation of this would be shameless plagiarism, although Terence's own interpretation would be that he has a very keen discernment for interesting sources as well as being an inspirational teacher. Since Terence was a highly intelligent man who was no intellectual, the notion of intellectual property perhaps had little meaning. And he was ruthless. Hobbs said: 'I love him rather than hate him, but I would *never* trust him.'

Yet there was another Terence, the one with babyish hair and very soft skin and a laddish giggle. He had only a slight beard and never wore scent, although the Havana aroma compensated for that loss. He mostly had soft-spoken speech and mannerisms, put unusual em*phas*is on strange syllables. He used archaisms such as 'in any event'. On a good day, Terence could be very, very charming. Or 'extremely' charming, as he would put it, with that word rather long drawn out.

Close acquaintances were usually 'm'dear'. He enjoyed smut. When I once recommended a restaurant in Cagnes-sur-Mer on the French Riviera whose chef was called Adrian Campo, he sniggered like a schoolboy.

He used to have an antiquarian book dealer in Bloomsbury, David Batterham, who would feed him volumes of the *belle époque* caricaturist, Georges Goursat, known as Sem, whose work he adored. Incongruously, perhaps, Sem's work was pretty rather than robust.

I never heard him refer to music. The New York novelist Reggie Nadelson described his musical taste as 'classics for dummies'. Terence was always able to balance indulgence with parsimony, never letting one get the advantage of the other. He once asked me to find a brothel. I did some lukewarm research, but failed. It was surprisingly difficult. Instead, I took him to a dreadful 'gentlemen's club' in Marylebone, where Brazilian girls did pole-dancing. I dare say they, by negotiation, offered other delights as well, but after a raucous evening with several bottles of £250 champagne, we left, virtue intact, in a battered Skoda minicab.

I never quite understood what that evening had been about. Was it a test of my initiative? I failed badly. Surely someone who had survived the sixties knew how to find a *maison de passe* in Marylebone. Evidently not. Similarly, Terence also claimed never once in his life to have been offered, still less used, cocaine. On occasions, he possessed an almost touching innocence.

But stories of his aggressive business style have become legend, and all of his business partnerships ended painfully. Those urbane manners disguised a man who could be a bully. He discarded people when they ceased to be useful or threatened to excel. The consensus is, as Keith Hobbs says, that he could not be trusted. Yet Terence was sentimental. He often avoided direct confrontation (whose brutal details offended his aesthetic) and found it hard to fire people when it was deserved, though he could be lethal and cold when it wasn't.

Yet there was still another Terence whom every designer who worked with him will describe with a mixture of awed respect and endocrine fear. He adored poring over sketches of projects or proofs of books. Here he was at his very best. And with an almost inhuman reliability he could spot errors, pomposities, silliness, pretension and cant. Very little got past him.

This had the effect of being both extremely scary and very stimulating. Designers in his studio would dread his approach, yet emerge from any encounter shocked and chastened, but determined to improve. If Terence approved something, you felt specially blessed because it was such a rarity. If Terence disapproved, you worked very hard to do better. In matters of the eye, if not of the mind, Terence was rarely wrong.

Since school and student days, Terence had very evident charisma. And often charm too, although this last function did have that on/off switch. While not a specially imposing figure physically, he nonetheless had real presence. People were attracted to him. Power, fame and wealth became elements of this attraction, but a strong spirit pre-existed these acquired attributes.

Terence's presence electrified both students and working designers with whom he could be painstaking in his critiques, recommendations and encouragement. These people respected him because, more than any other living person or dead soul, Terence represented 'design' in all its meanings. Moreover, he convincingly demonstrated its power to enrich him. He showed its beneficial influence on everyday life. To work for him was, for a while, to enter a world, not so much of fantasy, as of enchantment and opportunity. But many discovered that the enchantment and opportunity were not for sharing.

Terence was one of the few to have made a connection between the sometimes chaotic art-school culture and the testing disciplines of business. In him you could see the cash value of art. He was a designer's champion, not because he was a designer of original genius, but because he was a champion of creativity itself. He seemed to be saying 'I am design.' And he said it with quiet passion to textile and product designers, perfumers, cooks, furniture-makers, illustrators, architects, artists and graphic designers. These people enjoyed an inspirational aura that gave him an almost mystical status. To have been in his circle was to have been close to The Source. People wanted to touch him or be 'in touch' with him.

But Terence always found it hard to give credit. And he had the very greatest difficulty saying 'please' and 'thank you'. Reviewing Terence's *Q&A: A Sort of Autobiography*, a perhaps too self-adoring *auto-da-fé*, Justin de Blank, a refined architect and linguist who had worked for J. Walter Thompson as well as for Terence in the sixties, complained in a letter to me that John Stephenson, Terence's managing director who 'drove the Design Group so hard that its cash flow made possible the opening of the initial six Habitats', was never actually acknowledged.

Nor was Philip Pollock, the plastic-foam heir who invested substantially in the first Habitat. His Aerofoam business had been an important supplier and maybe certain obligations had been acquired in the course of this trade. Indeed, some would say that Pollock's involvement was such that he could reasonably be called a co-founder of the store. But Terence did not care to share creation myths. Like sharing money, sharing creation myths has a diluting effect.

Thus, when an opportunity presented itself, Terence saw a Brutus and Caesar moment. In a story that is so discreditable it might actually be true, Pollock was forced out of Habitat when he was discovered in a gay liaison. Consensual homosexuality only ceased to be illegal in the UK in 1967. But let us move swiftly on to more certain ground.

Another example. The designer Rodney Fitch, one of Terence's earliest collaborators and his heir apparent until he was ruthlessly sacrificed in a business manoeuvre which turned out to be a short-sighted one, spent the rest of his life plotting revenge.

To my question: 'Would you like to say anything for an obituary I am pre-emptively writing for the *Guardian?*', Fitch replied: 'Only something that would cause it to be published immediately.' In *Q&A*, Simon Hopkinson, who made Bibendum's gastronomic reputation and whose cooking was a dense reduction of the essence of the Conran concept of lunch – that often referenced, but not so often eaten, wild rabbit cooked on a blaze of Provençal olive wood – gets no mention at all.

That startling omission was as deliberate as the resonant name drop. Terence enjoyed fabricating stories about people who served his cause, but was ruthless in erasing memories of apostates. Fatigued by the heat in Terence's kitchen, Simon Hopkinson got out of Bibendum to become a successful author and television personality. His *Roast Chicken and Other Stories* is often said to be the best cookery book of the modern era. Once again, Terence was careless with a great talent.

He had a curiously unapproachable informality. Rarely the correct 'Sir Terence', never, ever, under any circumstances, the wince-makingly matey 'Terry'. He was always 'Terence', an appellation that nicely balanced the forces of strict reserve and apparent informality which comprised the conflicted personality of this very famous, yet unknown, man.

But there's more. Long before brand voodoo became part of the business-school curriculum, 'Terence' made himself a brand. In this sense, if in no other, he was similar to the father of renaissance architecture, Palladio. The name acquired associations and expectations which almost everyone alive in Britain today recognised and, very likely, enjoyed. Terence had an intuitive genius for this sort of me-first invention. He was his own greatest design.

Indeed, like other great enterprises, Ford and Gillette once upon a time, possibly even Apple or Dyson today, Conran was the brand, the dynasty, the household name, but it's 'Terence' that became an eponym for a world of values, mostly admirable ones. At least among his large circle, who appreciated the good deeds done on their behalf and returned the compliment by assuming a fictitious intimacy.

This Terence destroyed the suburban semi's brown moquette 'lounge suite' and made the travelling executive's ploughman's lunch a thing of the past. This Cheddar and pickle assemblage was a relic from the era when Terence established himself as a designer. A faux-rustic invention of J. Walter Thompson on behalf of the Cheese Board, it spoke to all those ideas of cute quaintness and bogus tradition that Terence detested. Additionally, a ploughman's is eaten in a pub. Terence, to put it no higher, was not a pub man.

So he gave us superior Continental alternatives. If Terence recognised chicken-in-the-basket, another pub staple, the fowl would not be breadcrumbed supermarket chook, but a French rare breed and the *panier* woven by nut-brown Ardéchois artisans wearing *bleu de travail*. This extremely talented middle-class boy wanted to annihilate middle-class normality.

He was also, like his contemporaries, John, Paul, George and Ringo, one of those rare beings immediately recognisable by the forename alone. It's a name people were keen to cite as a tool of social or professional promotion: 'I was speaking to Terence the other day,' you used to hear them say. Fifty years after he became famous, when his name occurs in conversation, no one – certainly no designer – ever says: 'Terence who?' It is not surprising, as Terence changed life in this country. And made it better.

There was an old belief that the horse- and dog-loving English – provincial, Protestant and insular – are philistines, wretchedly impervious to comfort. This might seem a strange insult to the countrymen of Wren, Turner and even Hockney, but for a long time the literature-drenched England was assumed to be as backward in matters of art and design as it was in dental hygiene. The Germans even had their own lofty and wounding expression for this despicable national trait: *'visuelle analphabeteten'* (visually illiterate).

And it was the same with food. English cooking was long held in derision. Again, this may seem incongruous in the culture that supported cookery writers Hannah Glasse and Charles Francatelli, not to mention César Ritz, Auguste Escoffier, pioneer telly-chef Marcel Boulestin, never mind Fanny and Johnnie Cradock, but reputations endure long after the circumstances that made them have changed. The poet Kenneth Rexroth, inspiration to the Beats, said that eating out in England in the fifties was so dreadful you'd be better off being fed intravenously, while as recently as 2005 a French president declared that 'one cannot trust people whose cuisine is so bad'.

Today it is very different. Walk past the window of any estate agent and study the pictures of property interiors. You soon become aware that the general standard of design awareness, of visual literacy, in England is very much higher than the general standard you find in France, Italy, Germany or the United States. And now England, or at least London, has the most varied and competitive food culture on the planet. The corner pub has abandoned the ploughman's and will serve you a tomato and basil *galette* with a properly dressed *roquette* salad when once you were offered only a mephitic pickled egg sunk in opaque brine. London's food is now much better than Paris's. It's what a better-informed French president might call *le monde à l'envers*.

Terence did not himself design the interiors of all the flats and houses you see in estate agents' windows. Nor did he even sell the occupants their furniture because, even at its height, the actual size of his business was much smaller than its swaggering profile suggested. Nor did he write the menus for the ambitious pubs, still less cook the *galettes* or make the *vinaigrette*. Instead, through protean myth-making, indefatigable publicity, persuasive example, ruthless deal-making, a cynical disregard for friendships or obligations and an absolutely genuine commitment to improving life by 'design', he became – unquestionably – the biggest benefactor of material life in post-war Britain.

But his businesses became moribund and his reputation suffered. One reason for this was that he meticulously maintained damaging disputes, even among his family. Terence was notoriously difficult. Everyone who worked for him above a certain level knew the horror of finding on your desk an envelope (previously used) with a scrawl in blue Pentel roller-ball saying 'Strictly Private'.

I once, early in my association, carelessly opened such a communication and found the words 'jumped-up', 'little' and 'prick' in the very first sentence. Soon afterwards, I said to him in circumstances I cannot quite recall: 'Terence, don't be such a cunt,' and he spontaneously warmed to me. He warmed to me even more when in one of his kitchens I was found tearing, rather than cutting, basil, one of many fine and absurd snobberies he (and indeed I) liked to maintain. It was acquired from Elizabeth David.

Terence was an enigma: a mild-mannered monster of vanity, a do-gooding misanthrope, a selfish socialist, a masculine termagant, occasional charmer, utter bastard, myopic visionary, inspirer, compelling ideas man, generous host, narcissist, gourmand, philanthropist; and evasive, possibly damaged, perhaps shop-soiled, certainly sensitive, soul. But most of all Terence was someone who committed himself to a very particular vision of how life should be.

We are somewhere sunny and lunch is in prospect. There is elegant, spare furniture all around and a distracting assembly of intelligent *bibelots* and interesting people. We may eat something very French and very vernacular. Even better if it has been foraged or shot or fished recently and locally. There will be a magnum of wine (because 'a magnum turns any wine into a luxury'). Then there will be another magnum.

The glasses will be large and handsome, since small glasses are prissy and common and betray suburban appetites. And cigars. There are books on the tables and art on the walls. There will be lots of animated talk and, before too long, the beds we will enjoy are made with river-washed, air-dried linen.

So many found this vision persuasive that, at the height of his influence, Terence was running what seemed more like a revivalist cult than a business. People who worked for him often felt they were on a missionary campaign, something he exploited when the same people asked for rises and were treated with the disdain appropriate to a disciple asking favours of a prophet. At one point, Terence started using the first person plural 'we' to explain new projects. This was a device intended not so much to suggest inclusion and collaboration, as to refuse the existence of egos other than his own.

It is proof of magisterial originality – or at least of magisterial powers of synthesis – that these simple ideas had never before been attempted, let alone realised. That these same ideas have now been absorbed into everyday assumptions about shopping and eating, while Terence's own businesses fell into desuetude, was a sign not of failure, but of success. Yet he became rueful rather than triumphant.

Above all, Terence had an astonishing drive – to do, to build, to create, to achieve, to be admired, but perhaps most of all to make money. Love him or loathe him – and most who knew him did both – the breadth of his activities and achievements is astounding. What fuelled such extraordinary energy and passion? Were they demons or angels?

PART 1
THE HABITAT YEARS

1

Thirty-Two Virgins from Surbiton

S.B.

Terence was born in 1931 in Esher, a quiet place in Surrey. Ever afterwards, he was on vectors of escape from suburban tedium. Because of – rather than despite – their frustrations, England's suburbs have been a rich source of genius, since misery and boredom are more powerful creative influences than the lassitude of contentment. Belgravia, for example, has produced few artists.

From a Liverpool semi-detached house in genteel surroundings – or, at least, genteel by Merseyside standards – John Lennon dreamt of elsewhere, using literature and art as stimulants. The Beatles were the result and rock 'n' roll changed for ever. David Bowie's Brixton was Starman's launchpad. J. G. Ballard's terrifying techno-surreal dystopia was imagined in a dreary and calm semi-detached house in leafy Twickenham.

That key text for understanding the mentality of post-war British sophisticates, Elizabeth David's *Mediterranean Food* (1950), a love story about lemons, oil, garlic and sunshine, was conceived and written in a dismaying, damp hotel room in Ross-on-Wye. And Esher gave us Terence, with his warming conviction that everyday life can be improved by 'design'. Of course, this definition of 'design' was limited to modernist furniture and household goods executed to his own taste, but it proved persuasive.

Who is to say what measure of melancholy existed in his youth that he yearned to escape? And he was escaping from sadness ever afterwards. Driving through a small town once, he pointed out a property and said: 'Look at that terrible, sad little house.' His attention had, I think, been specially taken by an old-fashioned pendant light hanging from a central fixture in the ceiling, casting a yellow-brown glow over the dreary interior.

In the religious cult Terence was soon to create, salvation from this sort of sadness could be achieved by the removal of pendant lampshades and their replacement by adjustable spots or downlighters. Illumination, as therapists know, can alleviate sadness.

Terence was never especially forthcoming about either of his parents, Christina Mabel Halstead and Gerard Rupert Conran, but was much more open about his mother, to whom he attributed his artistic sensibility. She had a taste for drawing and an awareness of the pleasantness of the gently *moderne* middle-class interiors being promoted by Heal's when Terence was a child. From Esher, the Conran family moved to a flat in Hampstead, where he recalled enjoying the polite and reticent environment, where beige dominated, established by his mother. Hampstead, of course, was where European émigrés, including Piet Mondrian and Walter Gropius, settled. Henry Moore was a long-term resident. Modernism was in the air.

His South African-born father never became a source of anecdote or example, although I once heard Terence claim for him a vague association with the sport of rugby. Instead, his father contributed very little to Terence's personality, other than the urgent desire to escape paternal influence. He had founded Conran & Co., a small City business trading in gum copal (an ingredient in varnish) in the days when real merchants selling real stuff still inhabited the Square Mile.

This business got into some sort of financial trouble about which Terence was never very specific. It was spoken of as a dark secret, but not, I think, without an occult element of pride; the reflected glamour of a City association was quite enjoyed, no matter how tarnished. Still, Terence never talked affectionately of his father. He once told Justin de Blank: 'My dad's in the gutter again.' Then he asked: 'Can't you find him anything to do?' That's typical Terence in that it initially suggests sympathy and concern, while simultaneously shifting the obligation elsewhere.

School at Bryanston in Dorset was not, perhaps, a great pleasure, although Terence always spoke affectionately of his teaching by Don Potter, a pupil of type-designer Eric Gill and acquaintance of ceramicist Bernard Leach. Charles Handley-Read, a pioneer in the study of the then unfashionable Victorian architecture, was also a teacher. For an English public school, it had an unusual focus on the visual arts. In this way, Terence was introduced to an essentially English and commonsensical tradition of design. This made him sophisticated, if not always cheerful. Terence's school friend Alexander Plunket Greene, later to marry Mary Quant, said: 'Terence was less of a child than the rest of us and I was rather in awe of him; he was a surly lad with some very strong ideas. He still is if you don't know him.'

Bryanston had a robustly liberal and tolerant reputation, but Terence was able to make decisive transgressions up to the point where he was expelled or, at least, invited to leave early. The cause of departure he always said was 'something to do with girls' although he never explained exactly what.

Thus, Terence was able to disprove that old dictum that the educational Establishment cannot recognise genius. It most certainly can. The educational Establishment spots genius unerringly and then removes it from the system.

In September 1947 Terence arrived at the Central School of Arts and Crafts on London's Southampton Row. This was a fine institution founded by the Arts and Crafts architect W. R. Lethaby in 1896, and its practice was rooted in the principle that the design of any artefact was inseparable from the making of it. The Bauhaus later adapted a version of this in its doctrine of learning by doing. This was an idea that remained enduringly influential with Terence.

At the Central School Terence, by all accounts, including his own, impressed his teachers including Dora Batty (the 'sensible Miss Batty') and Mary Kirby, although he perhaps made a less favourable mark on his student colleagues whom he unfavourably described as 'thirty-two virgins from Surbiton'. Surbiton being a neighbour of Esher, he continued to repeat this fine expression with a scornful snigger for the rest of his life.

It was at the Central that this surly boy, occasionally capable of great charm, began to make a distinctive reputation. Not just with his textile designs, which were polite, witty and contemporary, but with his whole persona, which was altogether more complicated. And out of this reputation emerged the first of the many and often-repeated stories whose presence in his narrative contributed to the myth about the man. At the Central, it was reported that Terence was so prodigally talented that – in order not to demoralise or shame others, or perhaps squander his own genius on worthless projects – he was paid £1,000 a year not to design (although it was unclear who was doing the paying).

However, despite, or perhaps because of this juvenile star status, Terence left the Central before actually graduating. Whether this was because of a transgression or his inability to contain his prodigious ambition has never been clear. His first job was as a designer at the Rayon Design Centre in Upper Grosvenor Street, rayon being a popular semi-synthetic fabric of the day. The creative director here was an architect, now rather forgotten, called Dennis Lennon, who also worked with modernist architects Maxwell Fry and Jane Drew, firmly anchoring the Rayon Design Centre in modernist truths as understood in the thirties. Fry and Drew had designed influential thirties' flats and houses, some of them in or near Hampstead, with bold simple lines, metal Crittall windows to let in healing sunshine and severe concrete structures to articulate a distance from the architectural past. This was Terence's nurturing culture.

And it was through Lennon that Terence found his way in 1951, aged just twenty, to working at the Festival of Britain, the Conservative government's carnival boost to battered national morale. Here, on the bombed-out South Bank of the Thames, a vast canvas was made available for architects and designers to develop ideas that had been essayed three years before at the Victoria & Albert Museum's 'Britain Can Make It' exhibition. Terence later confessed to being entirely unqualified, but there was a mood of delirious enthusiasm in 1951 and delirious enthusiasm was qualification enough.

The Lennon studio had several jobs on the South Bank site, and Terence was sent to work on the mock-up of an interior of the Saunders-Roe Princess flying boat, as well as furniture for the Homes and Gardens pavilion. He also produced signage for the Natural History pavilion made up of little shellfish suspended in clear plastic. Alas, none survives as a tribute.

The furniture was made of salvaged re-bar (the rods used in re-inforced concrete), ingeniously (and thriftily) scrounged from building sites, and Terence, using the principles of Lethaby and the Bauhaus, would apply first his welding torch, then his one good eye, to the matter of fabrication. In this one-eyed, but committed, way did Britain advance into the era of modern design. That Terence did the welding himself is a matter of symbolic significance. It was welding too that brought him into contact with the artist Eduardo Paolozzi, who was to become one of his few lifelong friends.

Paolozzi, seven years older than Terence, was at the time making his bold collages and montages featuring cartoon characters and commercial scraps which would eventually be identified as precursors of Pop Art. His yearning for the colour and freedom of American pop culture was the equivalent of Terence's more European modernity: each offered a vista of escape from drab life at home.

For the Festival, Paolozzi had devised a complex and idiosyncratic animated water sculpture with cascading buckets. It was always breaking down and Terence, in his own account, would rush up to repair fractured brackets and restore the mechanism to life with his ever-ready welding torch. Paolozzi is, alas, no longer alive to confirm this version of events.

So here was a favourite Terence principle emerging: his ability to remedy faults through the application of practical skill and mechanical intelligence, with a huge dash of added style. Additionally, hand work was a sacrament. The flying boat and the furniture also tell us something revealing and contradictory about Terence and his methods. And possibly contributing as well to his own emerging personality, construed as a zealously ambitious reformer not merely of art and design, but of industry as well.

The Princess flying boat, a ten-engined monster, was one of Britain's great aviation calamities, an outstanding failure in a very busy field of national duds. Its designers had failed to anticipate that overland jet routes were the future of air travel. Three were built, but only one flew before it was ignominiously scrapped in 1953. Describing its interior in 2007, Terence cheerfully said it seated six hundred. It actually seated a more modest one hundred and five.

Sometimes, Terence found facts sad and constraining. But with less aggrandisement, he did confess that his own Festival of Britain furniture had none of the elegance of Robin Day's designs for the Royal Festival Hall which will for ever be identified with 1951. In one sense, Terence never believed himself a first-rate designer. To his credit, he admitted this.

Still, the euphoria of the moment made a lasting impression. Never mind mere suburban dreariness, the South Bank site was a comprehensively blitzed devastation. Against this dismal background, the modern buildings achieved inspirational stand-out. Even if the famous Skylon and Dome of Discovery were in fact string and wire in the fashion of a Potemkin village, their uncontaminated, forward-looking optimism was thrilling. More so the impressive Royal Festival Hall itself, the most ambitious modern building yet attempted in Britain. Terence looked with wonder to see this majestic edifice made of fine materials (including his favourite Derbyshire fossil limestone) with *stuccatori* craftsmen shipped in from Italy to hand-finish the plaster columns.

As a symbol of redemption through design, an agent of new life in dead areas, a portent of a brighter future, the Royal Festival Hall was enduringly influential to Terence and, indeed, to the nation as a whole. But when the Conservative government cleared most of the site late in 1951, it was as if a fragile utopian vision had been exposed to harsh daylight. The disappearance of an exemplary dream was Terence's first big disappointment, and perhaps the origin of his messianic urge to create and build monuments of his own.

And it was the experience of the Festival of Britain that gave Terence the idea that exhibitions were the most effective medium for his didacticism. These were ideas ultimately realised, to a degree, in Habitat, but also in the Boilerhouse Project in the Victoria & Albert Museum and at the original Design Museum in Butler's Wharf.

But Terence was a practical man and inclined not to be long detained by philosophical pondering. After 1951, there was soon a studio of his own in Bethnal Green, which quickly moved to Sloane Court West, then to Notting Hill Gate (before it became fashionable), then Donne Place in Chelsea (when parts of Chelsea were still slums), ultimately to North End Road in Fulham. Additionally, there was a wood workshop in Camberwell.

He became a very busy young man and work does not seem to have been difficult to come by. And it was work of a sound, practical sort. Terence designed ticking for Myers Beds and sold over one million yards of it, although that figure may be as rhetorical as the £1 million worth of cigars. He did like seven-figure numbers. There was work for John Lewis and for the influential art director Natasha Kroll at Simpson's, Joseph Emberton's superlative modernist department store on Piccadilly.

At Simpson's he followed other star designers, including Bauhaus-meister László Moholy-Nagy and Ashley Havinden, a pioneer of British advertising art. Kroll was one of several mentor figures in Terence's early life: in her book *Shop Window Display* (1954), she showed how European standards of display might revive Britain's sleepy high streets, a lesson Terence learnt well.

With these contacts and associations whose culture was based in the thirties and its beliefs in clean lines and no-nonsense, Terence was justified in seeing himself as an authentic representative of high modernism. He even published a book on printed textile in 1957 when he was only twenty-five years old, but he never spoke of this, which made me – perhaps unworthily – suspect that he perhaps did not actually write it. Refusal to discuss an achievement being very out of character.

But in this youthful heroic mode, Terence designed textiles for David Whitehead and china for Midwinter. Conran fabrics were commissioned for the SS *Canberra*, a popular P&O cruise liner that entered service in 1961. His fabrics also appeared in some versions of the Vickers Viscount, the world's original turbo-prop passenger jet (which had first flown for BEA in 1950). Those not listening care-fully could sometimes get the impression that Terence designed the entire aircraft.

This work was sweet and polite: the *Canberra* and the Viscount, even if their names suggested a colonial capital and the peerage, were among Britain's most convincing tilts at the modern. Terence confidently mastered the idiom: admirers might call it accomplished synthesis, detractors might say pastiche.

Then there was Terence's own furniture: terracotta planters and conical cane chairs were both supported by frames of slender welded rods. Interestingly, none won Design Council awards, a slight that must have hurt, except that Terence might have been too busy to notice.

Even as his reputation grew, there was ever more evidence that Terence's own designs did not rise much above the stylishly derivative. Never one for harrowing self-analysis, he had realised early that as a designer plain and simple he would never win great esteem. Maybe this was the source of Terence's prodigal imperialism: he needed a larger canvas than his workshop or his studio.

East End playwright Wolf Mankowitz was Terence's partner in importing the woven basketware from Madeira, through a company called Basketweave. The association with Mankowitz is eloquent of Terence's milieu at the time. Mankowitz was a fifties character writ very large. A scholarly Wedgwood expert, he was also the author of *Expresso Bongo*, a satire on Soho's sleazy music business, whose film version in 1959 launched the career of Cliff Richard, who convincingly acted as a moron who played the bongos.

Mankowitz later became a celebrity on flickering black-and-white television panel shows. Meanwhile, Basketweave's first salesman was John Stephenson, a tall, elegant, well-mannered, polite, nervous, bespectacled, kindly, chain-smoking, likeable, occasionally irascible individual whose complicated relationship with Terence included marrying Shirley and thus becoming stepfather to Terence's eldest children, Sebastian and Jasper.

Stephenson's second wife was known as Ginty, thought to be an amiable contraction of 'gin and tonic', her declared preference in drinks enjoyed in their convivial lifestyle. Perhaps aware from time spent with Terence of the ever-present threat of violent conflagrations, metaphorical as well as actual, Stephenson always specified additional fire extinguishers in his cars. I once found him reduced to tears by Terence's bullying.

And in 1957, still only twenty-five, long before anybody else had thought of quite such a thing, Terence established the Conran Design

Group. True, America had had, in Raymond Loewy, Walter Dorwin Teague and Henry Dreyfuss, its own pioneer design consultants since the late twenties. True, in London, Milner Gray, Misha Black and Herbert Read had founded DRU, the Design Research Unit, in 1943.

Terence was never first, best or different . . . nor even claimed to be. Instead, he was a master of synthesis, a talented editor, an aggregator, an inspired leader and an authentic genius at self-promotion. Into the Conran Design Group went a unique combination of a craftsman's touch, a singular vision, a nearly feral instinct for opportunity, a sensibility that merged Scandinavian modern with Pop, middle-class ambition and, on a personal basis, an avid need to succeed. Also, if necessary, succeeding by ensuring that others failed, to adapt Gore Vidal's expression.

The Conran Design Group occupied a studio in Hanway Place, a dingy cut near the junction of Oxford Street and Tottenham Court Road. Hanway Place became a crucible: it was here that his closest collaborators, Oliver Gregory, Keith Hobbs and Rodney Fitch joined Terence as interior designers with a gifted knack for shopfitting. John Stephenson managed them. Terence added to its creative, sophisticated ambience by using the premises as an agency for the American and Finnish textile designers, Jack Lenor Larsen and Marimekko, always favourites of his. Keith Hobbs, thinking of how bleak and bereft London was at the time, said: 'It was one of the only places in London where you could work,' and added that, just like the Festival of Britain, it was 'a room full of people who didn't really know what they were doing.' But one of them did.

2

The Soup Kitchen

S.B.

It is not true that Terence invented soup. But perhaps the very first time Terence was referred to in the press as a 'young designer' was in the context of his Soup Kitchen. It was 1953.

The opening of this inspired little bistro was a signal event in the development of Terence as an entrepreneur. With a mixture of vision and opportunism he translated himself from being merely an ambitious designer of fabrics and furniture to a magus-like figure who conjured dreams of stylish well-being to entertain a demoralised and hungry public.

The Soup Kitchen was his very first restaurant venture, in fact his first signature venture of any sort, and soon became a part of his personal creation mythology.

From Chandos Place in Charing Cross, the Soup Kitchen expanded to Knightsbridge and then even unto Cambridge. The latter soon closed when Terence realised that feckless students, as opposed to busy office workers, would spend an entire day with a single cup of coffee. He might have been pleased that they were absorbing his taste, but he was dismayed that they were a burden to his overheads.

Terence understood food and drink well, but he understood publicity even better. On the Soup Kitchen's first day, tramps and vagrants were invited in and fed free of charge, and Terence made sure the story was all over the next day's newspapers.

But it is surprising how few survivors of the fifties actually remember the original Soup Kitchen. In their remarkable 1984 *Official Foodie Handbook*, a pop-anthropological account of modern English gastronomy, Ann Barr and Paul Levy, fifties survivors both, did not include the opening of Terence's Soup Kitchen in their comprehensive timeline of gastro phenomena. Meanwhile, Terence attributed to the Soup Kitchen a Suez-like significance in the history of the nation's alimentary canal.

And even though the Knightsbridge branch of the Soup Kitchen was next door to Esmeralda's Barn, the Kray brothers' notorious mob nightclub in Wilton Place, it nonetheless does not feature in contemporary diaries. Maybe the Krays and their associates were not interested in *vichyssoise*.

There was still rationing when Terence, with partner Ivan Storey, offered a menu of not only the vichyssoise which the Krays did not like, but minestrone, split pea, onion and tomato soups all made, with typical ingenuity and frugality and authenticity, from the same basic stock. For Terence, basic stock was a philosophical as well as a culinary proposition. Who, after all, would not make stock? Who would trust someone who did not? Stock is economical, useful and delicious. Or so the theory goes. Apple pies, however, were bought in from Mrs Trueman of Bethnal Green, a characteristic tilt at impressive provenance. Decent Cheddar and French bread were also available.

In a London restaurant scene where rissoles and Brown Windsor soup were still staples, when there was still rationing, Terence sensed the importance of the very same 'authenticity' that began to preoccupy serious cooks thirty years later. At some level, perhaps even an unconscious one, he realised that caring about food was philosophically similar to caring about design: the good cook and the good designer each needs quality ingredients to create an attractive result. Each has a concept, or, in the case of the cook, a recipe, and each intends to give pleasure. Or I suppose you could also say each gives you an element of control over other people.

It has been claimed, at least by Terence, that he drove to Milan in a borrowed Riley to buy a second-hand espresso machine and instal it in the Soup Kitchen. Thus, another signature example of unusual enterprise and a personal vision that anticipated popular taste, moderated by thrift, with a dash of adventure and self-mythologising evoked by the name of that modest, but sporty, little car.

This would have been one of the first commercial espresso machines in London. A rival claim is that of the Moka Bar in Frith Street, which was also early to offer coffee made in an Italian pressurised device. But the Moka Bar never had so persuasive a champion as the Soup Kitchen had in Terence.

European travel in search of authentic experience, good kitchen equipment and real food was a feature of cultural exploration in the fifties. Elizabeth David and Julia Child, of course, but there was also Chuck Williams, founder of the hugely successful Williams-Sonoma kitchenware business that stylised and commodified French food first for hip Californians, then for the whole of the altogether less hip continental United States. In some ways, Williams was the US equivalent of Terence. It was in that very same 1953 that Williams made his own pilgrimage to the great Parisian kitchen supply companies. One of them, Dehillerin, a little later also became an inspiration to Habitat.

If Terence did in fact go by Riley to Milan in 1953, it was for him a very busy period of European driving when European driving was not at all familiar. Especially for a twenty-one-year old, because – if I am calculating correctly – it was in the same year that he made his oft-recounted first trip to France in photographer Michael Wickham's Lagonda.

This was an adventure which ignited his Francophilia, that uncritical infatuation with an edition of France that completely shifted and influenced his whole outlook on everything, and given that he was the taste-maker of Britain, would change ours as well. Significantly,

Terence has never suffered from Italophilia. The Milan trip featured much less often in Terence's personal saga. So little does it feature that I sometimes wondered if it ever actually happened. Perhaps it was a journey made in the imagination rather than on the road, but as the Italians say *'ma, si non è vero, è bellissimo e immortale'*, even if it's not true, it's very beautiful and immortal.

The chosen name Soup Kitchen deserves a little deconstruction. At one level it suggests Orwellian queues of down-and-outs whose hunger and anguish are mocked by a smart-alecky public schoolboy in red braces. At another level, the middle class is invited to engage in an honest, no-frills experience, but, at the same time, given access to a quality of experience hitherto unavailable. The sense in which the Soup Kitchen anticipates Habitat is clear: it was a wholly designed environment.

Nostalgie de la boue and a Fabian sensibility are obvious here, but they are commingled with exotic luxury: after all, the very first restaurant was an eighteenth-century Paris soup kitchen. Soup was not always an impoverished option. The word 'restaurant' actually means a restorative broth. So, as with the removal of the sad pendant light and its replacement with cheerful adjustable spots, there were in the Soup Kitchen measures of nourishment that were spiritual as well as functional. It was a clever and knowing name.

And Terence's market sense was acute. His friend Alexander Plunket Greene said that at the time there was nowhere to eat in London between the stratospheric Savoy Grill with rising cloches, silver service and grovelling waiters, and the sort of greasy-spoon caff that would serve an evil egg and chips. Terence's single excellent eye for an unoccupied niche had achieved very sharp focus.

But more remarkable than the food was the interior design. The *Evening Standard* called it 'madly contemporary', intended as a compliment. The floor was chequered black-and-white tiles, the ceiling black, and one wall a vivid red. Below the black ceiling (which gave *trompe l'oeil* depth) there were suspended panels which masked the light. Some panels were white, grey, red and blue. Others were covered with giant pictures of egg whisks, lifted from antiquarian French books. The same source provided images of prawns, joints of meat – perhaps a *poitrine* or a *culotte* – and artichokes. Quarry tiles and tongue-and-groove anticipated Habitat, while soup eaters sat on a long bench with zebra-striped cushions. The soup arrived in blue-and-white striped bowls.

And then he lost interest. Terence sold to partner Ivan Storey, citing a difference of opinion about hot food. But, really, it was the first historical evidence of his intense, but fragile and temporary, concentration. Terence wanted to move on. He was bored. Was this evidence of prodigal creativity, an urgent need to do the next thing? Or was it simply an inability to concentrate? These questions would recur for the rest of Terence's active life.

3

1966 and All That

S.B.

The year 2016 saw the opening of the second generation Design Museum. But it was also the fiftieth birthday of 'Swinging London', an agenda-setting article that appeared in the US *Time* magazine on 15 April 1966. Terence had almost certainly frugged with Mary Quant, thus responding to the spirit of the age, but the *Time* journalist did not include the two-year-old Habitat in his list of Swinging London locations. Whether this was because *Time*'s criteria for swingingness were restricted to fashion and music, more than to kitchen utensils, or because Habitat perhaps swung less than some cannot now be determined.

Frug was a dance of the early sixties, a close relation to the Chicken and a distant relation to the Watusi. When not frugging, Quant popularised the miniskirt, a garment by which the era will always be remembered. In its combination of radical, modernist simplicity and frankly sexual, at least heterosexual, suggestion, the miniskirt rivals the Jaguar E-Type as a meaningful relic of the era.

Quant sold her miniskirts from a Chelsea boutique called Bazaar, which she had founded in 1957 with her husband and Terence's school friend, Alexander Plunket Greene. When she opened a second boutique on the King's Road later that year, Terence was asked to design it. He was twenty-six.

Post-1945 there was an almost psychopathological craving for colour. And by about 1960, Chelsea's King's Road was just beginning its career as a fashionable boulevard. After the Soup Kitchen closed, Terence opened a more ambitious restaurant called the Orrery near World's End, down the road from where Mary Quant would open her famed boutique, thus confirming Terence's knack of getting to topographical and career destinations first.

Again, the name is significant. An orrery is a mechanical model of the solar system, and Terence had always been fascinated by them. As a name for a restaurant it is suggestive of sophistication and a taste for fine things, with a nice cosmological emphasis. It also, of course, suggests that everything revolves around a central point: this could be understood to mean either the Sun or Terence.

A brief marriage to an architect called Brenda was now over and it was in the Orrery in 1955 that Terence met his second wife, Shirley Pearce, perhaps confirming a lifelong association with food and romance. She had arrived at the restaurant one day on the arm of David Douglas, the 12th Marquess of Queensberry, a distinguished ceramicist, Chelsea *flâneur* and hautest of the haut bohemians with family connections infamously involving Oscar Wilde.

Terence and Shirley married later that year and the process of systematic media flirtation and mythology soon began. Shirley was a journalist.

In nearby South Kensington, Terence would soon experiment with modish restaurant design, introducing the world to the decorative 'louvre' at Walter Baxter's Chanterelle on Brompton Road. With a good sense for a story the press would pick up, when the actress Vivien Leigh complained abut the lighting, Terence promptly had the light-bulbs painted pink to create a more flattering ambience. The louvre, a clever amalgam of the vernacular and the chic, predicted the Habitat proposition. It was a motif that would endure in interiors for at least another twenty years.

Baxter, a grey eminence in the London subculture where food and art mixed, had inherited a sausage fortune and became notorious when his purplishly gay books were showcased in obscenity trials. Christopher Isherwood described this client of Terence's as a 'tragic self-pitying drunken figure with a philosophy of failure', although his restaurants were great successes. Terence liked him a lot.

As the Francophone name suggests, Chanterelle's smart French cooking combined with Terence's clean lines and louvres to illuminate drab London. Here and elsewhere, Terence did not actually discover France, but he artfully sold an Englishman's interpretation of it. It was a short step from wanting to eat *frisée aux lardons* to wanting to buy a better salad bowl to put it in. That step would soon be taken.

A certain class of Englishman has always been exposed to France for education. In the eighteenth century, privileged youth was sent on the Grand Tour. They bought fancy clothes in Paris, did a spot of whoring, then moved on to Lyon, Grenoble and southwards. Often they would have tutors to accompany them.

The trip to France in Michael Wickham's Lagonda was Terence's Grand Tour. The make of car was always important in his cosmology. This detail gives credibility to a recollection that might otherwise seem fanciful. And minute gradients of snobbery are detectable in the citing of marques, as they so often were in Terence's pronouncements. A Riley was raffish while a Lagonda was grandly aristocratic. He often described this as his epochal introduction to European finesse, and the Lagonda is an essential part of the telling. If a Ford Popular had been involved, Terence might not, perhaps, have found the make and type worth mentioning.

The France-in-a-Lagonda trip was, if his Milan-in-a-Riley story is discounted as an anachronism or a fiction, Terence's very first encounter with European culture. In his telling of the tale, he casts Wickham as a Virgil to his Dante: a benign and inspired tutor. Other passengers included Wickham's own wife and, in a nice period touch,

Mrs Humphrey Lyttelton, wife of the jazz trombonist who was a fixture at the most popular nightclub of the day, 100 Oxford Street.

And there were telling details to support the character-building aspects of the trip: in the back of the car Terence was reading both Elizabeth David (volume unspecified), Sigfried Giedion's *Mechanisation Takes Command* and thrillers by Ellery Queen. That combination of the gastronomic and the technical and the entertaining is a clever little miniature autobiography which is exactly how the often repeated anecdote was intended. What precisely they did and saw, Terence never quite said and history does not reveal, but it is fair to assume that from the Lagonda's passenger window, when not reading, Terence saw the rows of plane trees, the spluttering *deux chevaux*, the roadside graphics, the sunny, sleepy villages that later populated his benign tunnel vision of France.

Perhaps Wickham kept a Michelin *Guide Rouge* on board to aid diversions towards lunch and dinner. In French provincial restaurants, Terence found the elegantly simple china, the robust glasses, the mannish carafes and the deluxe peasant food he later made his own. It was, and sounded, seductive, but that Fiona MacCarthy described Michael Wickham – a *bien pensant*, debonair CND activist and a man given to wearing berets – as a 'terrible old fraud' should not, perhaps, be seen as destructive of this happy idyll and the mythology that arose from it.

Fraud or no, as a photographer working for *House & Garden*, Wickham was in mid-fifties London at the centre of the most sophisticated and cosmopolitan source for ideas about interior design and, indeed, the entire *art de vivre*, at least as understood by glossy magazines. He gave Terence entry to this world. Elizabeth David, no less, was cookery correspondent of *Vogue*, *House & Garden*'s sister magazine. The milieu evidently appealed powerfully, and Wickham's mentoring soon became a fixed and often burnished part of Terence's life story.

Three years after the French Grand Tour, *House & Garden* was being edited by Robert Harling, an elegant and engaging character with special interests in typography and vernacular lettering, who later became a novelist of Fleet Street genre fiction. A friend of James Bond's creator, Ian Fleming, the well-liked Harling had eclectic taste; under his editorship the magazine specialised in a pictorial style juxtaposing old and new while emphasising, revolutionary at the time, the importance of colour and simplicity.

Of course, these very same characteristics later described Terence's own style and it is irresistible to speculate how much Harling's *House & Garden* might have influenced the development of his aesthetic. Certainly, the magazine accommodated Terence and his whims.

Harling said Terence's youthful spontaneous romantic appetites were often gratified by improvised assignations in cupboards. The brief occupation of the cupboards was not, one assumes, dominated by close design-based scrutiny of the brooms and dustpans. He was as busy in romance as in business, if a little less sophisticated.

In France Terence had found a nice combination of sensualism and earthy practicality which defined him: he would sniff the cleft in a peach and mutter about a woman's bottom. In the same way, his favourite shop in Paris was Deyrolle, whose speciality is taxidermy, which combines a delight in display with a certain refined cruelty. *Le style est l'homme.*

It is the France of long, convivial lunches in the sunshine, of nights in those very same beds with their river-washed, air-dried linen, and bowling down a D-road shadowed by *arbres de lineage* to search for breakfast in a classic Citroën *Traction Avant.* Terence's France was where he wanted to be and is the place we all want to be.

France and things French allowed Terence to assemble several pleasing anecdotes which, through loving repetition, have achieved the status of myth. For example, it was in 1954 that he first tasted *foie gras*, not in France, but with Mark Birley – whether before or after his trip to France with Wickham is not clear, but to be historically pedantic about dates does no honour to a charming memory.

Terence says he designed the Hermès shop in Piccadilly Arcade which Birley, twenty-four at the time, was managing. This may well be true, but it played no part in Birley's own highly polished personal mythology.

The same – evidently busy – year was perhaps when Terence first ate at Fernand Point's gastronomic shrine, La Pyramide in Vienne, near Lyon. Point's principles of excellence – 'a lot of little things done well', or 'marginal gains' as we might call it today – would later return to haunt Terence.

And he visited too Madame Barattero's Hôtel du Midi in Lamastre in the Ardèche, a redoubt of *cuisine ancienne*, where the *poularde en demi-deuil*, or 'chicken in mourning' became adopted into his personal story. The dish is so called because slices of truffle are inserted under the skin, making the fowl appear like a widow in weeds. The chronology here is interesting. If it was really 1954 when Terence visited Lamastre, then he was in advance of Elizabeth David who was to lionise the Barattero family. Always a possibility, but perhaps not a very likely one. (Mrs David's article 'Chez Barattero' was published in *Vogue*, September 1958).

Mrs David's wonderful account of the trip from Valence through the Ardèche to the Hôtel du Midi and the consequential rhapsody about French food was only published in her 1960 *French Provincial Cooking*. The cover photograph by Anthony Denney was taken in the Hôtel du Midi. Significantly, it looks like a prototype Conran lunch with its chequered tablecloth, crusty bread and rough carafes.

Vogue shared premises with *House & Garden*. This was Terence's London, where designers, journalists and photographers all mixed. It was in *Vogue* that Mrs David gives the full recipe: 'A 3lb Bresse chicken, stuffed with its own liver, a little foie gras and slices of truffle, is tied up inside a pig's bladder.' During the course of the cooking, a jelly forms between the carcass and the bladder. This, one notes with some bewilderment, is Terence's idea of simple food. But, then, Madame Barattero was herself married to a relation of Escoffier, the chef whose motto was: 'Faites simple.' Doing it simply became an article of faith for Terence.

Another mentor friend of Terence's at this period was Dickie Chopping, the illustrator of the classic trompe l'oeil James Bond dust jackets. Chopping's 1965 novel, The Fly, was described by its publisher as 'perfectly disgusting' and a calculated affront to good taste: the cultural revolution in which Terence participated had its grubby side, which he was philosophically suited to enjoy. 'Nothing wrong with a bit of buggery,' he once told me in a lift. I am as ambiguous about this assertion now as I was at the time. Meanwhile, Chopping might be found with their chum, Francis Bacon, in Soho's extremely louche drinking club, Madame Jojo's, or the equally decadent Colony Room.

But perhaps Chopping's most substantial contribution to the Conran story was the name 'Storehouse'. This was the Regency house in Wivenhoe, Essex, where Chopping lived with Dennis Wirth-Miller during the Second World War. Painted brick with blind windows, recesses and urns, it is now Grade II listed. When Terence merged Habitat with British Home Stores in 1986, the clumsy new group was called . . . Storehouse.

While Chopping wrote about sexual relations with plants, most media reporting of mid-sixties pop culture concentrated on the people with flowers in their hair, not their penises in a yucca plant. The Time magazine article said: 'In a decade dominated by youth, London has burst into bloom. It swings; it is the scene.' Playing catch-up, Esquire, another wide-eyed American magazine, confirmed that London is 'the only truly modern city'. Centre Point – described by the bow-tied, cheroot-smoking, fur-hat-wearing disciple of Le Corbusier, Erno Goldfinger, as 'London's Pop Art building' – was just being completed.

This was also a London inhabited by marvellous louche exotics including the embezzler Michael – 'Dandy Kim' – Caborn-Waterfield, the adman Jeremy Scott, and Michael Rainey, proprietor of Chelsea's Hung On You boutique, favoured by both the Beatles and the Rolling Stones. It featured in the original *Time* map of 'The Scene and Beyond', by a journalist R. M. Chain, whose knowledge of the city was less impressive than his enthusiasm: Belgrave Square is misleadingly represented as Belgrade Square. While Habitat was ignored, boutiques cited for their swingingness included Bazaar, Rainey's Hung on You, Top Gear, Countdown, Granny Takes a Trip in Chelsea, Hem and Fringe in Pimlico and, inevitably, Carnaby Street.

Ten years before Swinging London, the picture had been different, being chromatically duller and dynamically more static, as well as socially more stratified. Imagine Elizabeth David, now returned from travels in France, rather grandly riding her stately bicycle from her home in Chelsea to Soho. Her destination is Lina Stores on Brewer Street, a long-established source of authentic Italian produce . . . in the days when olive oil was sold in the pharmacy. Traffic is thin and olive oil is scarce. We do not yet have parking meters. Mrs David, as she is properly known, is buying oil. (It was not until the seventies that her local King's Road acquired a supermarket . . . known to posh locals as the common market.)

With olive oil, lemon and garlic (and a generous measure of upper-class revolutionary zeal), Mrs David's beautifully written, immaculately researched and provocatively stated books and journalism radicalised the dull English palate and, by extension, English taste. Her colourful Provençal or Tuscan dreams were a catalyst of desire among consumers, Terence included. His precise debt to Mrs David may be found in a close comparative reading of his own recipe for *pâté de campagne* in *The Cook Book* (1980) and Mrs David's own recipe in *French Country Cooking*. Inspiration or plagiarism? Who is to say?

Terence, after Quant and Baxter, was well prepared to help people dream the dream that Mrs David described. In time, his Habitat chicken brick would take its place alongside the Jarrow March or the Parisian barricades as a symbol of democratic engagement in the struggle for a better life. If any single object reveals the triumphs and absurdities of Terence's world, here it is.

The chicken brick is a truncated oviform terracotta container, split longitudinally into more-or-less symmetrical halves. Into this you place a seasoned chicken and, say, a bulb of garlic. The thermally efficient terracotta speeds the cooking and retains delicious aromas and juices. Moreover, the chicken brick is a form of packaging in itself: an oven-to-table container that gives off, as well as richly agreeable roast chicken smells, several pleasing associations with the hearty life of the peasant and his earthy, no-nonsense ways. 'Countryfying Fulham' was how Fiona MacCarthy acidly described it.

With great good sense, chicken bricks were adopted by suburban cooks everywhere, who followed the recipes not only for chicken, but pigeons, ham and roast pork with lemon and rosemary, which were printed on the utilitarian brown-paper instructions. They were tokens of practicality and, for a generation that remembered when spaghetti came ready-cooked in tins, tokens of sophistication too. It was an honourable thing, the chicken brick, but earned for Terence an undeserved amount of mockery. To the snide and the boorish, it seemed slick and fashionable.

Mrs David was not alone: revolution was in the kitchen air, food was becoming radicalised. Others were making a connection between food and design. In their 1957 *Plats du Jour*, Patience Gray and Primose Boyd wanted to create a new sort of cookbook. It was not for speculative reading, but for action with sleeves rolled up. It too was fearless in its promotion of 'foreign' food, but the advice went beyond a reliable recipe for *boeuf bourguignon* or *cotriade* and extended into what we would nowadays call 'design'. Accordingly, *Plats du Jour* was illustrated by David Gentleman, his first major commission. Gentleman became the outstanding illustrator of the day.

Gray and Boyd even recommended actual pots and pans to their readers. Seven years before Habitat, they comment on a Danish casserole: 'This design expresses clearly, in terms of use, the abolition of the barrier between kitchen and dining-room in the open-planning of a modern house or flat.' This was because 'one cannot separate the *plat du jour* from the vessel it is cooked in'.

Nonetheless, they were keenly aware that the retail trade had not caught up with the ambitions of a new middle class that was beginning to enjoy European travel. Significantly, the 1962 Ford Cortina was named after a Dolomite ski resort, not after an ancient university town as Austin and Morris had done with the Cambridge and the Oxford. Its brochure used passport stamps as a motif, intended to suggest sophistication. The next step was to bring this Euro-sophistication indoors.

Horizons were broadening: the taste inspirations for *Plats du Jour* came from a little railway inn at Coutances in Normandy, from a *trattoria* in the Piazza della Signoria in Florence, from an oleander-swathed courtyard in Siena and from a Calabrian *albergo* with an impressive colonnade. If that sounds like a summary of the features pages of a Sunday newspaper supplement, then that is because Boyd and Gray were newspaper journalists.

Five years after *Plats du Jour*, the *Sunday Times* launched its magazine where many of these ideas were synthesised (and very brightly polished) by the brilliant Mark Boxer, husband of Arabella Boxer, soon to become a celebrity cookery writer herself. That first edition – 4 February 1962 – included Mary Quant and Alexander Plunket Greene, as well as photographer David Bailey, model Jean Shrimpton and painter Peter Blake. Terence was yet to be a national figure, but he was only thirty and the *Sunday Times Magazine* would eventually become his essential promotional tool.

As if they were conceptualising the business plan of Habitat, Boyd and Gray write: 'We know perfectly well that many people live in far from modern homes and are cooking daily with ancient but serviceable weapons.' To remedy this problem, they suggested shopping at Cadec Ltd at 27 Greek Street (just up the road from Lina Stores). Later, Terence would frequently – with the air of someone having single-handedly untangled the human genome sequence – rhapsodise about the pure flame of inspiration provided by Madame Cadec's simple, white French porcelain.

Terence would also talk about the importance of the *batterie de cuisine*, a term popularised by Boyd and Gray. This is the French cook's term for absolutely everything you need to establish a working kitchen, thus a *beau idéal* for Terence as a merchant. Indeed, though he was not a notable royalist, in the year he was knighted, Prince Charles and Lady Diana Spencer were offered a Conran-sourced *batterie de cuisine* as a wedding present. It was refused. Perhaps better domestic harmony would have been the royal result had they accepted the gift for a future Buckingham Habitat.

The class element in all of this is inescapable. Michael Rainey, for example, might have been an Australian shopkeeper, but he was married to Jane Ormsby-Gore of the political dynasty. Jeremy Scott might have been an adman, but he was ineffably posh. Michael – Dandy Kim – Caborn-Waterfield was rumoured to have illegally landed his helicopter in Hyde Park when dating Princess Margaret, resident at the time in Buckingham Palace.

On a holiday trip to Sousse in Tunisia, Shirley Conran, looking around a restaurant and considering the package tourists, said to her travelling companion Celia Brayfield: 'The working class is coming on very well, don't you think?' This sort of tone-deaf superiority was typical of Terence and was passed onto wives and family. He could present as self-effacing, but who is to say that a strategy of self-effacement is not, in fact, an efficient way to achieve ambitious goals? He thought himself *different*.

One of the stubborn clichés about the sixties is that the downtrodden working classes (that is, Michael Caine, Terence Stamp, Twiggy, David Bailey and Len Deighton) rose up, became creative, and demanded and won respect, getting rich in the process. This is obviously true, but not a wholly accurate reflection of the composition of culture. That Elizabeth David was the granddaughter of a viscount and Arabella Boxer the daughter of an earl was not at the time emphasised.

Mary Quant may have come from a Welsh mining family, but both her parents had first-class university degrees. Eventually, Terence would, after lunch, claim in his Berkshire home that he was descended from local gentry. That was probably fantasy, but he was a well-spoken public schoolboy whose fear of social demotion may have been an influence on his frenetic sixties lifestyle.

Terence's own achievement has a basis in this awareness of social class: he was to make liberal, educated, middle-class taste available to the first Robbins Report university graduates who, perforce, had to buy their own furniture for student digs or starter homes.

Another market was the ever more un-closeted gay community. It was said that the King's Road Habitat benefited especially from the high gay count in the Chelsea milieu. Gay men, in the highly objectified theory of the day, being both house-proud and design-conscious, as well as notably promiscuous and in volatile partnerships, thus stimulated demand for household goods because of a high turnover of property and the consequential need to refurnish on a regular basis.

Be that as it may, an entire generation benefited from a new awareness of design, but the leaders of the popular revolt were an exclusive bunch, not a newly unchained proletariat. Terence was in this exclusive bunch. It wasn't democracy, it was a club. As Jonathan Aitken explained in *The Young Meteors* (1967): 'Swinging

London consisted of a few hundred exhibitionists with a flair for self-promotion.'

Perhaps none became as successful as Terence. He had already been busy making impressions and self-promoting. No one had ever said: 'Terence Conran? What a bore.' or: 'I don't have an opinion about Terence Conran.'

The young student Min Hogg, who later cruised majestically through the world of interiors as an influential magazine editor and expert conversationalist, described her first encounter with Terence, when he was teaching on Hugh Casson's interiors course at the Royal College of Art, as the experience of 'an incredible man' who was 'quite fun'. However, a few weeks later she wrote 'had a beastly evening with Terence Conran'. Min Hogg discovered that Terence was often able to excite completely contradictory responses in the same person at the same time.

4

A Better Salad Bowl

S.B.

Imagine London in 1964. Or even just a few years before. In 1959 Colin MacInnes published his novel *Absolute Beginners*. It is a first-person account of a young photographer trying to make his mark in the aftermath of the Notting Hill race riots.

MacInnes is rightly acclaimed for his historical identification of that new phenomenon: the teenager. Here we find ambition, design, restlessness, an energetic need to reverse the status quo. Strangely, I never heard Terence mention MacInnes. He was no longer a teenager when the book was published, but maintained a lot of the abrasive ambition of this new tribe.

In London during the early sixties, the only store selling modern furniture was Woollands on Knightsbridge. Everything else was sad and brown. Set up by brothers from Devon, Woollands had success-fully promoted itself, at least socially, from a proletarian below-stairs drapers to a coruscating department store: duchesses and royal mistresses were, it was said, amongst its customers.

But another clientele was identified by its managing director, the urbane Martin Moss, a retailer with a finger on the pulse of the spirit of the age, later claimed by the *New York Times* as the man who made Knightsbridge fashionable. Moss's wife was the *Observer* photographer Jane Bown: the media are ever present in the story of design in London.

In Woollands, Moss opened both an attention-getting furniture floor and a kitchenware department, as well as a 'boutique' called the 21 Shop which, with its midnight parties and catwalk fashion shows, and assistants with Vidal Sassoon bobs, became a sensation.

On the furniture floor you would find Terence Conran's furniture, not arranged in dreary martial ranks, but in credible and attractive room sets. And it was Terence who designed the 21 Shop installation. In more senses than one, the origin of Habitat was in Knightsbridge.

Here Terence plotted the defeat of sadness and brownness. Woollands was the exception to the rule that sallow-faced buyers in bad suits were not interested in Terence's modern furniture. A range of, at the time revolutionary, CKD (completely knocked-down, or self-assembly) furniture called 'Summa', which Terence had designed himself, appeared in 1962 and Woollands stocked it.

Eventually, Woollands itself would be defeated; following Terence and others, the urban dynamic shifted from Knightsbridge to neighbouring Chelsea. In 1969, Woollands' owners Debenhams closed the store and demolished the building. The dire Richard Seifert-designed Park Tower Hotel now stands on the site, a dour reminder of the other spirit of the age.

As Napoleon explained when asked what he thought about circumstances, Terence made circumstances. While the 21 Shop flourished, there was a Conran factory in Thetford, Norfolk, built under a GLC incentive scheme. An outlet was needed for its production and a larger stage was required for Terence's vision. Thus, Habitat.

The opening of the first Habitat at the junction of the Fulham Road and Sloane Avenue brought together all the different parts of Terence's life, artistic, business and social; although with Terence, conventional distinctions in these areas are not always observed. Many tributaries of sixties culture came together as well into one cheerful, spotlit, colourful stream flowing through tongue-and-groove and white-painted brick and quarry tile.

Key staff had joined from Woollands and their training included dinner in Terence's flat where he demonstrated, for example, a *mouli* to boggle-eyed and blinking watchers. One of them touchingly said: 'There we saw a lifestyle we'd never experienced.' This was the Terence Effect: almost Messianic, he soon attracted loyal followers. Woollands had never had music. But in Habitat they played the Beatles on the in-store sound system. Because 'Terence in-SIST-ed' according to Kate Currie, the first Habitat manager.

Later, if a Dieter Rams record player – the perfect expression of Germany's white-box *Gute Form* – had needed to be shown anywhere, it was here . . . next to a red enamel Polish coffee pot, butchers' aprons, butchers' blocks, china, rugs, a Conran-designed Chesterfield, a Mogensen sofa, a Magistretti chair. At the time, no museum had such a daring display of design.

This was Habitat. It was to become not only a showcase for Terence's existing furniture designs, but also a showcase for an eclectic range of products which he admired: the kitchenware of Paris's Dehillerin, for example. Caroline Conran was the kitchenware buyer. Habitat presented itself a little more like a didactic exhibition than a mere shop.

Searching for synonyms of 'home', Pagan Gregory, an ex-model and married to Oliver, Terence's closest collaborator, had chosen the name 'Habitat' from *Roget's Thesaurus*. Although not a great reader and never one for highfalutin' literary references, a singular element of Terence's genius is his synoptic flair for names. While the Soup Kitchen perfectly caught the idea of vernacular chic and a surprise offer, Habitat had clarity, precision and, best of all, seemed modern. The successful name is an important element in the successful story.

Certainly, Habitat brought a very middle-class educated eye to the grubby and constipated world of British retail. Hitherto, the 'once-in-a-lifetime grand slam' of domesticity had, according to the novelist Angela Carter, been marriage, a good set of china and a serviceable three-piece suite. But Habitat was directed at what its first press release described as 'young moderns with lively tastes'. These were people who lived with their furniture, not in spite of it.

And the moment was good: a generation of first-time buyers emerging from the new glass-and-concrete universities provided a ready market. Yes, these were people who bought their own furniture, but when they did so it was informed by a sense of style, even of lifestyle, as well as for something to sit upon.

At first, Terence wanted to be in the background so as not to alert the important contract clients that his concentration was being distracted. But soon he was able to overcome such uncharacteristic diffidence and it became apparent that Habitat was all about him. Pagan Gregory described it as a hard fall from a galloping horse.

An already well-exercised flair for self-promotion was now ready to take impressive form: with a characteristic mixture of dash and optimism, invigorated by amazing drive applied indiscriminately to both himself and others.

By every account, by every single breathless account, Habitat was a sensation. As much a sensation, perhaps, as the first sighting of a mini-skirt. The sun shone in. The interior design and its spotlights put the merchandise on display, as if it were in an art exhibition or a memory of the Festival of Britain. The wholly designed environment dignified mere dry goods: ordinary stuff was given celebrity treatment. But it was a celebrity product available for those young modern Londoners to buy and enjoy. Hard to appreciate now, but there was a moment when a modern sofa and a Paris goblet seemed like an entry ticket to a world of optimism and promise that had been alien to drab Britain.

Habitat was a place of wonder: modern furniture that was once only seen in the glossy international architectural magazines which both taunted and titillated educated British consumers, now was available at home. The film director Stanley Kubrick was a well-publicised Habitat customer. Novelists Kingsley Amis and Elizabeth Jane Howard were seen dallying in the basement.

Despite its enthusiastic reception, Habitat always had difficulty making money: its first year net profit was less than £2,000, a modest sum even in the sixties, but Terence has always known the benefits of good accountants and vivid PR, so uncomfortable truths – commercial or conceptual – might be beneficially disguised. So Habitat expanded.

From countrifying cottages in Fulham, the campaign to make the provinces more cosmopolitan began. The progress of Habitat across the nation reads like a Messianic programme of provincial enlightenment and awakening. Manchester 1967, Burnley 1968, Brighton 1969, Bristol 1971, Liverpool 1973. Then on to larger horizons: Paris 1973, New York 1977 (where the store had to be called Conran's as 'Habitat' was already trademarked). There was a Habitat in Bromley by 1968, perhaps an unlikely centre of modernist enterprise, but it was here that Bernie Ecclestone had built a spotlit white box of a car showroom and sold MGBs to Sandie Shaw and Lulu.

By 1975, Habitat had become so established in the national imagination that Malcolm Bradbury used its products as satirical weapons in his knockabout novel of university campus life, *The History Man*. Here the Kirk family practises 'conspicuous thrift', deploying the kind of furniture that 'inflated, or folded-up, or fitted into this or that'. The expression 'conspicuous thrift' is Bradbury's knowing take on Thorstein Veblen's 1899 coinage 'conspicuous consumption'. The sociologist Veblen had meant to suggest that, at a certain stage in society's development, goods were acquired not for utility, but to project status. Yes, indeed.

Habitat became a media spectacular through both merit and plotting. The term did not exist at the time, but Terence was a print-media *influencer* of original genius.

In 1961, when twenty-nine, he had married his third wife, Caroline Herbert, a journalist seven years younger. Three years later Caroline was writing the first Habitat catalogue, a charming conceit printed on brown wrapping paper with New York-influenced graphics and charming illustrations by Juliet Glynn-Smith, suggestive of a relaxed sophistication.

This alone was evidence of a new approach to the idea of shopping. It was no longer a chore, it was entertainment. It was sociable. But Caroline was more than a simple copywriter, she was an authentic joint source of the Habitat idea; she was an investor, not a staff member, an uncomfortable truth that Terence was reluctant to acknowledge. Even later on in court.

It was all collective endeavour on a broad front. Never mind the distinctions between kitchen and dining room alluded to by Boyd and Gray, in Habitat the distinctions between shopping and education, commerce and culture, business and entertainment were being ever so slightly eroded. This was the essence of Habitat: at once elitist and democratic, stylish and opportunistic. Idealistic, but good sense too. 'Yes, I can identify excellence,' Terence seemed to be saying. 'And you can share my taste if you buy from my shop.' You can join my tribe. Or perhaps my cult. You can buy 'design'.

Visitors to early Habitats, including the always very perceptive Fiona MacCarthy, explained that while individual items of merchandise were often unremarkable, the store as a whole was able to generate a sort of frenzy among its customers with made the ordinary covetable. Frothing like revivalists as they clutched a thirteen-shilling pepper mill or contemplated the mysteries of a *mouli*, people were overwhelmed by Terence's mystique.

Like many creation narratives it is not always possible, or even appropriate, to separate fact from fiction in the Habitat story. Terence says he made furniture deliveries on a scooter, but this seems implausible. Scooters are poorly balanced in any event, but dangerously so when carrying a sofa. There was the thesaurus story. If Pagan Gregory actually made the choice from Roget, Terence never bothered to mention it. The logo, in the English classic Baskerville font, was by Dudley

Bootes-Johns and presented in lower case. Characteristically, it looked both modern and somewhat traditional.

With a mixture of art and artisan shopfitting, Oliver Gregory had created the original Habitat interior for £6,000. Indeed, the inspiration for Habitat had come from territory beyond Terence, which he had been clever enough to scope with his beady monocular vision: he had admired a store called Design Research which had opened on Brattle Street in Boston in 1953.

The proprietor here was Harvard-trained architect Benjamin Thompson: to imagine a Design Research store, think of scrubbed brick and Marcel Breuer chairs. Later, Thompson's eighties redevelopment of South Street Seaport in New York and Quincy Market in Boston would inspire Terence's Butler's Wharf development. Terence has always been a brilliant aggregator of other people's ideas.

There had even been local precedents. In October 1963, Sir Charles Chadwyck-Healey, baronet, had opened a store called Abacus in Great Dunmow, Essex, with his business partner, the photographer, John Hedgecoe. Another store opened in Chelmsford in autumn the following year. Abacus sold furniture that Terence had designed so was not a hostile competitor, but when Sir Charles visited Habitat, he conceded defeat. He told *The Times*: 'I realised the sheer scale of Conran's vision and his professionalism ... [Terence] had a unique capacity to absorb everything around him and recreate it in his own original vision.' Abacus soon went out of business.

The consumers' experience of Habitat was influenced by Terence's knowledge of and fascination with exhibitions. Working at the Festival of Britain had taught him how powerful a medium an exhibition can be. It is a summary of the designer's art, a mixture of architecture and graphics. The convictions of 1951 had been enhanced when he had been commissioned to create travelling exhibitions for the Design Council. Additionally, despite a distaste for 'trade shows', the Conran Design Group worked on motor-show stands for Ford. Here, Terence learnt to display products with respect and even affection. He learnt also to present information with economy and clarity.

Further influences on the Habitat experience were derived from that time spent in the fifties at photoshoots for Robert Harling's *House & Garden*. Here Terence had seen how photographers lit their subjects and how photoshoot stylists assembled meaningful objects in meaningful ways. Like (Sir) Jack Cohen's Tesco, which opened its first supermarket in Essex in 1956, Terence learnt how to pile it high, if not sell it specially cheap. Stacking merchandise in impressive piles had, according to Terence, 'that irresistible feeling of plenty you find on market stalls'. What Tesco had done with detergent, Terence now did, for example, with Habitat's Polish glass and enamel.

But if the feeling was of a French *quincaillerie*, the influences on the character of Habitat were Italian. Terence had admired the Milan Triennales, design exhibitions created by Gio Ponti, the great architect who had also founded the magazine *Domus*. On the stands at a Milan Triennale or on the pages of *Domus*, Terence would have seen, for example, the work of Franco Albini, whose interiors were boldly austere. Albini would, for example, display a baroque painting out of its frame and attached to a simple grey wall. In a similar way, Habitat made the products a celebrity. As you would find in an exhibition or a gallery, special attention was paid to the lighting.

But savour again for a while Habitat's 1964 moment. Robert Brownjohn's titles for *Goldfinger* astonished with their style and sexiness. The Dangerous Drugs Act was drafted in response to wide-spread misbehaviour. Ken Kesey's Merry Pranksters took their school bus around the USA. In London, 1964 was also the year of the quin-tessentially sixties Dennison Hall 'Happenings' of which Jean-Jacques Lebel said: 'The barrier between artist and audience is destroyed.' A lot of barriers were being destroyed at the time. In Terence's case, between shopping and entertainment. When a Habitat pepper mill selling for thirteen shillings found its way onto the pages of a *Queen* fashion shoot, it seemed like an epiphany. That never happened with Grandma's cruet.

Others caught the mood of what Lebel called an 'ecstatic community'. Eric Clapton shared a house with the Australian pop artist and album sleeve designer Martin Sharp in the King's Road's Pheasantry. This building now houses a Pizza Express, a restaurant chain founded in 1965. BIBA opened in Kensington, while Ossie Clarke and Alice Pollock launched Quorum, a shop backed by impresario Michael White.

The Israeli architect Zev Aram began selling classic modern furniture by Le Corbusier, Breuer and Castiglioni from his own shop on the King's Road. Miss Selfridge opened in 1966 and Harrods' Way In appeared in 1967. The Chelsea Drugstore opened the following year. There was much swirling, as well as swinging, especially in London SW.

Habitat might have been a perfect expression of the mood of 1964, but the remarkable thing about Terence was that he did not, like so many contemporaries, get stuck in the sixties. Instead, he restlessly continued to influence national taste for another half-century. Terence was soon driving an E-Type into the future.

PART 2

THE COAST OF BOHEMIA

5

West Central Bohemia

S.B.

Less than a mile from London's frenetic Oxford Circus, Covent Garden was no one's idea of a true bohemian wasteland, but circa 1970 it was an area on the cusp: in an unsteady state between decay and revival.

The decay was all too obvious, but very few people had a vision of how a revival might actually take place. Thus, the circumstances were ideal for an intervention by Terence. Property was cheap, so there were good deals to be done. And, equally, the general crappiness of the area was a fabulous setting for making a decisive statement about progress. Or, more particularly, of 'progress by design'.

Neal Street in Covent Garden was for many years the spiritual home of Terence and his design religion: the best expression of his energy and style. It was here, long before Covent Garden began a revival that has now led to catastrophic popularity and the worst expressions of urban tourism, with artless buskers and generic shops and clueless conga-lines of bewildered visitors, that Terence established a remarkable restaurant and the headquarters of his design consultancy, now called Conran Associates.

Very cleverly, and typically, he had found a frontier, a border, a twilight zone, a changing room. Covent Garden was poised just between its old identity as London's gor-blimey fruit and vegetable market and its new identity as the place to be. All the scents and associations were appropriate: interesting fungus and bright, fresh fruit. Opportunity was not so much in the air as the entire environment. It was in Neal Street in 1971 that Terence opened his very finest restaurant. Its purpose was partly to impress clients, but mostly to provide pleasure for the partners.

These partners were Kasmin and Oliver Gregory. The former, London's most successful modern art dealer of the sixties. The latter, Terence's most trusted fixer, whose own particular design vision contributed almost as much to the public perception of Habitat as Terence's. I have never had the opportunity to do this, but if Terence had been manacled to a white tiled wall, bright lights shone in his eyes and a truth serum administered, his answer to the question: 'Who has helped you most?' would probably have been: 'Oliver Gregory'.

In the early years, up to the flotation of Habitat, Oliver Gregory was one of Terence's very closest collaborators, his man of business, his *consigliere*, as they say in the Mafia. Oliver knew, among many other impressive arcana, about 'Jewish lightning', those mysterious conflagrations which occur in buildings whose development is stalled by planning constraints. A destructive fire, Oliver explained, could put an end to business frustrations.

His extraordinary character and way of life are deeply revealing of the personalities to whom Terence was drawn and upon whom he depended so heavily, if acknowledged so lightly. Oliver lived a rambunctious life and once was tempted to push Terence over the edge of the Tour Saint-Jacques in Paris because he was so annoying.

He was both very similar to, and very different from, Terence. Oliver was a tough artisan from a working-class background with calloused hands and robust appetites. He spoke with a class-less accent, but a slight lisp. He was an argumentative autodidact and prankster, a shamelessly mischievous raconteur, and his friends loved him for it.

Everything with Oliver was achieved from first principles. He knew about the craft of making things and understood the nature of materials. His boyhood home was a council house in Leicester. While not especially amenable to discipline, he spent National Service as an RAF policeman. Here, like Rodney Fitch, thriller writer Len Deighton and artist Joe Tilson, he discovered a world very distant from the mediocrity of the English suburbs. He studied cabinetmaking, went to Australia, joined an architectural practice and learnt an elegant simplicity in design because raw materials were so rare.

Back in England, he settled in Richmond and joined a small firm of architects. He was in the circle of the architect James Stirling. In the office, a girl said she knew someone who made furniture: 'He's just like you – interesting and difficult.' This was 1960 and that someone was, of course, Terence. Their liaison now began.

It was in this haut-bohemian environment that the Habitat idea was born. Terence's eye for detail, missionary zeal and commercial sense were a perfect stimulus to, and foil for, Oliver's practical approach. Show Oliver Gregory a depressing, abandoned building and he would come up with real-world ideas about how to convert it. He would and could and did, on occasion, pick up the tools and do it himself.

It was in a house Kasmin rented in France, the Château de Carennac, where detailed planning of the Neal Street Restaurant had begun. In 1969 Kas was sleeping on publisher Tom Maschler's sofa after the break-up of his marriage. It was at this point that he met Terence at a dinner given by Philip Pollock, the foam-rubber entrepreneur now reconciled with Terence after their dispute. Pollock's Aerofoam had been a supplier to Terence's furniture business, and he had been the chief backer, perhaps in some eyes even a founder, of Habitat. His wife, Venetia, had a popular Primrose Hill bookshop of the day.

The then bibulous Kas, now a teetotaller, spilt his drink over Terence and wrapped him in loo roll as a remedy. Thus drink made them friends. Kas explained that his relationship with Terence was always vexed, although enduring. Terence, meaning to be funny, had told Michael Likierman, a Habitat director: 'I want a clever Jew in the business.' And this he was fond of repeating. For his part, Kas, being Jewish as well, said: 'I have a lot of friends who are grumpy and difficult,' and felt he did not need any more, but soon added Terence and Caroline to his circle because of shared passions for wine, food and France, and because he found Terence's enthusiasm attractive. Indeed, he found him an 'extremely engaging person'.

'What we had in common,' Kas explained, 'was cooking and idolising Elizabeth David,' not least because she smoked while at work in the kitchen. Their French sojourns must have been idyllic. Kas did the shopping and at this point may have known more about French food than Terence. It was Kas who introduced Terence to Lameloise, the famous restaurant in Chagny. Indeed, Burgundy was a shared fetish: through his Lameloise connections, Kas got to know and bought from the great *vignerons* and once a year would have a fine-wine sale in his gallery. In Terence's culture, food and art are a part of the same whole.

Kas and Caroline cooked competitively, fusing ideas from Mrs David with recipes from the Maison Arabe in Marrakech. Once, Kas and Caroline caught turkey-cocks and slit their throats, intending to show their respective children the reality of real food. One day in a café, over a less bloody meal of an *omelette aux truffes*, they decided to open a restaurant. Terence offered the space below the Neal Street offices. They agreed a deal over many bottles of Alsace. Kas would have 10 per cent, Oliver Gregory the same. Terence put up the capital and had the remainder of the shares.

Kas supplied the gorgeous art, mostly prints, and Oliver committed himself to be serious about running a restaurant. Charles Campbell, a family friend, was the first manager and Kas mischievously poached the cook from Mayfair's Clermont Club to work in the Neal Street kitchen.

As a restaurant design, Neal Street was remarkable and unique. When Terence found the property there was already a new façade by Max Clendinning (designer of the slot-together Maxima chair of 1965, a classic of sixties *modernismo*). Oliver Gregory and Keith Hobbs then created an interior. A long narrow space of raw brick was painted cream and brightly lit. The floor was cream tiles. It was a world away from the crepuscular norm of classic French or ethnic restaurants with guttering candles or unhygienic flock. There were 'Bauhaus' chairs and art on loan from Kasmin's collection. Kas's art was always an inspiration to Terence. He once sent a designer to Kas's gallery to look at a Kenneth Noland painting. And, ultimately, to reproduce it. The idea here was not to create a cynical copy, but to benefit from inspiration.

Be that as it may, there were mischievous rumours that Kas lent original art on approval to the restaurant, which Terence then copied, retaining the original and returning the reproductions. Indeed, Terence's inclusive vision legitimised this inspired form of piracy. His attitude to the furniture was exactly the same. Marcel Breuer's 'Bauhaus' chairs were so good, the idea had to be passed on through unlicensed reproductions sold in Habitat. The Breuer estate received no royalties. Meanwhile, Neal Street's zinc counters had bold bull-nose edges and there was a neat little bar in the basement. David Hockney illustrated the menu and, rather later, Gennaro Contaldo and Jamie Oliver cooked here. Its royal-blue façade was a modern landmark helping define the personality of a Covent Garden emerging from fruit market to bohemian chic and then, less happily, into its descent into cynical tourist trap.

The mood was extremely confident, relaxed and comfortingly expensive: London had never had so smart a restaurant that paid no attention to lazy clubland traditions or half-understood European cliché. Even at its great moment of pomp, the River Café could not compare for glamour with the Neal Street Restaurant. Eventually,

Antonio Carluccio became its last manager, using it as a launch pad for his own stellar career as cuddly avuncular Italian telly chef. It became a popular media haunt and tabloid names walked in and ordered lunch every day. As Terence's interests drifted elsewhere, Carluccio was ever more able to impose his own personality on Neal Street.

The connections are again revealing of Terence's culture. Carluccio had arrived in London from Italy via Germany, and had become known in the restaurant trade as a wine importer. One day Terence showed me snaps of a family holiday in, perhaps it was Sardinia, and said, 'My sister Priscilla brought along this exceedingly good Italian cook.' That was Antonio. In rapid order Carluccio won the *Sunday Times* Amateur Cook competition in 1981 and married Priscilla, extending the reach and range of the Conran dynasty. Somewhat regretfully, Carluccio, a man in possession of a deliciously plump ego all his own, explained that he had hoped to add a little sun-dried, extra-virgin 'humanity' to the Conran family. The Neal Street Restaurant closed in 2007. If English Heritage had any sense, which it did not, the Neal Street Restaurant would have been listed as an exquisite monument to London style in the seventies.

The design consultancy's offices were in the warren of rooms above the restaurant. It was here that I first met Terence in 1977, whom I found slouched and weary in gardening cords on soft furnishing, having just driven up from Berkshire. And it was here that I was installed in a bunker in the basement in 1980, sitting at my electric typewriter and planning what became perhaps the biggest part of Terence's legacy.

The mood was exciting, especially for someone whose norm was a provincial university with a local-authority sense of style and the architectural character of a communist asylum. In Neal Street there were fresh flowers, real soap and fluffy white towels in the loos. The air was scented with money. Well-dressed, important-looking people came and went. The lighting was good.

There were smartly turned-out pretty girls (allowable at that time) and, long before decent coffee was available absolutely everywhere (as late as 1981 the only place you could get a decent *cappuccino* in all of Covent Garden was at Ponti's in the Piazza), Terence mandated that truly excellent coffee from the Algerian Coffee Store on Old Compton Street should be served amply and free from classic, battered and patinated Neapolitan canisters. This was the job of a dear old thing called Gladys. Except there was a condition, typical of Terence: the coffee was ample and free only before nine o'clock in the morning, at which point the kitchen was closed. It would open again very briefly at eleven.

People felt motivated. There was a real *esprit de corps* and a population of bright young designers felt engaged on a mission. The internal weather changed in Neal Street depending on Terence's own presence, but his spirit was always felt even as he came and went on important journeys.

Here I saw wonderful, ineradicable things: Doreen, the office manageress, a delightful woman with few affectations, being manhandled, squealing, down the stairs by Terence who was hissing: 'Gypsophila is fine. Daffodils are lovely. But not in the same fucking vase!' In its mixture of manic attention to detail, a keen sense of style, snobbery, humour and cruelty, this seemed a perfect miniature of the man's personality.

At this time, there was perhaps no such thing as a typical working day for Terence. However, he always made 'work', or, at least, the appearance of it, a sort of sacrament. Monday mornings he would be driven in from the country to Neal Street by Reg, his faithful chauffeur and general fixer, an amiable cove who played in a jazz band and was once blown off his moped (which Terence had provided) by a passing truck on the Medway Bridge.

Terence's arrival was always noticed. Up the stairs he would huff and puff in a David Chambers suit and carrying a boxy pigskin briefcase. On reaching his office, there would be strong coffee and perhaps the first cigar of the day. He would scrutinise, head low to the table like an old biblical scholar, the press cuttings still, in those days, clipped from the newspapers. The quality and quantity of these would affect the tone of the day.

If he was planning a foreign trip, a personal assistant would sometimes have bought new underwear and new shirts from Turnbull & Asser, and arranged them in a display for his consideration, a little bit like The Judgement of Paris, but more fundamental.

At some point in the morning, Terence turned to correspondence both formal and informal, the latter including his explosive messages on used envelopes in autograph blue Pentel, which he used to abuse and to motivate staff. Senior people would come and go, discussing new projects. There would be lunch in the Neal Street Restaurant, never a frugal affair. Clients would arrive. Before clamping, on-road parking was commonplace and the presence of a large car outside Neal Street was a general alert that important business was being done, upstairs and behind closed doors.

Often in the afternoons, Terence would disappear. Many were the visits he made to Habitat stores where the cleverer managers soon learnt to include a deliberate mistake in advance of his arrival, a cigarette end on a tiled floor, for example, to draw Terence's watchful and angry beam away from more serious flaws.

He would return, unpredictably, late afternoon or early evening. This patron saint of domesticity never showed any very marked inclination to go home. He lingered in Neal Street after hours: there were often drinks in the office. Here, amazing decisions were made. I called by Terence's office once and got involved in a discussion about what to call a new chain of clothing stores. That was Next. And dinner was often out somewhere because, in the early eighties, there were always more deals to be done.

Terence would often arrive late to keep the staff on edge. He would disappear and reappear. Things changed according to his presence.

Terence met his second wife Shirley (Pearce) on Chelsea's King's Road. When she became superwoman in 1975, Shirley became too busy to stuff a mushroom and almost certainly too feminist to assist with a bow-tie, as she did at their 1955 wedding. *(Thurston Hopkins/Stringer/ Getty Images)*

Caroline (Herbert) became the third Mrs Conran in 1963 and the first Lady Conran twenty years later. She was a substantial investor in Habitat as well as its influential kitchenware buyer. With her translations of Guérard and Troisgros, Caroline introduced the British to *nouvelle cuisine*, helpfully reinforcing a Conran connection to good food. At their 1996 divorce hearing, Terence told the judge she had merely supplied some 'domestic help'. *(Stuart Ramson/Daily Mail/ Shutterstock)*

In 2000, Terence married Vicki (Davis), a divorced mother of three. *(Richard Young Shutterstock)*

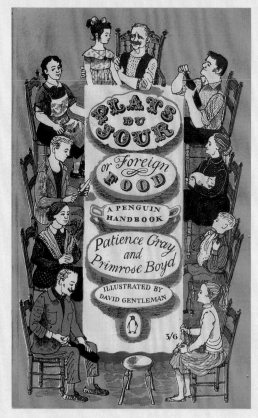

Patience Gray and Primrose Boyd's *Plats du Jour*, with distinctive illustrations by David Gentleman, was published in 1957. It was a guide not just to French recipes, but to French kitchenware ... and to cosmopolitanism in general. The introduction reads like a manifesto for Terence's Habitat.
(Peters Fraser & Dunlop)

French Provincial Cooking.
(Anthony Denney)

John Minton's illustrations and Anthony Denney's photographs for Elizabeth David's serial classic cookbooks – with their rustic pots and pans – were Habitat *avant le mot*. *(The Stapleton Collection /Bridgeman Images)*

With a grandeur that was both charitable and condescending, Terence would declare that semi-detached houses were 'sad'. Pebble-dashed suburbia was the target for his uncompromising taste. *(Allan Cash Picture Library/Alamy Stock Photo)*

Without irony, his friend the art dealer John Kasmin said, 'Terence's problem is he wants the whole world to have a better salad bowl'. *(Design Museum)*

habitat

1977/78 CATALOGUE 50p

TWENTY-SEVEN STORES AND BY POST

The Habitat catalogue became more than a simple sales tool. It presented an entire domestic philosophy. Customers cheerfully left their catalogues on display – possibly on 'coffee tables' – to demonstrate their smart credentials. And here you can see Terence's famous duvets which, he said, enhanced everyone's sex life during the seventies. *(Author collection)*

Terence had an oneiric vision of France. It was eccentric graphics, a rural Hôtel de Champagne and a couple either contemplating or recovering from lunch or the love-making of the *cinq-à-sept*. *(Author collection)*

The reality, of a stately Citroën DS, the 'Goddess', weaving through a dreary brick town in the Pas-de-Calais, he ignored . . . or chose not to observe. *(Author collection)*

Le Grand Véfour was opened in Paris's Palais-Royal in 1784. It was a favourite of Terence's, even if *de luxe haute cuisine* and plush *art décoratif* seem at odds with his mantra of 'plain, simple, useful'. *(Hemis/Alamy Stock Photo)*

The illustrator Georges Goursat, known to all as Sem, was also a favourite of Terence's. His singular vision of Parisian life was populated by the cultural heroes of the day at lunch: Chanel, D'Annunzio, Blériot and Massenet. Here was a bar for Terence to leap. *(Archivart/Alamy Photo Library)*

The enduring tin snail that was the Citroën *deux chevaux* proved Terence's maxim that functional things can be charming too. *(Author collection)*

Although early publicity photographs show Habitat as a team effort, Terence was never reluctant to place himself front and centre when journalists were present. Caroline Conran is on the left. On the right is Philip Pollock, an early investor who soon fell out with Terence.
(*Photograph by Terence Donovan, Camera Press London.*)

And his moods were unpredictable. I stayed late in any case because, this being the centre of the world, there were not many other places I wanted to be. Sometimes Terence could be found scroffling around in the restaurant's pig bin, looking for broken china and hoping to find someone to blame.

One evening he came down to see me and asked what I was writing. I showed him something for the *Sunday Times* and he soon became angry, saying I had no business to be writing such things (although I forget what they actually were). I said something like: 'Oh, for God's sake, Terence, leave me alone. I know what I'm doing.' He insisted, so eventually, in a melodramatic gesture, I ripped the sheet of paper out of the machine and threw it away. Smugly and promptly, Terence then said: 'Why do I employ you if you don't know your own mind?'

That was a very good question, but like many others, I was often too busy trying to inhabit Terence's mind to have quite enough time to explore my own.

6

An Englishman's Home Is His Habitat

S.B.

The year before the Neal Street Restaurant opened, Terence had bought Barton Court, a fine eighteenth-century house in lush and generous grounds in West Berkshire, hitherto a school.

Barton Court lies an hour or so west from London on the M4. I have turned off the old Bath Road many, many times with a mixture of cheerful anticipation and morbid dread. Cheerful anticipation because there will be very good food and wine and, eventually, a comfortable bed. And an inevitable hangover to follow. Besides, I liked Terence very much. Morbid dread because there would sometimes also be painful *longueurs* in the conversation, or black moods and a brittle sense that all is not quite right in the magic kingdom. Always, you were made to feel you had underperformed.

Anyway, you turn left down a narrow road and then right into Barton Court's approach road, an event signalled by a once-immaculate sign, blue on white, nowadays a little careworn and faded, in upper- and lower-case Helvetica Neue Light. The handsome red-brick house stands in what must once have been water meadows. There always were and still are fine cars outside. A Porsche or an Aston Martin, for example. And, on my own first visit, my flashy and plebeian Ford Capri.

It was Kas who had told Terence it was his duty to buy a large house, the better to entertain all the friends he expected would visit. Neal

Street and Barton Court were perfectly complementary – indeed, their interiors had much in common – but only the latter remains. On my very first weekend visit I had cautiously and naively taken a dinner jacket, being uncertain what might be expected, socially speaking. Instead, all was informality. One thing I soon learnt: visitors always entered Barton Court through the kitchen.

If ever you wanted an architectural metaphor to describe Terence's maddening contradictions, here it was: a magnificent and grand house making all-too-obvious claims to the status and privilege of great wealth, but visitors were required to acknowledge democratic principles by using the tradesmen's entrance. This was 'below stairs' valorised for the modern liberal. The kitchen, whose table came from Kas's home in Quercy, soon revealed itself to be the most comfortable room in the house.

It is a vast space and at some point becomes a sitting room with a wood fire. Huge Georgian sash windows look out over the lush greenery. The floors are wood and the bull-nosed shelves, reminiscent of the Neal Street Restaurant, were crowded with artful clutter. I have since learnt that Terence would put on an apron in anticipation of guests arriving so as to give a pleasingly democratic and liberated impression of the toiling artisan cook, now exposed as something of a fiction.

Still, food and wine were the main events here. You almost always ate in the kitchen; there is a small room off it which was sometimes the arena for lunch and dinner, although not in later life when less mobile Terence commandeered it for a study. A maid and – if Terence were not a status-conscious socialist – a man who would normally be described as a butler, were active in the scullery-pantry area.

Entering by that kitchen door, in daylight you rarely got beyond this vast room, with a range and copper pots at one end, a huge refectory table in the middle and a lounging area, agreeably littered with newspapers, with a fireplace at the other. That is unless, as often bidden, you visited the vegetable garden or potting sheds. These were capacious. Here you learned about the sparmania and Japanese artichokes, which Terence gleefully explained as the cause of preposterous flatulence.

The house's corridors, somewhat chilly, led to a vast drawing room, but before arrival there you passed Terence's huge collection of quarter-size model Bugatti T35s all, naturally, in French Racing Blue, arranged on the wall, the better to be perceived as sculpture, perhaps as Ettore Bugatti himself intended. Merchandise and art have not always been distinguished in either Terence's shops, homes or museums.

From these corridors the institutional ghosts of the past have not been entirely eradicated. Nor is the actual drawing room a place of great warmth, despite its over-stuffed sofas and eclectic range of conversation pieces. Somehow, while beautiful, it feels dead. The beat of the house's heart was in the kitchen.

On the staircase, lush dusty-blue carpet was worn to threadbare on some of the treads. There is one significant guest bedroom, as big as a tennis court. You find a white bedspread, Moghul prints and a view through the windows of the embracing greenness, sculptor Nick Munro's red plastic deer standing knee high in the tall grass, blocking the vista to the river and the canal. Outside was once the scene of generously catered staff cricket matches.

Barton Court was, at least in theory, an ideal family home. With his architect first wife, Brenda, Terence had lived, childlessly and very briefly, in a flat so apparently unremarkable that he has never bothered to describe it to anyone, still less have it photographed.

With his second wife, Shirley, home had been Regent's Park Terrace: a handsome and comfortable house that camouflaged an uncomfortable way of life. Sebastian and Jasper, Shirley's children, were brought up here.

Caroline Conran presided in the Baron Court kitchen for nearly thirty years, and she and Terence were often photographed together over the vast range with copper pans hanging from above. The images look almost heraldic. Wives necessarily influence husbands, but Caroline's influence on Terence was exceptional. She knew France and spoke French. Terence did not.

This grand house became the home of their three children, Tom, Sophie and Ned. It was the theatre of the family business. Actually, it was the theatre of business.

Indeed, she translated and promoted the first generation of *nouvelle cuisine* chefs, including Michel Guérard and the Troisgros brothers. Terence continued to visit Guérard's restaurant at Eugénie-les-Bains, but never, I believe, personally poached an oyster.

In this way her food connections enhanced Terence's credibility at life's great table. Not at all one for her own self-promotion, Caroline's media connections were impeccable and had been useful to Terence. As she was Home Editor of *House & Garden*, they shared a common culture. So enchanted was Jocelyn Stevens that he named the first pirate radio station 'Radio Caroline'.

At some point in the image-obsessed eighties, I wrote a Sunday newspaper article about Bulgarian wine. This was predicted to become modish by someone, as they say, with knowledge of the situation. It was filthy, but I protected the identity of my sources by writing that the only rationale for its sale was that the 'distinguished widow' who brought us the stuff was having an affair with the Bulgarian truck driver who was delivering it. She was outraged in response to my mischievousness and was not afraid to say so.

I was telling the ludicrous story to Terence and Caroline over lunch at Barton Court, emphasising my own bewilderment at such a reaction, when Terence got himself into a familiar position. Head down, shoulders up, leaning forward. He said, probably wagging a finger: 'My dear Stephen, can you not understand that no one would wish to be described as a "distinguished widow"?' Caroline immediately said: 'I would!' Theatre, indeed.

Divorce is rarely very pretty, but Terence's third was specially ugly.

It was ironic that an individual who placed so much emphasis on ease and delight, who understood both the semantics and practice of pleasure so well, should have made separation from Caroline very difficult for himself. So *extremely* difficult he would have said, with 'extremely' very attenuated.

In 1968, Caroline had distanced herself from Habitat to concentrate on family life and writing on food for the *Sunday Times*. This was the year of Terence's calamitous merger with the Ryman stationery business, a very poor fit of cultures. It lasted only eighteen months, but netted the couple a million. In 1968, a Mini cost about £600. Today, a Mini costs about £30,000. Calamities can have their upside.

In 1983, Terence and Caroline bought Brunelys, a fine house in two hundred acres at Maussane-les-Alpilles in Provence, close to one of his favourite restaurants, the distinctly undemocratic Baumanières at Les Baux-de-Provence (*prix fixe* €240) where the only person in *bleu de travail* is, indeed, the struggling binman. Caroline paid a fifth of the £300,000 purchase price. They spent £650,000 on redecorations to create a superb house, a deluxe version of *la vie paysanne*. Magnificent, but also a little absurd.

That same year, Caroline became seriously ill, but after diligent attention to the Bristol Diet, happily recovered. During her illness I recall Terence rather treating her life-threatening condition as a selfish intrusion on his own way of life. 'Has she got no idea how busy I am?' he seemed to be saying. But I also think Terence was very squeamish about illness or anything which reminded him of the fragility of existence. Whatever, Caroline became a changed woman. She earned an Open University degree in psychology and in 1986 bought a house in Dorset without consulting her husband.

The sensational divorce trial was a classic, not only of family law, but of conflicting personal styles (not excluding the judge's), exposing many of the tensions that visitors to Barton Court had often suspected lay beneath the surface of great calm and comfort usually enjoyed there. Caroline, a friendly, if reserved, woman of great charm and ability, often seemed ill at ease at home. By the mid-eighties, it did not take much imagination, nor even an OU degree in psychology, to infer that her vectors were becoming no longer quite Terence's own.

For example, it was always typical of Terence to make no distinction between work and play, thus Barton Court was often used for catalogue and interior shoots. And there was a boardroom above the kitchen. The excellent accountants Terence always insisted on hiring could find tax benefits in such arrangements, although Caroline condemned it as turning her home into 'a sort of conference centre'.

True, at a Barton Court lunch, no matter how indulgent and loquacious, it was almost impossible to know whether it was in fact a meeting. This was because Terence's milieu comprised the designers, writers, cooks and bankers who were also fundamental to his businesses. In a very modern way, life and art were as one.

Terence was devastated by Caroline's departure, perhaps not least because his ego was damaged by an unfamiliar act of rejection. Very few people ever said: 'Terence, no!' He had also warned me, in 1981, at the Esso petrol station on New King's Road, that 'divorce can be very expensive, you know'. But I soon got married anyway, taking a more optimistic view of wedding outcomes.

Around the separation and the divorce, here was a man who had influenced the taste of a generation, but was now demonstrated to have no control of his own personal crisis: this was the only occasion I ever saw him affected by any strong emotion other than anger. Visibly upset over a lunch I bought him at La Famigilia, a pleasant Chelsea backwater favoured by footballers and elderly rock stars, the stated reasons for the split were: 'I forgot her birthday. But I didn't forget. It was just that I was too busy.' That is, of course, much worse. But in

Terence's view it was exculpatory. He told me she left without taking any possessions. Not even underwear. Whether this was his sense of melodrama I cannot say, but it made a strong point.

Keith Hobbs advised Terence that the way to make it up to Caroline was to take over his most glamorous restaurant for an entire night, empty it of customers, give her dinner alone in its cavernous spaces and say: 'I am sorry.' This was a magnificent and stylish conceit, which might even have worked. Terence refused because it would have been too expensive.

The judge at the divorce hearing was Mr Justice Wilson, now Lord Wilson of Culworth, latterly of the Supreme Court (who has subsequently become a friend of mine). Like Terence, he too had been at Bryanston, but some fourteen years later.

In his judgment, he described Caroline as a 'beautiful, creative, energetic and instinctively stylish woman'. He added she was 'neither grasping nor dishonest' in her intentions. Judges are human and Mr Justice Wilson may have found more sympathy for a beautiful, wounded woman than an unsentimental, bullying millionaire.

Following the judgment, and to the judge's surprise, Terence publicly disputed his generous, possibly even too generous account of Caroline's contribution to his business. And here we enter disputatious territory, because Terence was ever reluctant to distinguish *philosophically* between domestic and professional activities . . . until a distinction suited his *practical* purposes.

Terence only conceded that Caroline had offered 'active home support', perhaps not realising the absurdity that a man who founded a successful business whose name is a synonym for 'home' might be delighted by such a contribution. He denied that Caroline made any substantial contribution to that success. The facts are that on their marriage he gave her 26 per cent of Conran & Co and, with a £200 loan from her father, she later acquired one-eighth of Habitat Designs. Her kitchenware buying for Habitat was astute and important.

But Terence disputed any contribution to the business. He was, Mr Justice Wilson said, 'totally convinced that the wife made no such contributions and that any award against him constructed even in part by reference to them would be perverse'.

The 'healthy ego' question then arose. 'It can be difficult,' the judge said, 'for a man with a healthy ego who has achieved vertiginous success to look down and discern a contribution other than his own.' This, let's admit, is a judgement of Terence's personality that many outside his domestic arena will recognise.

And the court heard a dispute about who, between Terence and Caroline, taught whom to cook. 'Notwithstanding the husband's vehement denial,' Wilson found that Caroline's food writing 'represented an important contribution by the wife to the public perception that linked him with fine food. Her renewed links with journalism enabled the wife to introduce the other food journalists and indeed journalists in the field of design who, captivated by his charm and energy and by the quality of his products, wrote glowingly of him and them.'

Indeed, this was precisely the MO of the Barton Court 'conference centre': to hundreds of (very happy and well-fed) visitors, it was a beguiling real-time demonstration of Terence's world-view. And visiting journalists' accounts of it blurred the distinction between reportage and sales promotion. Mr Justice Wilson explained, 'The husband's friends were his colleagues in business. He brought them home. The wife cooked a superb supper or he did so himself. Fine wine was drunk. At these times there were lengthy, energetic discussions about current projects and the wife was a full participator.'

The hearing and the twenty-six-page judgement were reported in *The Times* on 4 July 1997, the same day as other headlines read, 'Sleaze report condemns Hamilton'. Neil Hamilton was the former Conservative MP for Tatton who had been fingered for being generously sponsored by Mohamed Al Fayed to ask questions in Parliament.

Mr Justice Wilson said: 'In many respects the size of the husband's fortune eases my task.' For which we can perhaps read 'rich bastard'. *The Times* estimated Terence's fortune to be £80 million and Caroline won a then-record settlement of £10.5 million, comprising: £5.3 million lump sum, £900,000 for a house in France and £1.9 million for houses in London and the one in Dorset, £400,000 for jewellery and cars, £2 million representing a share of liquid capital and there was an allowance of £230,000 per annum. Caroline had asked for £319,000 and Terence had offered £185,000.

Terence, clasping a cigar, told the papers: 'I feel very upset that something that was perfectly amicable has escalated into this. She left me. That does not come out in the judgement. I was extremely upset after a long period of marriage. She took off on the thirtieth anniversary of our wedding.'

There can be no doubt that Terence's healthy, even belligerent, ego had an effect on the judge, who clearly felt that Caroline had been a woman slighted. Terence said, 'The figure is unbelievable. Just because she cooked a few meals now and again and wrote a few books. I taught her how to cook. I felt the judge was trying to make a name for himself. I think it reads like a Mills and Boon novel. I find it offensive a judge should write in that sort of language.'

Terence could have gone to the Court of Appeal, but, no doubt on advice, he did not. Instead, he made a misleading remark to the media that Mr Justice Wilson had prevented such a thing. Meanwhile, *The Times* reported that, 'Lady Conran was said by friends to be delighted with the award.'

After the judgement, and to the judge's surprise, Terence made an unusual public attack on Mr Justice Wilson who, a judge for only four years, was taken aback by accusations of factual errors which Terence never actually explained. Wilson called it an 'extraordinary outburst'.

He was tempted to respond, but decided not to condescend.

For his part, Terence soon departed on a series of sloppy and ill-judged affairs, gleefully reported by the gossip columns.

7

Getting into Terence's Head

S.B.

'Not life,' as someone once said, 'but.' And they were not intending to be kind. For much of the seventies and eighties, the Conran Shop was London's outstanding lifestyle store. Its clientele was more like a discriminating club, an ambulant constituency who gathered on Saturday mornings for what sometimes felt like a private view. The Conran Shop was where you would expect to find design classics on display. As well as less essential curiosities, that elusive asparagus kettle, for example. This was consumerism raised to the level of cultural enquiry and social competition.

The Conran Shop came into existence because by 1973, Habitat had outgrown its original site at the junction of Sloane Avenue and Fulham Road. The area has advanced considerably since: today, opposite this original Habitat site, are Chanel and Carolina Herrera. It was Terence's presence in the area that brought them here.

Habitat moved half a mile away, installing itself in a handsome classic art deco cinema on the King's Road. And Habitat's original premises, an undistinguished speculative building subsequently found to be stuffed with 1960s asbestos, became the first location for the Conran Shop.

By the seventies Habitat's expansion was greater than geographical; as well as Bromley and Paris it was also present more intimately, subconsciously, in bedrooms and bathrooms and, deeper still, Habitat had invaded the cultural consciousness. And Habitat's cultural reach had been extended by the publication of Terence's popular *House Book* of 1974, followed by *The Kitchen Book* in 1977 and *The Bed and Bath Book* in 1978. Modern in style, sumptuously illustrated and gently didactic in tone, these handsome titles worked as religious texts in a messianic canon. They took Terence's vision to places Habitat would never go. And, at the same time, they established a new genre of publishing.

Still, Habitat was an epoch-defining phenomenon. By 1973 it retained a novel vitality, sometimes of a mischievous sort. The store was, for example, proposing the Sagbag Collection (inspired by – which is to say cheerfully ripped off from – the 1968 Sacco chair by Italian designers Gatti, Paolini and Teodoro).

If you bought a chicken brick or a duvet from Habitat, you somehow felt you had surer access to the agreeable Conran way of life that he had so diligently promoted in the social media of the day: magazines. The 1973 edition of the Habitat catalogue shows the celebrity-stroking Chinese restaurateur Mr Michael Chow at ease on an OMK sofa (designed by Terence's friend, Rodney Kinsman). This seemed to give an ordinary piece of furniture a special sanction for those – and there were many of them – keen on social promotion through the acquisition of approved artefacts.

Or take the Palaset storage system, admired in the catalogue by Muppet-fringed men in aviator glasses and heavily ribbed Shetland wool polo necks. These units seemed to offer an exciting promise that transcended the emotional limitations of ordinary shelving. In addition, there were jumbo floor cushions (which somehow suggested sexual licence and a glass of Beaujolais), and the catalogue of that year included a 'How to' section on the duvet. Yes. In those days, people needed to be told.

Terence first sold a 'continental quilt' in 1964 and was careful to give consumers bewildered by the exotic sophistication of this hypnotic innovation some helpful advice. 'Give it a bit of a shake,' his managers advised.

There is no true historical record of who exactly was the first to import a duvet into Britain, so, in the absence of any competitive claim, Terence easily assumed his priority in the matter and no one stepped up to deny it. But selling bedding, even of an avant-garde continental sort, was not enough. The scope of Terence's ambition required that a merchant be more than a mere salesman and more, instead, of what Stalin called an engineer of the soul.

Thus, the duvet did not merely replace sheets and blankets, but restructured domestic behaviour in its entirety, at least in Terence's telling. And, of course, in the frank public acknowledgement of sleeping arrangements, there was a sexual frisson which Terence was helpless to ignore.

The French too had a problem with the duvet, but it was more practical than romantic. In the French shops the time-saving promotion '20 secondes pour faire un lit' was, according to Terence, 'a huge success and undoubtedly changed the sex life of Europe'. Quite how the duvet achieved this was never fully explained, but the claim was often repeated, although the role of the contraceptive pill and women's liberation may have been underestimated.

Indeed, as ever, Terence's was not a research-based claim. It was a characteristically witty, megalomaniac and untested assertion with a little undertow of smut. Still, it was a powerful reputational device. The duvet was positioned somewhere between bed linen and sex toy. To emphasise the erotic potential of this liberated age, a mixed-race couple is shown with expressions of scarcely contained yearning next to their duvet in the Habitat catalogue of 1973.

The Habitat adventure, primed perhaps by Eros, was now ready to evolve. A great deal of the stuff Terence found interesting on frequent buying trips was beyond the acceptable 'price points' of the new Habitat customers. But rather than pass up the opportunity to sell interesting merchandise, Terence opened the more exclusive shop. Its gorgeous mixture of high modernism and fascinating vernacular perhaps more accurately reflected his own taste and budget than the more *mondaine* merchandise in Habitat. The Conran Shop offered customers their very first opportunity to enter Terence's head: it was like being in his home.

Here you could find the very best that the material world could offer, irrespective of budget. Chairs by Charles Eames and (Terence's own favourite) Yrjö Kukkapuro. Antique bentwood Thonet furniture, fine kilims and dhurries, proper linen, professional kitchenware, fine glass, decorative pots, bolts of fabric, eighteenth-century antiques, French country furniture and gorgeous dressing gowns. It was eclectic, smart, cosmopolitan, chic and satisfyingly expensive. You could buy a Kilner jar for £2 or a chaise longue for £2,000. There was nothing else like it in London. For a while, it was perhaps the best shop in the world. You heard French, Italian and Spanish spoken as often as you heard English. Its customers were united not by budget constraints, but by luxurious appetites and a sense of privileged clubbiness.

8

Mr Conran Trades on the Premises

S.B.

So close in time, the eighties also now seem a distant, historically remote era when innocent people performed inspiring tasks. Perhaps a bit like the marriage ceremonies of the Incas or the breakfasts of the Plantagenets.

The decade began without mobile phones or computers, while quaintly unthreatening stockbrokers were yet to be replaced by feral and rapacious merchants of baffling financial commodities.

Impossible, from this distance, to say whether Terence's activities were a cause or effect of a decade when 'design' became a matter of popular debate. Various factors were involved. Mrs Thatcher's policy of running down ugly, old, inconvenient, worker-friendly manufacturing industries had the effect of promoting services and, before deregulation of the City in 1987, 'design' was the most glittering and promising of these.

Mrs Thatcher's decade was, if nothing else, characterised by optimism. In a culture where people were demoralised by the experience of continuous decline, the lures of profit and privatisation seemed like the treasure of El Dorado.

Populated by a continuous stream of bright youth from Britain's uniquely sophisticated art education system, 'design' was the shiny representative of the Knowledge Economy, a new order of doing things.

Never mind that design alone was no more effective in saving a troubled economy than strapping a powerful outboard motor onto a waterlogged and sinking raft, the rhetoric was persuasive. And so too was the evidence on the street. While Britain shamefully abandoned the manufacture of most of the products an advanced civilisation needs to survive, it enjoyed, instead, a 'retail revolution'. Mass-market print magazines had their last hurrah. There was a sense of excitement like the sixties, but with worse music.

By contrast, in the late seventies, official awareness of design in Britain, such as it was, remained stuck in the early sixties, if not before. The government's Design Council was the official body charged with its promotion. This was an evolution of the old Council of Industrial Design (CoID), established by the 1945 Labour government, which perceived, no matter how dimly, that prosperity depended on manu-facturing industry that would be invigorated by this magic property of 'design'.

Attempts to modernise its outlook began in 1956, when the Duke of Edinburgh opened the Design Centre on the Haymarket. This, in the days when Britain still had vertically and horizontally integrated industries, was a hot shop of excellence, as identified by the duke and other 'experts', intended to inspire industry. Approved examples were displayed with little triangular black-and-white swing tags.

It was later shown that most Design Council Awards were given to manufacturers who were distinctly unable to make it (and went bust). Still, it was a remarkable exercise in media-centric populism. Across town, at the Whitechapel Art Gallery, that same year, a renegade group of artists, designers and writers – including Terence's friend Eduardo Paolozzi, Richard Hamilton, Toni del Renzio and Reyner Banham – put on the 'This Is Tomorrow' exhibition, which defined what became known as 'pop art'. Just up the road in Charing Cross, making his own contribution to the zeitgeist, Terence had been serving soup and baguettes.

In 1972, the CoID became the tighter-and-brighter sounding Design Council. But bureaucracy and an outdated and narrow-minded vision of design had become its province. The Design Council was negligently slack in ignoring America, Japan and Italy and preferring, shall we say, to exhibit an unsuccessful and unpopular British trowel if it was felt to embody 'good' design, while ignoring a Ford Mustang, an astonishing commercial success, because it was 'vulgarian'.

In the mid- to late seventies, official attitudes to design were still insistently elitist. Only Reyner Banham and Fiona MacCarthy wrote about the subject with style and authority. So newspapers and magazines largely ignored it, other than to deal with it occasionally on the women's pages, where it jostled for space with advice on pruning and recipes for Victoria sponge.

Terence had, inevitably, been in and out of the Design Council for many years, advising on this and that, occasionally designing exhibitions that travelled around Europe, but never much enamoured of it. To the bureaucrats, he was a token of all that was fresh and bright. There was one occasion when Paul Reilly, the modernist director of the Design Council, son of C.H. Reilly, designer of Peter Jones's modernist Chelsea store, had asked Terence to chair a Design Council committee 'to liven things up when they were getting a bit staid'.

But committees are perhaps not the best forum for the independent-minded. Still, when Reilly retired from the Design Council, Terence offered him a directorship of Conran Associates, the design consultancy. This was an appointment whereby each might expect material as well as social and professional benefits. Reilly would bring lustre to the board and make useful introductions, Terence would pay him for them.

Although Terence often found the avuncular Reilly's taste for triangulation, shall we say, exasperating, they were close and fond. At some point, Terence had said to Reilly that he wanted to start a collection of design to do for contemporary students what the Victoria

& Albert Museum had once done for him, which is to say provide sources of inspiration. This was the germ of a larger idea. Terence was inventing a newer and more influential version of design: his scope was no longer the high street, but high culture.

These trails now became interestingly mixed. In 1977, my first book *In Good Shape* was being prepared for publication by the Design Council. This had come about after I had met Reilly at a dinner in Bedford Park; my enthusiasm and volubility were so evident, he commissioned the book. Reilly later recalled that at the dinner: 'Stephen had an idea much the same as Terence's and he was looking for a rich man to sponsor it. So when Terence mentioned his idea to me it seemed sensible to put the two in touch with each other.'

Reilly called me during a seminar I was conducting on a wet University of Kent campus in Canterbury. 'I want you to come to meet Terence Conran,' he said with mischievous insistence. I cancelled my teaching for the rest of the week and drove up from Kent in my turquoise Citroën GS Break with its (Design Council approved, but ridiculously clunky) Raleigh folding bicycle in the boot and sheepskin cover on the seat.

It was not, actually, my very first meeting with Terence. That had been in early 1977 when I interviewed Terence in Neal Street for the Jubilee Edition of the *Architectural Review*, which I was guest editing. Anthony Burgess was another contributor I commissioned. Such a pity now not to have found an opportunity to introduce Terence to Burgess. Stanley Kubrick's 1971 cinema adaptation of *A Clockwork Orange* used the modernist Thamesmead to suggest dystopia. It would have been an interesting conversation ...

I was respectful, fascinated and awestruck; Terence was tired and bored, but the interview was predictably polished and inoffensive. Terence was never rude to journalists. Then, as a result of Reilly's reintroduction, three years later I was back in Neal Street. I had left the university behind, was planning Terence's design legacy and, on the side, writing about the meaning of the Bauhaus in the Habitat catalogue.

This reintroduction was in Alexander Place, Reilly's house near the Victoria & Albert Museum with its unforgettable salmon-pink front door. I recall that Terence's Porsche was already parked outside with two wheels on the pavement, but he later denied this suggestion of antisocial behaviour.

Certainly, he was stomping around Reilly's drawing room making the polite stainless-steel Swedish platters rattle in their display cabinets. The house, with sixteen nudes in the bathroom, exuded an atmosphere which Fiona MacCarthy helpfully described as genial risquéness. It seemed very exciting. Memory plays tricks, but I think Terence was smoking a cigar.

Without much preamble, he said: 'I've made a lot of money. I don't want to leave it all to the children and the Inland Revenue. I want a collection to inspire students and young designers.' And, happily, on a whim, he had decided I was the person to collect for him. It was a perfect fit of my ambition and education with Terence's authority and influence. I returned to Kent exhilarated and restless. I thought of little else than how to create a 'design museum'.

Terence wrote to me in December of that year expressing his amused bewilderment at my nomadic existence, wondering whether he might find me at provincial universities, London clubs, Suzy Slesin's New York apartment, or – an asterisk was added and footnoted in Terence's very recognisable scrawl – 'even Fawlty Towers'. He asked me to ring him.

So I rang him and that led to my being given £1,200 to fund a world tour to check the state of design awareness and see if there was any competition for the idea we were discussing. This translated me from nomadic student-type backpacker to business-class swell, travelling throughout Europe and the United States, visiting The Cooper Hewitt Museum in New York, the Neue Sammlung in Munich, the

Kunstgewerbe Museum in Zürich, the Kunstindustrimuseet in Oslo, and so on, as well as meeting Philip Johnson, George Nelson and Arthur Drexler in Manhattan, all of the latter holding very lofty positions in America's design aristocracy. Twelve hundred pounds went a long way in 1979.

I wrote a report for the Charity Commissioners, explaining our plans, and this gave rise to the creation of the Conran Foundation, an educational charity. I became its director. This was breathtaking promotion for me and persuasive evidence of Terence's bravery, or, at least, his ability to back a hunch.

In creating the foundation, I think Terence was – even unconsciously – emulating the Sarabhai family of Ahmedabad, textile suppliers to Habitat and the Conran Shop. Their own patronage extended to commissioning Le Corbusier, so was rather grander than Terence commissioning me. However, the Sarabhai example of benign, paternalistic capitalism with a strong top note of adventurous artistic patronage was an enduring influence on Terence's view of the world.

Tangible progress, however, depended on the flotation of Habitat, an event continuously delayed, but I continued to research possibilities for our nameless venture. My own conviction was to create a 'museum' of design, but Terence was not at the time keen on the term, thinking it antiquarian in an unhelpful way. But there was no other suggestion forthcoming. Still, in November 1979, I lectured on 'The Need for a British Design Museum' at an academic conference in Oslo. This was the first public airing of the idea.

This moment was, despite the frustrations with the funding, one I vividly recall as extraordinarily exciting. I felt enormously empowered by the promise and prestige of Conran millions, although, passionate and committed as I might have been, I was a poor salesman.

I visited Neil Cossons at the Science Museum and asked him if he wanted a Conran-sponsored design department. Cossons most certainly did not, as he was already rather of the opinion that the Science Museum – with its rockets and engines and looms – was all about design in any case. To my mind this was an example of that atrocious form of English pseudo-intellectual snobbery that saw a pyrometer and variable geometry jet intakes as worthy of study, but a chicken brick not.

A similar version of the same snobbery existed at the Tate Gallery, then a sleepy and dark museum of polite British art on Millbank, sucking up the disabling humours emanating from the old Bentham-era penitentiary on the site, whence crims were once transported to Australia.

I offered Alan Bowness, its director, a zippy design wing, citing the example of New York's Museum of Modern Art, where cars and food mixers sat, as they should, side by side with Picasso and Braque. Bowness, an elegant man related by marriage to Barbara Hepworth's family, and thus awash with St Ives School genteel sensibility, looked exquisitely pained and told me that he did not think Terence's lampshades were very exalting and that design, therefore, had no place in the Tate. Thus in this careless, pursed-lip fashion was a subject that engaged Alberti, Edison, Eames and, later, Ive dismissed from British culture. Cossons and Bowness have been proved wrong. Terence has been proved right.

We had alternatives.

At the time, Terence was discussing moving Habitat's HQ from Wallingford in Oxfordshire to Milton Keynes. The new city was admired for its idealism and vision and commitment to making things new. Since then the concept of atomised settlements linked by roads has gone in and out of fashion, but in 1979 it was revelatory, if divisive. To commit to Milton Keynes was to commit to being modern.

Milton Keynes was also the seat of the Open University, an optimistic and successful experiment in public education. I had worked there for two years and rather enthusiastically identified with the spirit of the place. Milton Keynes was many things, but certainly not 'sad'. Terence may have felt a similar enthusiasm, but was also alert to the prospect of a deal. Not least because Milton Keynes residents were people who bought their own furniture and, therefore, potential Habitat customers.

And, as if to confirm the benign *genius loci*, on 25 September 1979, Mrs Thatcher opened the Central Milton Keynes Shopping Centre. This vast structure was inspired by Mies van der Rohe. Among the Milton Keynes Development Corporation team was Stuart Mosscrop, later architect of the Design Museum. He had worked in Chicago and was an outspoken, sometimes even combative, modernist. Lasers were used to line up the unflinching horizontals. Mies's design principle was *beinahe nichts* (nearly nothing). This was that, except for nearly two million square feet of retail space. And for this democratic palace of shopping, Mies's favourite travertine marble was used. It all seemed very propitious.

Fred Lloyd Roche, Milton Keynes's chief executive, showed us an available site next to Willen Lake. Here the vision was to build an accessible warehouse of design classics stacked on Dexion shelving which could be retrieved by intelligent robots for study by curious students. An additional benefit would be, in the event of Habitat moving to Milton Keynes, the stimulus afforded to neighbouring staff by the presence of so much exemplary design and so much creative interaction with visiting students.

Terence's friend, *New York Times* journalist Suzy Slesin, had published her epochal *High Tech* in 1978 and industrial finishes were not yet a lazy cliché. In fact, they were rather exciting, but Habitat HQ did not move. And the high-tech vision faded.

Instead, a more inspired and stylish museum director intervened decisively. This was Roy Strong of the V&A. I had known Roy Strong by reputation since my school days and admired him from afar, not least because of his cheeky populism, scholarship, camp posturing and bold, imperious self-invention. I especially liked his idea when at the National Portrait Gallery, wanting to serve 'Martinis with Bellinis', referring to gin and vermouth cocktails and a Venetian painter, in the days before the latter's name had been hijacked for a prosecco and peach juice aperitivo. Once, as an item in its regular Pseuds' Corner feature, *Private Eye* had simply published a photograph of Roy with no accompanying text, assuming the readers would find the image alone sufficiently pseud-ish to merit inclusion. For his part, Terence had known Roy since his time on the Advisory Committee of the V&A, the body that preceded the trustees.

With the exception of his sometimes dramatic Tommy Nutter suits and his flirtatious relationship with popular media, Roy was uneasy with modern life. He did not, for example, know how to drive. Still, he was alert to pressures that the V&A should acknowledge contemporary life. With a mixture of stylish opportunism and political opportunism, he said: 'Why don't you get started here?' This seemed ideal since Henry Cole had established the V&A's campaigning traditions that Terence and I wanted to think we were continuing.

Cole's Chamber of Horrors had put on display horrible examples of mid-Victorian mass-produced rubbish in order to humiliate the cynical manufacturers and educate the ignorant public. Or that was the theory. The notoriety of Cole's finger-wagging Chamber of Horrors, an astonishing exercise in patrician superiority, was something we were keen to emulate, not least because Habitat was itself a lecture about taste. And Terence was good at finger-wagging.

With Oliver Gregory, I started wandering the V&A's neglected underbelly, through sordid underground rooms, some untouched since 1945, perhaps earlier. We identified two spaces, one gloriously known as Clinch's Hole, the other as the Old Boilerhouse Yard. I think we were standing in half an inch of water. Knowing Roy Strong's occasional inclination to petulance and intellectual snobbismo, I asked Terence if the gruff and artisanal Gregory could cope with any possible foot-stamping from the highly strung Strong. Terence said very softly and certainly: 'You'll find Oliver well able to cope with most things.'

Negotiations began over occupancy of the Old Boilerhouse Yard, whose name euphoniously suggested Bauhaus, hinted at a ferment of activity, and also referred back to Henry Cole's Brompton Boilers, a forerunner of the V&A. I had to acquire a licence from the Treasury Solicitor to occupy the place, a long-drawn-out process.

Eventually, a letter arrived, typed on an old machine with a brown ribbon and jumping characters, granting us our request. The sole proviso was that Mr Conran would not be allowed to 'trade' on the premises. That the word 'trade' really was in inverted commas is powerfully illustrative of how disdainful and suspicious was the establishment's attitude to design. This we now set out to violate.

When I told Terence about the Old Boilerhouse Yard, he promptly said: 'We must call it the Boilerhouse *Project*.' That emphasis on the last word was made with the slightly camp manner he sometimes adopts, italics being his only second language. Then he laughed and said the name sounded like an effortful Boston coffee bar. I think the choice of 'Project' revealed a psychological truth, a liking for the idea of an evolving work-in-progress.

For my part, intoxicated by the new religion of corporate identity, I wanted a strong graphic presence for the project. The Design Council had published Wally Olins's influential *The Corporate Personality*, the best book on what's now called 'branding', in the same season as my *In Good Shape* and, in a warm bath of mutual admiration, Olins and I had got to know each other.

Wally and Terence were true opposites, in that Wally had an educated and intellectualised attitude to design, but no taste whatsoever. Whereas Terence was wilful and intuitive to a maddening degree, but had an exquisite eye and flawless judgement of the visual. Be that as it may, Wally had taught me the importance of meaningful identity.

When I spoke to Terence about the need for coherent graphics that would work in all media, he said: 'Go to see Stafford,' meaning Stafford Cliff, the softly spoken, but pleasantly insistent, director of the light and airy graphics studio in Neal Street. Stafford, who only ever wore green, pointed me to a table with two very attractive young women at work upon it. One was dark, the other fair. The latter eventually married David Hillman, who redesigned the *Guardian* in 1988. This is what Terence's connections were in those days. The former eventually married me, but only after she had designed a striking identity for the Boilerhouse Project: a red grid was cleverly laid over the upper- and lower-case Gill Bold font to suggest our analytical purposes. When, later that year, Terence came to our wedding at the Hurlingham Club, he complained insistently about the food. This was perhaps inelegant, but I was flattered he was there.

Terence had mixed feelings about the marriage. On the one hand, I was 'fraternising' with a member of staff. This required all sorts of obfuscation and subterfuge about simultaneously leaving the flat we shared, but arriving at Neal Street at different times. On the other hand, amused, Terence said: 'I have always "fraternised" [actually, it was another f-word] with anyone I liked in the office, so I don't see why you shouldn't.' Later, he was to ask, 'You do know how expensive divorce can be, don't you?' Terence saw romance as a P&L.

Architecturally, looking back now, the design of the Boilerhouse seems to have anticipated fashionable minimalism: it was an uncompromising white box whose subterranean entrance Terence was pleased to say looked like a *club privé*. The whiteness was startling and, underfoot, glazed white tiles were of quite shocking impracticality. Cleaners had to come and go several times a day. Yet it looked fabulous, a real empty canvas. So in tune was it with the zeitgeist that scenes shot in my dramatic corner office were used as titles for a popular BBC series called *The Money Programme*, and so stressful was it to occupy that it was used as a location for a headache-cure advertisement.

The architect in charge was David Salter, who had trained with Yorke Rosenberg and Mardall, Britain's first 'modernist' practice: F. R. S. Yorke's *The Modern House in England* (1937) was, and remains, a sacred text for those who adore concrete, metal and geometry in a domestic setting. YRM, as it was always called, was run by Terence's friend Brian Henderson. It had become well known for its handsome, classic buildings: not just Gatwick, but London's St Thomas' Hospital and Liverpool University's Electrical Engineering Building as well. And it had become notorious when white cladding tiles began falling off these buildings at some danger to the passing public. This white tile motif may have influenced Salter who recalled:

'We knew what we wanted: a large, airy, well-lit, clear exhibition space, and our initial inspection was not encouraging. The only way to establish the potential in what we had been offered was to strip everything back to the fundamental structural shell. The result was the emergence of a much larger space than had been initially apparent and we were able to see that it would be reasonably straightforward to create a space to match our original vision. The space should be minimal in order to act as a foil to a programme of differing exhibitions over a period of about five years. It should showcase the principles of modern design that we had pioneered.'

Salter continued: 'We had created the ultimate modern, minimal exhibition space – but perhaps not quite "ultimate". We were nearly ready for business, but what was missing was a small hint of humour, something to take us beyond the functional elegance we had achieved. So in one corner we built a large fully glazed cube and there, in that box, long before Damien Hirst, in minimal splendour, at his minimal desk with the ultimate eighties accessory, an Olivetti typewriter, sat Stephen Bayley, the ultimate exquisite exhibit in his own gleaming crystal cage.'

This was my life for five years.

9

Nunc Est Bibendum

S.B.

Terence had always coveted the Michelin Building which sat, temptingly under-used, just opposite the original Habitat and, after 1973, what became the Conran Shop. A structure more synoptic of his interests and enthusiasms could not be imagined: an impressive corner site in smart London, adventurous architecture, swaggering self-advertisement, cheerful idiosyncrasy and reeking of France, as if steeped in a rich marinade of Vosne-Romanée, Boyards and pungent Époisses.

He had often written to Michelin wondering if it were for sale, but the secretive company rebuffed him. By 1984, at the height of Terence's business dynamic, the Michelin Building eventually came onto the market. Terence persuaded the publisher Paul Hamlyn into a joint venture that involved a radical refurbishment of the interior. A shabby industrial core was to be translated into a bright symbol of London's ambitious eighties. Can there be a more eloquent token of a decade's weird hedonism and thirst for style than a tyre bay becoming an Oyster Bar?

Hamlyn moved his publishing businesses into the bulk of the building. Conran-Octopus, since 1985 the joint Hamlyn-Conran venture devoted to illustrated books, was a part of the move. Terence moved the Conran Shop into the ground floor and basement and would build a restaurant in a beautiful room illuminated by stained-glass advertisements for pneumatic tyres. Hamlyn, an immensely rich but modest man, who resisted publicity, never received credit equivalent to his investment.

Terence had always been interested in the restaurant-as-a-concept and often cited textile designer Alexander Girard's 1960 La Fonda del Sol in New York's Time-Life Building as an inspiration.

Here Girard drew eighty different sun motifs and used pirated samples of bold vernacular typography as decoration. Eames chairs were covered with colourful fabrics. At a time when smart Manhattan restaurants were epicene in grey and beige and the politesse of *haute cuisine*, La Fonda del Sol's shrieking colours and ceviche, chilli, *mole* and *cerveza* hinted at new possibilities in dining. In all, La Fonda del Sol was a designed whole: Girard did the books of matches, the fabrics, the décor, the menu. To enter La Fonda del Sol was a little like entering Alexander Girard's head. Terence liked this idea.

Thus, to enter Bibendum was to enter Terence's head, even more so than the Conran Shop. Perhaps the hypothalamus rather than the frontal lobes.

We cannot say what was in his dreams, but subsequently it was amusing to see how Terence began to assume the identity of both the Michelin family as patrons of art and design and of Monsieur Bibendum himself, their lovable cigar-smoking homunculus. This was Francophilia and demonic possession mixed.

Still, it would be a dull person who did not enjoy the astonishing charm of the Michelin building. Terence adored the entire ethic of the place. It was a response to a fundamental problem Michelin suffered. That's to say, tyres are boring. They have no emotional attributes. No one, at least no healthy person, fantasises about tyres.

So, long before Terence discovered France, Michelin played to the strengths of Frenchness and inventiveness which he later identified as his own. These Clermont-Ferrand industrialists construed the whole of France as a vast dining table, laid out with delicious dishes which changed region by region. This regionality was a significant part of France's own identity and Michelin decided that meals should be the rationale of a road journey. Excite the desire to travel on gastro-journeys and you will sell more tyres.

Tyres were thus not disposable rubber products, but connections to pleasure. The first device that was a response to this epic insight was Monsieur Bibendum, a cartoonish hominid made of tyres. He was drawn following a vision seen by the Michelin brothers at the 1894 Colonial Exhibition in Lyon, where a pile of tyres morphed into a person. In 1898 Marius Rossillon (also known as O'Galop) drew the familiar figure we still know today.

Monsieur Bibendum had an ego inflated to a pressure similar to that of the tyres which comprised him. He smirked, he kicked, he smoked, he drank. He was unforgettable.

At first Monsieur Bibendum was a graphic, a poster-boy, but he soon evolved into a company symbol. In 1900 there appeared the first edition of the Michelin *Guide Rouge*, a gazetteer of French towns with driving tips and the vital addresses of garages and hotels. The Hôtel de France in Montreuil-sur-Mer was given five stars, so it was that same town's Monsieur Nivert who could repair your bicycle and pump up your tyres. Thus there was practicality as well as pleasure.

At first it was distributed free. So there was business sense too. In 1920, the *Guide Rouge* went on sale and became, and remains, an encyclopedia of dreams, many of them Terence's. Just open an old or new *Guide Rouge* at random and it kick-starts a reverie. Maubeuge may in truth be a terrible dump, but its neat street plan in the *Rouge* invites you to stroll from the Étang Monier to the Place de Wattignies and imagine that wonderful little charcuterie, bar or bistro you might find. It is suggestive pornography for the hardcore Francophile. Terence said this was 'a marketing campaign that . . . had never been bettered'. Michelin House was designed by François Espinasse (1880–1925), an obscure technician in Michelin's civil engineering department.

It opened on 20 January 1911. He used François Hennebique's radical new ferro-concrete for the structure, but this is disguised by the undefinable style that is an alloy of art nouveau and art deco and wholly Michelin. It is a building with a narrative: the famous encaustic tiles were made by Gilardoni Fils of Paris using drawings by Ernest Montaut. His subject was the great road races of the late nineteenth century, the Paris–Bordeaux, for example, in which the Michelin brothers had themselves competed, to have flesh in the game of proving their products.

It was a magnificent example of architecture as advertising. Not just for Michelin, but for France itself, as well as the romance of travel. Michelin helped create the gastro-nomad. Thus it helped create Terence. No wonder he thought that when he acquired the building, it absolutely had to have a restaurant in it. It was, he said, 'madness' not to.

The dining experience in Bibendum gave visitors an immediate impression of the Conran ideal, a cerebral bypass of cognition. The combination of astonishingly bright, airy, temple-like space and dramatic stained glass, combined with bespoke bucket chairs (changing cover colours seasonally, at least at first) with hardwood, chrome-and-glass details and plush carpet, created a sense of stripped-back deluxe, an artistically inclined theatre of pleasures which was both timeless and out-of-time. Easing back in the cosseting bucket chairs, customers could consult a commodious wine list and ponder a menu of classics-inclined-to-richness of flavour and effect, but simplified in presentation.

Sydney Smith, the great Victorian churchman, reviewer and opinion-former, once said that the secret of happiness was to think no further than lunch or dinner. Here was a stage on which to act out that fantasy. Terence always had a favourite table: the one in the corner furthest away on the left after you enter the space.

The first cook at Bibendum was Simon Hopkinson, who had been a youthful prodigy-chef in his native Lancashire, then an inspector for the Egon Ronay Guides and, latterly, a cook in private service to a well-known and slightly raffish eighties financier. London's progression to the lead in the competition for the world's outstanding food city had several starting points. One of them was Brompton Road where, one day in 1983, an undistinguished hamburger joint reopened as Hilaire, and Hopkinson was cooking. It was a revelation. I took Terence there as soon as I could.

Hopkinson's epicurean passions were, inevitably, directed by his avid reading of Elizabeth David, as most cooks were at the time. But he was also close to Richard Olney, the American journalist whose part-works for Time-Life had, after Mrs David and Julia Child, accelerated popular appreciation of French food. Olney took Valerie Eliot, the poet's widow, to Hilaire, and David herself often accompanied him. It was that good. Then, in an event of perfect symmetry, Mrs David became a Bibendum regular. Hopkinson is mentioned warmly in Olney's 1999 autobiography *Reflexions*, where it is also ungenerously noted that, late in life, Mrs David was 'nourishing herself more on conversation and wine and less on food'.

This, then, was the culture of Bibendum. Hopkinson's favourites were: Piedmontese peppers, *escargots à la Bourguignonne*, onion tart, *poulet de Bresse* with tarragon, *steak au poivre* and fish and chips. Ideally, lubricated with a big red burgundy after a glass or two of Meursault or Chablis to quicken the palate. These too were Terence's favourite dishes, and for twenty years he was a regular customer.

For those same twenty years Bibendum was one of London's outstanding restaurants, where sophisticates would pay astonishing prices to enjoy simple food, superbly executed. Terence was always fond of citing Escoffier's principle: '*Faites simple.*' And as for undemocratic pricing, we all know that Elizabeth David believed a 'bad meal is always expensive'.

Then Bibendum began to deflate. On its twentieth birthday in 2007, the influential restaurant critic Jay Rayner visited to pay *hommage*.

He was badly disappointed and complained that overcrowded tables resulted in a waiter dipping his arse in the condiment. The bread was stale and the service lacked both urgency and style. A fish soup tasted of oxtail; portions were miserly. Rayner felt he had been scalped rather than fed, concluding a lacerating review with that same reference to Fernand Point, the famous proprietor of the celebrated Pyramide restaurant in Vienne. Point said success is the sum of a lot of small things done correctly. Rayner added that failure is the sum of a lot of small things done badly.

From the beginning, Bibendum had established a new standard in London restaurants: simple, honest food of high quality, French rustic-bourgeois, with an Anglo angle, served in an environment that buffered dreams of European romance in grey London. 'Gastro-retro, reactionary chic' was the way *Foodie* author Paul Levy had it. Without Bibendum's example, the Wolseley's supremely successful Viennese retro-kitsch would never have been possible.

But twenty years on, Bibendum's sky-high reputation was losing height. Terence himself blamed the desertification of Chelsea and the dark-windows-at-night phenomenon that's evidence of an absent local population of ex-pat itinerant property investors, not hungry neighbours keen to eat out in a busy *restaurant du quartier*. But the real cause of Bibendum's desertification was fashion. The high standards it once set were now higher elsewhere. And Basque *pintxos* became more popular than a French peasant's *coq au vin*.

In early 2017, the founding chef and one-third owner Simon Hopkinson, the man who cooked masterpiece fish and chips at caviar prices, sold his Bibendum shares for undisclosed reasons, although it's reasonable to speculate that this proud and very sensitive man – he broke down and cried after refusing to give Alain Ducasse his recipe for steamed ginger pudding – was becoming disenchanted by association with a restaurant whose best days seemed past. Then, London's busy tribe of restaurant-watchers was astonished to learn that Claude Bosi, a Frenchman of great artifice, a prince of culinary frou-frou, who made his reputation first in Ludlow and then in Mayfair at the small but serious Hibiscus, was acquiring Hopkinson's shares and putting his own name above Monsieur Bibendum's.

Bosi's Hibiscus was admired, but had been eased out of Mayfair by competition from the mega-watt seven-figure-budget, new wave of restaurants-as-entertainment, including Novikov, Sexy Fish and Parc Chinois, each in their way successors to Quaglino's hyper-restaurant concept. At Hibiscus, Bosi had been admired for the altitudinously attenuated sophistication of his kitchen. There was none of Escoffier's, or indeed Terence's, *faites simple* in Bosi's vocabulary; instead great complication was his marque, as was precise execution.

The popular restaurateur Russell Norman called Bosi's style 'fancy pants' cooking. Perhaps aware that a man whose dishes included halibut and grapefruit in a pork pie sauce needed explanation in a restaurant whose culinary roots had their origin in the purism of Elizabeth David and Richard Olney and their scholarly enthusiasm for French cuisine, Terence wrote an open letter on Bibendum stationery. After explaining the need for an expensive refit at Bibendum, Terence said, 'Then Claude Bosi, a two-star Michelin chef, approached us having just sold his Mayfair restaurant. He loved Bibendum and the Michelin building and was keen to do a deal with us as chef and equal shareholder.'

Otherwise, the open letter is as remarkable for what it does not say as for what it does.

Terence had offered the Frenchman a consultancy, but Bosi demanded more, which perhaps explains Terence's rather grudging and ungenerous tone. In this Bibendum retrospective, no thanks or credit are given to the influential founder-chef Simon Hopkinson, only reference to the 'Hopkinson team'. Nor is there any mention of why the traditional style of cooking once presented as a Conran article of faith was now to compete with fashionable innovation. A chef who can conceptualise, still less actually serve 'pork pie sauce' does not sit well in the David Olney tradition that valorises peasant craft.

Many people admire Claude Bosi's cooking, though some do not. No one, however, disputes that sophisticated invention is more his métier than tradition. The curiosity here is that it was the philosophical connection between simple food and simple design that formed the basis of the young Terence's world-view, a link that nourished all his activities. Bibendum acquiring a fancy-pants chef-patron was as if the Conran Shop had begun to stock gilt and velour furniture in the style known as Jewish Renaissance.

Terence did, however, concede that 'Claude had played a major role in bringing it up to date.' Bosi later made alterations to his menu. Maybe the restaurant has kept pace with the times, but that was never the point at Bibendum – it was designed to be timeless. Timeless cooking, it seems, is no more secure than timeless design. And, faced with a decision between priorities and profit, Terence blinked.

Additionally, Terence was irked by the graphics on the restaurant and menu cards that clearly stated CLAUDE BOSI at Bibendum, which was not a hierarchy he recognised. He had neither experience of nor taste for a background role. But he was also keenly aware that Bosi's wife, Lucy, was very *branchée* indeed in the food culture. As a senior figure in the Open Table website, she was influential in creating the reputations of restaurants.

As the prospect of Michelin recognition became a real one, Terence modified his views. Never much given to athleticism, Terence was here able to perform an energetically baroque pivot, leaving him facing two ways at once. Soon he was able to tell Peter Prescott: 'It's not my sort of food, but we've got two stars!' Again, the 'we' does not signify acceptance of a joint effort, but rather a way of dominating that effort. Despite this version of success, the decline and fall of Bibendum was the darkest moment in Terence's autumn.

The Neal Street Restaurant, the Conran Shop and Bibendum were all remarkably bold and stylish endeavours that each, for a moment, dramatically raised consumers' expectations. A truly modern restaurant! A shop more beautiful than a museum! Another restaurant that was a Francophile's dream world. In each case, London had never experienced anything so good before. And London learnt from what it saw. Soon there were competitors. But Terence got bored and moved on, leaving behind only broken promises, haphazardly corrected.

Ingvar Kamprad, the founder of IKEA, once asked Terence in charmingly stilted English: 'When shall you learn to take care of what you already have and not only put new activities on your desk?' The honest answer would have been 'never'.

PART 3

A FALL FROM GRACE

10

Greek Myths and British High Streets

R.M.

In Greek myth, the lustful Pasiphaë had a carnal urge to be mounted by a bull. The better to fulfil this bizarre desire, she enlisted the help of the famous craftsman, Daedalus, who fashioned a hollow wooden cow in which she hid. The bull (presumably somewhat short-sighted) mounted Daedalus's contraption and impregnated the passionate Pasiphaë.

Not surprisingly, Pasiphaë's husband, King Minos, was angered by his wife's deviant antics, and so built a huge labyrinth in which she and Daedalus were both imprisoned. For good measure, Icarus, the son of Daedalus, was thrown in too.

Escape by any conventional means was impossible. But the cunning Daedalus used his craftsman's skills to make wings from feathers and wax, for himself and his son, so that they could fly, literally, from their captivity.

Daedalus warned Icarus not to go too near the sun; and Icarus, like most children, ignored his father's sound advice. The tragic result was that the wax on Icarus's wings melted, the wings disintegrated, and Icarus fell into the sea and was drowned.

Thus the legend of Icarus has become a metaphor for all those who overreach themselves, who 'fly too near the sun'.

Terence had his Icarus moment when the Storehouse vision was created.

By the early eighties, Habitat had been built into a big business, a brand, almost a way of life in Britain. It had been set up in the USA too, and had stores in Paris that were both admired and successful. Terence had built something extraordinary, and now was the time to nurture his creation. But Terence was an innovator, not a nurturer. The question on his lips, figuratively if not literally, was always: 'What next?'

And the answer to that question was to jump from the single-minded simplicity of Habitat to an astonishing and far-reaching new adventure that was to be known as Storehouse.

The idea of Storehouse was simple in concept, but colossal in scale. It was to transform the kingdom of Habitat into a great retail empire, whose scope went far beyond sofas and chicken bricks, into the heartland of mainstream Britain. Terence would take over great swathes of Britain's high street and impose his own passion and taste; and on a far, far wider range of products. For all his (very justifiable) pride in the success of Habitat, Terence knew that it meant much to readers of the *Guardian* or the *Sunday Times*, but little to readers of the *Mirror* or the *News of the World*. His new vision was to create a retail momentum that would touch the lives of all of us.

The Storehouse saga is one in which every strand of Terence's complex character became woven into a tale of passionate ambition and painful disappointment. We can see his remarkable vision; his intense belief in the power of design; his vaunting ambition; his adventurous sense of what might be possible. But we can also see a blindness to risk; a certain naivety; and no sense of what might not be possible.

To many, Terence might appear to have been a retailer, or a designer, or a strange amalgam of both, but deep down, Terence was an evangelist. Rather like his contemporary Maggie Thatcher (whom he admired yet abhorred), he had a vision of how Britain should be, and he wanted to share it with everyone.

The journey began when Terence, endlessly restless for new adventure, began to study Mothercare, the high-street chain specialising in products for mothers and babies. Mothercare had spotted – and filled – a real gap in the market. And their leader, Selim Zilkha, was an innovative entrepreneur and a shrewd retailer. But his chain never quite had the design vibrancy of Habitat. So Terence and Selim decided to join forces. Habitat Mothercare was formed in 1982, and Terence had made his first step from a single business towards colonising the high street.

Many commercial marriages start with desire and end with divorce, but Habitat Mothercare flourished. Terence's eldest son, Sebastian, a gifted product designer in his own right, was given the lead role on the redesign of Mothercare's products. Sebastian has a gift for thinking how mundane, everyday objects could be reimagined to work better. He was thrilled to explore how, with imagination, a pushchair or a baby bottle could be made more functional, more friendly to use.

Habitat Mothercare became a success – and a significant strategic step forward for Terence. He was already Mr Habitat; now he was that and more.

But for Terence, one step was never enough. He wanted more than Habitat Mothercare. He wanted to be where everyone shopped, and he wanted his designs to be for everyone.

I saw this made flesh at a Habitat Marketing Committee meeting; a ritual normally carried out over most of a day in the magnificence of Terence's home, Barton Court. On one occasion, however, Terence had a lunch date in London so he moved the meeting venue to his offices at Neal Street.

We had a perfectly normal discussion in the morning, then Terence excused himself for his lunch appointment, leaving the rest of us munching sandwiches in the boardroom.

'We've already covered most of the agenda. Is there anything you want to add this afternoon?' asked Michael Tyson, then Terence's number two.

'There is one thing . . .' I chipped in.

'Yes?' said Michael.

'I'm a bit worried by the look of the furniture in the Habitat window,' I continued. 'Terence is so preoccupied with the idea that everything has to be affordable for anybody, that all the stuff in the window is very good value, but it's a bit unexciting. People come to Habitat for stylish as well as for cheap – we need a few things in the window which give us a bit of sex appeal.'

'Such as?' asked Michael.

'I was thinking about the Wassily chair,' I replied.

The Wassily chair is a classic design by Marcel Breuer, from the Bauhaus period. All stainless-steel tubing and taut leather straps, it is strikingly sculptural, at the same time both singular and austere. Compared to other statement pieces it is inexpensive, as it uses no upholstery but, being made in modest numbers, it was still more costly than most Habitat stock. As soon as I mentioned it, Michael leapt forward, wagging his finger at me.

'No, you must not mention that!' he shouted. 'I suggested it to Terence the other day and it provoked an outburst. He thinks it's much too elitist, too costly; it undermines the democratic ethic of Habitat. He just won't contemplate it. I forbid you to mention it.'

Powerful people are often surrounded by others who are too frightened of them to say what they think, so they end up saying nothing. I didn't want to be one of them, so I nodded to Michael (in apparent agreement).

A few minutes later, Terence came back from his lunch, sat himself down opposite me on the far side of his monstrously large boardroom table, and asked what we'd been gossiping about while he was away.

'Well,' I said, 'there's been an attempt to gag me because my view may be provocative . . .'

I knew Terence would then be itching to hear what my view was.

'Let's hear it,' he said.

'I think the windows need a bit more sex appeal – I wonder if it would be good to put some kind of statement piece in the window display, like the Wassily chair . . .'

Terence's response was immediate, and it was startling. He lurched forward and swung a clenched fist violently towards my chin. His action was so sudden that I had no time to avoid the punch. But I was saved by the grandiose size of his boardroom table: he couldn't quite reach me, and the threatening fist swung past, missing me by inches.

There was an astonished silence: no one knew what to say.

Eventually I said, a tad nervously: 'So that would be a "No" then?'

'It would,' confirmed Terence.

I realised then that there was no doubting the passion of Terence's convictions. He wanted his vision to be shared by everybody, everywhere. He had driven a Porsche 911, a car which epitomises original design, much of his life: but the car maker who characterised Terence's dream was not Ferdinand Porsche, but Henry Ford. For it was Ford's Model T that brought the car within the means of most of us, and so made the motor car the defining technology of the twentieth century. In much the same way, Terence did not want to influence a design-conscious elite, he wanted to influence the whole of middle England.

I remember once, in the glory days of Habitat, asking Terence which retailer (apart from his own beloved Habitat, of course) he particularly admired. I expected him to choose something stylish, something design-led. But to my astonishment, without even an infinitesimal pause for thought, he said: 'Marks and Spencer.' The store which was the spiritual home of middle England. That, to Terence, defined the heartland of British retail.

I was wrong to be surprised: M&S represents perfectly two of Terence's most profound preoccupations. Firstly, it is big, very big, and Terence was intoxicated by scale. Secondly, it had become a bit boring, and Terence was endlessly excited by the opportunity of revitalisation. To own M&S would give Terence an unimaginably powerful springboard for his talent and energy. But even to a man of his unstoppable ambition, buying something as huge and established as M&S didn't seem realistic. It was impregnable.

Alongside M&S, however, was a sleeping giant – British Home Stores. BHS, as everyone knew it, was a blurred carbon copy of M&S. Its stores were often sited alongside M&S, and were on an equally grand scale. It sold very similar products: mass-market clothing and household products. It was aimed at the same mainstream, price-competitive market.

But there was one crucially important difference: M&S always had a certain cachet, a sense of doing ordinary things well, of being the mass-market store that still had a brand reputation. The legend was that everyone from royalty to rag-and-bone men bought their underwear from M&S. It was that peculiarly English thing, a national treasure. BHS was not. It was known like Marks & Spencer, but it was not loved like Marks & Spencer. And that huge limitation was, to Terence, a huge attraction.

Terence was endlessly fascinated by the themes of restoration and transformation. Typically that passion expressed itself in the restoration of an old building, which re-emerged with new life as a restaurant, and more. The rebirth of the once-neglected, now-stunning, Michelin building in Chelsea is one celebrated example. The transformation of the once-derelict riverside at Butler's Wharf is another. But with BHS, Terence could do more than transform a building: he could transform an institution. BHS would no longer be a chain of shops, it would be a brand. It would challenge the might of M&S.

Of course, Habitat was already a brand, and a highly successful one. But its appeal was skewed to the young, to the aware, to London. A thirty-year-old adman in Fulham might have a Habitat sofa, but Terence wanted a middle-aged mum in Rochdale to share his taste too. With BHS he could do that: if she bought her knickers from M&S

today, she could buy better-designed knickers from BHS tomorrow. Terence wanted to democratise design. He wanted his vision to be experienced and enjoyed by everybody.

Nothing could have been more 'for everybody' than BHS. In principle, nothing could have been riper for a Terence transformation than BHS. But in practice, how could the lean, modern Habitat become master of the lumbering giant that was BHS? It would be like a gazelle attempting to mount a rhinoceros.

Enter, stage right, Roger Seelig. He was the archetypal investment banker: charming, impeccably dressed, urbane, and unswervingly ambitious. He was a high-flying banker at prestigious Morgan Grenfell, and he and Terence hit it off immediately: it was an attraction of opposites.

Terence might have known a thing or two about design (in contrast to Seelig, whose taste was unrepentantly traditional), but when it came to money, no one knew more than Seelig. Different though they were in other ways, the pair shared one crucial characteristic – undiluted hunger for success.

Together, the plan was formed. Habitat Mothercare would use their shares to acquire BHS and create an overwhelming new force on the high street. In the Asian jungle, a python can kill and swallow a much larger animal such as a deer or an antelope. In the commercial jungle, Terence would swallow whole the much larger, but less athletic, BHS. However, naturalists will tell you that once the python has swallowed the much larger prey, the process of digestion can take several weeks. That might have been a nature lesson for Terence and Roger Seelig to reflect on.

Uninhibited by caution, their plan grew. And as their plan grew, so did their appetite. They developed their own shopping list of shops.

Richard Shops – a mainstream high-street women's clothes chain – would be added to the group. Like BHS, this was a chain with plenty of stores but very little charisma. The next target was Blazer, a smart, new, men's clothes chain. The kind of man who bought his chinos there was likely to be the same man who bought his sofa from Habitat. The icing on this massive cake was Heal's, a long-established London furniture store with a huge site in Tottenham Court Road. But Heal's wasn't just big; it had history on its side. The store dated back to Victorian times, but it was Ambrose Heal, the great-grandson of the founder, who gave Heal's its distinct character. Ambrose Heal was both a designer and a businessman. Influenced by John Ruskin and William Morris, he was a kind of prototype Terence. In between the two world wars, he established Heal's as a flagship of good, simple modernity.

Long before the Habitat years, Heal's was the only major store in London selling modern furniture with any sense of design integrity. If modernism was the new God, then the massive Tottenham Court Road store was the cathedral.

Heal's had lost its way in recent years and was no longer the force it had been, but the Heal's heritage still stood for something. For Terence to possess it, and then bring back its sparkle, was more than just a commercial opportunity; it was also a personal fulfilment, a way of etching his name more deeply in the history of British design.

The new group of businesses was to be named 'Storehouse' – a fitting name for a powerhouse of retail: Habitat, Mothercare, Heal's, Richard Shops, Blazer, and the behemoth that was BHS. The sheer scale of the adventure was startling; and the audacity and brute pace with which Terence and Roger Seelig had put it together was equally staggering.

Terence and Seelig took a few days off at Brunelys, the gracious country house Terence owned in Les Alpilles, an unspoilt part of Provence. They decided to celebrate their achievement by enjoying a grand dinner at L'Oustau de Baumanière, a celebrated three-rosette Michelin restaurant in the neighbouring, and extremely picturesque, village of Les Baux. The occasion called for a truly fine wine. After a survey of the magnificent wine list, Roger Seelig suggested two alternatives – one cost a breathtaking £900, but an even finer vintage from the same vineyard was a frightening £9,000. The latter, Terence decreed after much debate with the sommelier, was too extravagant even for this special moment. Seelig duly ordered the £900 bottle. It arrived, was ceremoniously opened, decanted, and poured.

Terence and Seelig sipped this exceptional vintage. It surpassed their expectations even of a £900 bottle. Seelig looked at the label on the bottle, and checked the wine list again. The sommelier's enthusiasm had got the better of him: he had opened the £9,000 bottle by mistake. Faced with this error, the restaurant had no choice but to let Terence and Roger enjoy the superb bottle, and charge a mere £900 for the privilege.

It seemed to be a metaphor for Terence's life at the time: fate was always on his side.

Back in London, Terence was now confidently at the helm of this retail supertanker. To make this possible, he had been obliged to dilute his own personal shareholding so there was a risk that his level of control might also be reduced. But this risk seemed insignificant when set alongside the reward. Terence was now chairman of an extraordinary spread of retail businesses. Half of Britain's shopping was under his control. The new empire, with some touches of Terence's design magic, could not fail to expand. Or so it seemed.

Terence was entranced by his new power. When asked by a journalist if this new role would change his life in any way, Terence grandly replied that he would simply have to get a driver to chauffeur him around his empire.

As it transpired, Terence's life was to change rather more than that.

Terence had fewer shares, but in a much, much larger business; he no longer had the despotic degree of control he had always coveted. Of course, that wouldn't matter as long as the businesses traded well. The executive chairman has free rein while the results are good.

Shareholders only start interfering when things fail to make money. Which, of course, just wouldn't happen. The businesses already had scale, and soon they would have style as well.

What could possibly go wrong? A thought also shared by Icarus, when he took off into the sun.

11

In the Court of King Conran

R.M.

Life with Terence was astonishingly like that in a medieval court. King Terence dominated – and few other personalities could demonstrate a belief in the divine rights of monarchs as forcefully.

He was surrounded by courtiers, who slipped in and out of favour with alarming speed. The family were interwoven with the courtiers, and equally at risk of being embraced one moment, cast aside the next.

In the seventies and eighties, the heyday of Habitat, the formal court proceedings were conducted through the infamous marketing committee meetings. Tediously long, these occasions were not without moments of surprise. At my very first of these events, Terence was being particularly difficult, for no apparent reason. One of his most senior courtiers at the time was Michael Tyson, then his second-in-command. (This, as I later discovered for myself, is a role which can carry a great deal of power, or none at all, depending on the whim of the first-in-command.) Terence's behaviour was making Michael perceptibly irate: eventually he turned to him and said: 'Terence, you're being fucking irksome. Stop it.'

I was amazed. I'd never heard anyone answer back to Terence quite like that. I just didn't imagine it was allowed, though it did have the desired effect at the time. It certainly engraved 'irksome' on my mind as an adjective of disproportionate power.

Subsequently Michael was 'promoted' to head of the business in America, so perhaps this gold-plated exile was Terence's revenge.

Another of Terence's most senior courtiers was the urbane and intelligent John Stephenson. He, in quick succession, worked closely with Terence, left Terence to marry Terence's second wife Shirley shortly after they divorced, divorced her himself, and was then reunited to work closely with Terence again.

One of John's gifts was his sensitivity to Terence's moods. At yet another Habitat marketing committee, some market research was being presented by Giles Keeble, an earnest young man from the advertising agency. I was Giles's boss, and therefore responsible for his performance, which seemed to me perfectly adequate though rather long-winded. John thought otherwise: he sensed Terence was getting bored by this overly thorough peroration. He scribbled a message on a scrap of paper and passed it to me.

On it were written six words of startling simplicity. It just said: 'Stop this man speaking at once.'

I looked at John, puzzled. 'Terence is getting bored,' he whispered.

I stood up, put my hand on Giles's shoulder and said: 'Thank you, Giles, this has been a most interesting presentation.'

Giles, looking perplexed, said: 'I haven't finished yet.'

'Oh, yes, you have,' I responded, pushing Giles firmly down into his chair.

The meeting resumed, Terence relaxed, and John had done his good deed for the day.

At another Habitat meeting, I had to present a new advertising campaign. My agency had already produced several proposals which were clearly not good enough, and I was feeling vulnerable. At last we had some ideas I thought were genuinely strong, so I asked Terence for the opportunity to show them to him in private the day before the full meeting. I knew that if he was happy, the larger meeting would be a formality.

Terence was enthusiastic about the ads. 'You've got it, at last,' he said. 'Show them tomorrow. Well done.'

At the meeting the next day, I made my presentation to the team, knowing that Terence had already decided. It was an easy sale. I put the ads back in my portfolio.

'Anything else, Roger?' enquired Terence.

Elated by my success, I replied rather cockily: 'No, thanks, I think I'll quit while I'm ahead.'

As soon as I'd said it, I realised I had committed the crime of lèse-majesté.

Terence was not going to allow my arrogance to go unpunished. 'No,' he said, speaking even more slowly than usual, 'I don't think you are ahead.'

At which point he produced a design for a minor trade advertisement we had drafted. It wasn't good enough, which Terence knew all too well; and it gave him the ammunition he needed. He spent the next half-hour deconstructing the ad, demonstrating its inadequacies with merciless forensic skill, and humiliating me in the process. He punctured my balloon of confidence with surgical ruthlessness. I was, in spite of my earlier success, sent home with my tail between my legs.

I learnt my lesson: a courtier can be a successful courtier, but never – not even for a moment – should he try to usurp the focus on the monarch.

A medieval court depends on an all-powerful king, and during the Storehouse years it became clear that Terence was no longer in that position: his potency was eroded quickly by money men behind the scenes. So the court evaporated, along with Terence's influence. But during the restaurant revival of the 1990s, the court returned. When Terence was there, we were affectionately deferential; when he was not, we were endlessly gossipy.

Terence himself consistently maintained a lugubrious presence in the group. On one much more recent occasion, I had warned him I would be late for an important meeting, as I had to get the result of a biopsy which would show whether or not I had cancer: clearly a serious moment for me. He grunted, which was his way of acknowledging receipt of information without committing himself to a position.

In the event, the result of the test was all clear, and I bounced cheerfully into the meeting five minutes late.

'Sorry I'm late,' I said, 'but at least I'm not dying.'

Terence looked at me mournfully, then pronounced: 'Roger, we are all dying.'

I hesitated. 'I realise that, Terence,' I said. 'I just thought I might have been on an accelerated programme.'

Another grunt from Terence, and the meeting continued.

It would have been easy to dismiss his response as the workings of a dry sense of humour. But I felt it was more than that: it was indicative of Terence's unease in confronting difficult conversations. More significantly, it was indicative of his anxieties about his own mortality.

It was ungracious of him not to share my enthusiasm, but in a morbid sense he was right. We are all dying. And since he was eighty then, he was all too aware that he might be closer to that quietus than the rest of us.

In medieval courts, the rhythms of Church and State were interwoven – not surprising, given that these courts were underpinned by a belief in the divine right of kings. Life in Terence's court was little different. The politics of day-by-day business management were underscored by a certain sense of evangelism.

Habitat was, of course, a business, but it was much more than that: it was a personal vision. It was not so much *managed* by Terence as *driven* by him. He was (usually) a benevolent despot, never a conventional chairman. The people he recruited didn't expect to be led in a usual way – they knew that, under this tyrant of taste, life would be more difficult, but also more inspiring.

Habitat was not just a corporation, it was a belief system.

A fine example of this was a moment at another Habitat marketing committee meeting. This group, about fifteen strong, included anyone and everyone in Habitat management who might ever have something to do with marketing. The meetings took place every two months at Barton Court, Terence's grand country mansion. They ran earnestly from 10 a.m. till lunch, which was cooked splendidly by Terence's then wife Caroline, with Terence liberally distributing red wine. Unsurprisingly, the meetings continued after lunch in a more desultory way.

We were all overawed by Terence's home. It was a Georgian building of significant style and size, furnished in the eclectic mixture of old and new, grand and plain, which was the Terence trademark. Its prep-school origins, which gives an idea of its size, and the imposing setting conferred on the meetings a sense of occasion. It did feel a bit like an encounter between the junior prefects and the headmaster.

The purpose of the meetings was for each of us to brief the others on what we were doing; and to give Terence the opportunity to approve (hopefully), to cajole, applaud, shout down, or go wherever his mood led him – always in a pall of expensive cigar smoke.

One day, Peter Hope, who was then in charge of the day-to-day management of the shops, was outlining his plans for new staff uniforms. Uniforms for female staff were described and approved without demur; and then Peter started to explain how the men would be wearing jackets, in a specially chosen artificial fabric. This would last longer, look crisper, be easier to keep clean . . . at which point Terence interjected with a firm and simple: 'No.'

Peter protested, and attempted to defend the practicality of his choice.

'No,' repeated Terence, more loudly and ferociously this time. 'No, no, no.'

'But, Terence . . .' Peter stuttered.

'No!' shouted Terence again. He got out of his chair, walked to the window, turned his back on us, and stared out at his acres of land. He then unleashed an impassioned speech, lasting a good twenty minutes. It cannot have been prepared – he didn't know that artificial fabric for staff jackets was even on the agenda. Yet it was a speech of extraordinary eloquence.

His theme was that Habitat was not just about making money, it was a vision of a better world: a world where things were designed lovingly, with care and intelligence, and then made with craftsmanship and a respect for natural materials. Habitat furniture would be made from real wood, not laminates; upholstery would be in leather, not vinyl. And staff jackets would be tailored from pure wool, not some nasty artificial substitute.

When Terence started his diatribe at 12.30, Habitat was a business: by the time he'd finished at 12.50, Habitat was a philosophy.

We were not mere furniture salesmen; we walked in the shadows of John Ruskin and William Morris.

This outpouring of passion was utterly unexpected, and even Terence himself seemed slightly embarrassed by the strength of his own emotion.

'I think we should all go down for lunch,' he said in a quiet, almost shy, voice.

As we filed out of the room, I sensed that many of the others, though slightly perplexed and uncomfortable after Terence's outburst, were still tending to dismiss the episode as just another Terence rant. They'd seen them before, and they'd see them again. But I reacted differently: I was uplifted. I was working for a man who believed in something much deeper than the profit-and-loss account. Of course, Terence was massively motivated by profit too – I knew him well enough to be vividly clear about that. But he had a bigger mission: he wanted Britain to live in a better way, which valued design and respected the authenticity of natural materials.

It was a glimpse of Terence as an evangelist for a certain way of life: a preacher as well as a profiteer.

This then was the mood and mindset of Terence and his team, as they set about transforming the monolith that was BHS.

But it certainly wasn't the mood and mindset of the team at BHS. They were in personality uncannily like the shop they worked for – solid citizens, well-meaning, middle of the road, but unimaginative and a bit behind the times.

Of course, BHS was in trouble: far outflanked in reputation by its more famous rival, Marks & Spencer, it had a thin future to look forward to. It needed to change. But the people who worked there were slow to acknowledge that. For the management, arriving in London's Marylebone Road each morning at the very large, slightly dull headquarters building (itself a perfect metaphor for the style of the company) it would be hard to imagine that the business was under any threat. Denial is always a problem in a large corporation when it has run out of energy and ideas. A ship with a hole in it will sink eventually, but a very big ship will take a long time to sink, and often the crew take a while to notice that something has gone wrong.

So when Terence's angry brigade of Habitat-inspired reformers started to change things at BHS, the BHS team tended to regard them as over-promoted upstarts who didn't understand the traditional values of their more conservative customer. So the BHS team would agree to make changes (because that was politically easier) but they wouldn't enact change (because they didn't believe it was what their customers wanted).

Habitat managers and Habitat designers had already been working with Mothercare for a while. That had been a more fruitful relationship, and one in which each partner wanted the other: more of a love affair and less of an arranged marriage. So when the Habitat team swept into BHS, they failed to anticipate the stone wall that would greet them. Try as they might, they just couldn't make happen the changes they thought necessary.

In theory, Terence – as chairman – was in charge. But in practice, if the troops won't carry out the orders of the generals, then no one is in charge. Decisions were made, instructions were given, but not enough of this was translated into action. The BHS team were not consciously seeking to rebel; they simply didn't see the problems in the same way, so they didn't have the same motivation.

Subconsciously they were trying to protect their conservative customers from an onslaught of Conran good taste. Management was in stasis. Instead of battling to win over new customers, Terence found himself battling to win over his own staff.

While Terence was struggling with BHS, he still had Richard Shops, Heal's, Mothercare and Blazer to worry about. Blazer wasn't a problem: it was a much smaller business than the others, and its own management were entrepreneurial, style-sensitive and sympathetic to the Conran ethic. Mothercare had been in the family for longer, and was gradually being integrated. But Heal's was big, and in spite of its design heritage was living in the past. And Richard Shops was the kind of clothes store you might send your mum to, but almost certainly wouldn't go to yourself. So Heal's and Richard Shops started to manifest the same grudging resistance to change that was slowing down BHS.

Terence's energy, drive and work rate couldn't be faulted. But in the past, he'd applied those virtues to a business he had created, with staff he had hired. The staff were his people; they understood and shared his vision. Habitat was one business with a clear sense of its own identity. During the time in which Terence had created it, grown it, expanded it across Britain, and taken it to France and the USA, it had retained its sense of purpose. It was always a business rooted firmly in Terence's uncompromising vision.

Suddenly, it was all very different. There were several businesses, not one, so the sheer workload needed to create change was daunting. But the problem was not just the size of the challenge, it was the character of the challenge. Terence was no longer designing on a blank sheet of paper, no longer creating a culture from first principles. The businesses he was now running had their own history, their own culture, their own way of doing things. The staff he had inherited were not *disciples*, they were merely *employees*. Growing Habitat had been like erecting a beautiful new building on a clear site. But with BHS and Richard Shops, an ugly old building had to be dismantled first. And the tenants didn't want to leave.

Purity and commitment became overwhelmed by politics and compromise.

The consequences of this were simple, but serious. It took much longer than expected to make the changes Terence wanted. Very often, when the changes did happen, they seemed to have been watered down. Behind the scenes there was huge energy to innovate. But what the customer saw was not yet that much different from what the customer had been seeing for a long, long time. As the shops weren't changing as fast as Terence wanted, so the sales weren't rising as fast as Terence wanted.

That meant, inevitably, that higher profits were not coming through anything like as quickly or as generously as expected.

The banks behind Storehouse were not getting the easy win they had been promised. The grand plan wasn't working.

Terence had to explain this to critical investors: analytical, joyless people (or so Terence thought) who didn't relate to his passion for design, nor to his mercurial temperament. They had been happy to be beguiled by Terence's charisma when it came with the lure of huge profits. But when the profits didn't come in on schedule, they started to fall out of love very quickly.

They decided that Terence's flair needed to be balanced by some hard-headed business skill.

This 'balance' came in the form of Michael Julien, a rational and respected finance man with a track record at large corporations like Guinness and the Midland Bank. Against Terence's preference, Julien was imposed on him as the new chief executive of the Storehouse Group, with Terence remaining as chairman.

The Storehouse businesses were not making the money Terence had wanted; their managements seemed impervious to any ideas of creativity or innovation; and now he had to run it all with a very proper accountant half a pace behind him.

Terence was starting to feel what Icarus felt, when the wax began to melt.

12

Nemesis

R.M.

In the late eighties, Terence was suddenly struggling with the many-headed Hydra that was Storehouse. A tyrant (and Terence has sometimes earned that epithet) might be able to sort it out, but a two-man committee never would. Only a City investor, who understood the management of money but didn't understand the management of people, could have imagined that Terence Conran and Michael Julien would remain as partners for any productive stretch of time. They weren't like each other, and they didn't like each other.

Moreover, if it was right to impose someone on Terence, Michael Julien was not the right someone to impose. What was needed was a driver who could make Terence's vision a reality, someone who could force through a new feel to these outdated businesses in the face of entrenched interests and innate conservatism. Julien had walked into a deadlock between imagination and caution, and no amount of financial analysis would change that. What was needed was someone to radiate Terence's vision, not dilute it. The crisis demanded a bruiser, not an accountant.

Of course, the City felt comfortable with Julien because he understood finance, cash flow, all that good stuff. Unlike Terence, he spoke their language. But good cash flow doesn't just grow from astute financial control: first you need people walking into stores and spending money. Without their cash, there's nothing to flow.

But the pace of change was constipated by the cultural clash between the old guard and Terence's shock troops. So there wasn't enough new excitement in the shops to generate new spending.

As pressure mounted, Terence's own demeanour – at least on the surface – seemed remarkably unchanged. Yet as the forces gathered against him, it became clear to others that he no longer had the stranglehold on power that had always been so much a part of his charisma. In the past, when a decision was needed, it was Terence who made it. That was the rule, and his staff knew it. Now decisions were beginning to be made by people behind the scenes, people he didn't know. Terence's persona was starting to take on a two-dimensional character: the puppet master was in danger of becoming one of the marionettes.

We will never know whether Terence's vision, particularly for BHS, would have worked, if he had been able to deliver it in practice. Sceptics might think that Terence's own taste was way ahead of a typical BHS shopper. That might be right. But it's notable now, a generation later, that Marks & Spencer are fighting to add excitement to their offer in order to keep their share of the market. Today M&S are trying to do what Terence was trying to do years ago.

What is certain is that Terence's vision never did get properly articulated in the shops he'd taken over. In the early years of Habitat, every Habitat branch looked thrillingly different from anything we'd seen before. But BHS, after Terence, looked disturbingly like BHS before Terence. Better perhaps, but only better at the margins – not fundamentally changed. No wonder the customers stayed away in droves.

With no growth in trade, the City lost patience.

Predictably, the first scapegoat was the ideas man, not the bean-counter. In 1990, Terence was ousted from the throne of the empire he had engineered. Storehouse was barely four years old.

Michael Julien didn't last much longer. He left 'on medical grounds' in 1992. And Storehouse collapsed. The unravelling of the dream was tragic to behold.

BHS lumbered on ineffectually, and eventually in 2000 it was sold to the entrepreneurial Philip Green, boss of Topshop. Green, unlike Terence, didn't concentrate on redesigning the products: he concentrated on redesigning the profit margins instead. With calculated ruthlessness, he invited in his suppliers, and offered them the choice of being dropped by BHS or giving BHS much lower prices. Their financial pain was to be Green's financial pleasure. For the most part, they caved in. They had little choice. Half a loaf is better than none.

So Green increased his profit margins dramatically, and made himself a great deal of money as a consequence. Yet the underlying disease of BHS – its lack of excitement – remained untreated. The margins might have grown but the trade didn't.

In March 2015, Green sold the BHS business. The price? He received the not-so-princely sum of £1 for his troubles. To make a bad situation worse, within little more than a year the new owners were forced to put BHS into administration, leaving 10,000 workers not just without a job but without a proper pension either. *Sic transit gloria mundi.*

As a consequence of the pensions catastrophe, Parliament debated whether Sir (as he now was) Philip Green, the asset-stripper par excellence, should be stripped of one of his own assets – his knighthood. Then the government's Pensions Regulator successfully pressured Green to pay £363 million of his own money into the under-nourished BHS pension fund. Ian Wright, one of the MPs who led the inquiry into the collapse of BHS, said that the payment of that large sum should not enable Green to keep his knighthood. 'It would,' he said, 'be like rewarding an arsonist who put his own fire out.'

Terence's original view, all those years ago, was that the BHS stores needed a huge shot of design adrenalin. It looks now as if he might have been right after all. Certainly, those thousands of loyal employees who nearly lost their pension would agree with him.

Richard Shops was first bought by the then owners of Selfridges, and in turn was acquired, ironically, by Philip Green. He used the sites for his other brands, and the Richard Shops brand (if it had ever really been a brand) died in obscurity. The company name is still registered at Companies House, but it doesn't trade any more, and effectively it no longer exists.

Similarly, Blazer has disappeared from view.

Heal's, once the spiritual home of good British furniture design, staggered on and was bought by an investment company in 2001. The new owners have said publicly that they cherish its 'unique character'. Cynics may say that evidence of this is, to put it politely, somewhat limited. For sure, there is no one at Heal's today with Terence's style, or his heart, to bring that 'unique character' to life.

For Terence, the jewel in his crown was Habitat. This was the brand through which he had made his reputation and his fortune. This was the brand which had changed the way we live. And the fate of Habitat was particularly poignant.

In 1992, with Terence gone, Julien on his way out, and Storehouse in collapse, Habitat was put up for sale. This was by far the deepest wound. Terence had bought the other businesses, albeit with ambitious hopes of a dramatic and design-driven turnaround. But he had not bought Habitat: he had invented it, created it, built it brick by brick. It was his child. Now it was to be snatched away. Nothing could be worse. Except it could, because in the event the foster parent who stole his offspring was his deadliest rival – IKEA, the only other business in the world with a vision that could compare with that of Habitat.

No ending could, for Terence, have been more humiliating. Yet what followed made matters more painful still.

As IKEA grew to be a massive worldwide business, Habitat was seemingly neglected by the IKEA management. It lost its sparkle, and soon started losing money too. In 2001, Terence and I made an attempt to buy the business back, but Ingvar Kamprad, the immensely successful founder of IKEA, rebuffed the offer.

It might have been one of the few bad decisions made by Kamprad. Losses continued, and then got worse. In 2009, Habitat was sold to Hilco, a company which specialises in buying businesses that are in trouble and 'restructuring' them. (In practice, that often means stripping out the assets and closing down everything else.) Hilco paid €15 million for the business – but first IKEA had to write off big debts and provide Hilco with €50 million of working capital. In effect, IKEA had *given* the business to Hilco, debt-free, along with a Christmas present of €35 million.

Only two years later, in 2011, all but three UK Habitat stores were put into administration.

Fragments of Habitat continue to exist, but the scale and charisma of the brand Terence created are in the past. The dream is over. What a sad end to an ambitious adventure.

Fuelled with the confidence of Habitat's success, Terence had been persuaded to launch a full-frontal assault on British retail. It was an astonishingly audacious bid to dominate the landscape of high-street Britain, and to revitalise it with his design vision. But the result had been a catastrophe.

Terence had failed to make a success of the behemoth that was BHS, and the other businesses he'd taken over. Worse than that – much worse indeed – his beloved Habitat was no longer in his control. He then had to watch it gradually turn to dust.

The Greeks taught us that hubris is inevitably followed by nemesis. The tale of Storehouse is a particularly vivid example of that truth. It's a tale that tells us much about the complexities and contradictions of Terence's character.

It tells us of his unbounded ambition. In a few years, having created Habitat with great élan, he embraced Mothercare, then BHS, then Richard Shops, Blazer, and even Heal's. He appeared to have taken over half the high street. There seems to be an inevitability that someone of such huge ambition would eventually overreach himself.

It tells us of his passion for design. He believed, without a scintilla of doubt, that – with design energy behind it – the lifeless BHS could be made great again. At the time, many ridiculed this, yet the 2016 collapse of BHS to the point where it had to be sold for £1 makes us wonder, after all, whether it was Terence who had called it right, and it was the rest of us who were out of step.

And when it came to dealing with the City, Terence was their hero at the stage when the vision was expressed: but when that vision didn't turn quickly into money, he became their villain. That's partly because the City allowed their greed to blind them to the risks, but it's also because Terence's mercurial manner was much too much for them.

It tells us of Terence's creativity, and the temperament that goes with that. There is a theory that creativity is linked to a childlike quality. As children we express ourselves freely and imaginatively, sometimes even wildly. But as we mature into adults we learn to control our urges. Babies cry when they are hungry; adults don't. But with this maturity comes a loss of imaginative expression. The restraint that comes with adulthood may be socially desirable, but it stifles creativity. Adults who are highly creative, so the theory goes, never escape the uncontrolled emotional surges of childhood. That is why they are more imaginative as adults, and it is also why they can be petulant and wilful as adults. Like all generalised theories, they are plenty of exceptions to test this rule, but it still has an underlying truth. Einstein said: 'To stimulate our creativity one must develop the childlike inclination for play.' Even more eloquently, Picasso said: 'It took me four years to paint like Raphael but a lifetime to paint like a child.'

Certainly the theory matched much of Terence's behaviour: he was undoubtedly highly creative, but he could be wilful and childlike when thwarted. With that childlike quality came a certain guilelessness. While Terence was highly sophisticated in his tastes, he could still react with the simple naivety of a child.

That begins to explain his attitude to the transformation of dull businesses like BHS and Richard Shops. He assumed that once the design of the product was changed for the better, everything else would change for the better too. Equally he assumed that the staff who had chosen to work for these staid companies would embrace new design with the same excitement that he did.

Terence started Habitat in 1964. It took him quarter of a century to build it into an international force. But within four short years of the launch of Storehouse, Habitat and Terence had been torn apart, only for Habitat to crumble gradually away.

Terence was a man hugely conscious of his public reputation, who worked hard to manipulate it for the better. Every week the press cuttings about Conran were put on Terence's desk, and he read them with obsessive concentration, irrationally delighted by each and every mention. Imagine how he must have felt when – on 17 February 1989 – he saw in *The Times* the cruel headline: 'Conran's ailing empire reaches breaking point.'

The article continued in the same merciless vein: 'Conran's reputation as a master of style and arbiter of fashion has suffered irreparably.' It questioned Terence's strategy and his management ability. 'Style is one thing, substance quite another,' it harrumphed.

You might have expected Terence to emerge from this disaster a sadder and wiser man. And you might have expected him to have lost some of his obsessive hunger to achieve. But Terence had a knack of not conforming to expectations.

The failure that was Storehouse was a huge blow to Terence. But he was a pugilist at heart: he was down, but he was not out.

PART 4

REDESIGN

13

Conran and Contradictions

R.M.

Superficially, Terence's character might seem straightforward. Certainly there were some important constants. He had always been a man of great ambition, unwavering drive and determination, endlessly fixated by the power of design. The sense of steely focus was always there.

And yet his temperament was shot through with perplexing contradictions. Take, for example, the small plaque which sat on his desk. It carried the rubric: 'Plain, simple, useful.' These are the values, Terence believed, to which any design should aspire. He has even written a book with the title *Plain Simple Useful*. He talked about this three-word mantra with a kind of religious fervour, as if he were a member of a Shaker community, or one of the Amish.

Habitat stands as one of his great achievements. And most of the products sold there, whether a sofa or a soup spoon, would qualify as plain, simple and useful, albeit they were often delightfully stylish as well.

Yet over the road from the first Habitat stood its grander cousin, the first Conran Shop. While the underlying aesthetic – a respect for modernity at its best – might have been similar, the way that aesthetic was interpreted could not have been more different.

You won't find many Shakers or Amish here: the Conran Shop is a temple to luxurious living. The prices are high and the mood is one of extravagant good taste. Sumptuous leather sofas are displayed alongside distressed quasi-industrial antiques. All kinds of whimsical oddities are hidden amongst the more practical pieces. A candidate for a job was once asked by Terence what he particularly liked about the Conran Shop.

'It's the only furniture store I know which also sells unicycles,' was the reply.

You might just about get away with describing a unicycle as plain or simple, but useful doesn't seem remotely right.

The first time I was invited to Barton Court for a Habitat meeting, I rang a friend, Ray Gillman, who worked for Terence, and asked him what to expect.

'Exactly what you'd predict,' he replied. 'A magnificent house, with bare floorboards and the cheapest spotlights in the Habitat catalogue.'

Ray had captured in a sentence a pivotal component in Terence's aesthetic vision: the combination of the splendid and the simple. Barton Court, under Terence's tenure, was just that. Entering from the backyard, one stood in a long austere corridor, unfurnished and uncarpeted. Bizarrely, on the walls hung a stunning collection of toy Bugatti pedal cars.

Beyond was the main room of the ground floor: a vast space, running the full width of the mansion. It was furnished with a startling mix of the highest of high-end modern designs juxtaposed with beautiful, rare and quirky antiques. It was theatrically striking. And no one ever went there. Instead we congregated in the kitchen – the dining room had been removed, so cooking and eating happened in the same room. That's a commonplace now, but it was revolutionary then. It all felt as if Terence had wanted the space and grace of a grand country house but with the pomposity stripped out, along with the wallpaper. It was Georgian elegance, democratised.

Life at Barton Court (or Terence Towers, as I nicknamed it) was often taxing, but it was never dull. On one occasion, Sir James

Dyson, one of Terence's closest friends, came for a business meeting with Terence: they were both investors in a small furniture design business which Terence had set up. Dyson lived in Malmesbury, a modest 38 miles from Terence in Kintbury, a short and comfortable drive in his chauffeur-driven car. But Dyson does things in style, so he came by helicopter. Except that it had been raining heavily, and apparently if you land a helicopter on wet grass it can sink in, and when the grass dries the wheels get glued in so you can't take off again. Accordingly, Dyson had rented a concrete hard from a nearby farmer so he could not only land, but take off again. But that still left a mile of muddy fields to traverse. So Dyson's chauffeur was duly despatched (presumably from Malmesbury too) in Dyson's elegant Maserati saloon to escort the great man precisely one mile from farm to Terence. As Scott Fitzgerald famously said, the rich are different from you and me.

Barton Court was one example of the interweaving of simple and splendid that was so central to Terence's personality; but there were others. His startling riverside London office was a huge penthouse, with a light-filled atrium, limestone floors, elegant furniture and valuable modern art on the walls. Yet by the wood-burning stove in the main living area was a large wicker basket overflowing with faded copies of the *Financial Times* – which Terence used as low-cost firelighters. On a shelf, there was a ziggurat of Terence's empty cigar boxes: waste transformed into a kind of sculpture. Nothing should be thrown away.

This hatred of waste, interwoven with his love of the simple, expressed itself in other ways. As we've observed, the handwritten notes he churned out were usually written on the back of a letter retrieved from his waste-paper basket. A bottle of Scotch kept in the office used a chinagraph plimsoll line to discourage uninvited consumption.

His lunchtime habits at his London office were equally extreme: he either went for a fine meal at a serious restaurant, or he stayed in his office and ate nothing whatsoever. It was an extraordinary regime: most people who eat out regularly would still have a sandwich or perhaps some fruit if they weren't going out for lunch. But Terence would go through the day, from a light breakfast to dinner, with absolutely nothing in between, save copious amounts of coffee, several large cigars, and perhaps an early evening whisky. Alternatively, he would eat a rich three-course lunch, washed down by plenty of good white burgundy with the starter, and rather more good red burgundy with the main course. All this for a man whose idea of exercise was to instruct someone else to bring him an ashtray when he lit yet another cigar. I never saw him do anything more physically taxing than walk slowly from his limousine to the door of Bibendum. Yet he lived till eighty-eight, so maybe a diet of self-indulgence and Santenay is better for you than your doctor thinks.

Terence's own furniture design work reflected his mantra of 'plain, simple, useful'. Yet alongside this puritan straightforwardness, there was the flamboyance of the impresario. The swirling marble staircase at Quaglino's, with its glistening brass balustrade, might be useful, but it is neither plain nor simple. The chairs at Quaglino's were a design originally created for the US Navy to use in its submarines; and you can't get much more functional than that. But each chair was decorated with a brightly coloured tassel that served no purpose other than to delight the eye and hint at the frivolous.

Ever the contrarian, Terence's belief in the beauty of the unadorned was only matched by his sense of theatre. His seventy-fifth birthday party took place at Le Pont de la Tour; a grand dinner for the great and good of London culturati, followed by a firework display of captivating flamboyance, launched from a barge on the river. It was a great and spectacular occasion, but was it plain or simple?

Alongside his mingling of the beautiful with the basic, Terence loved to mix ancient with modern. Beside the art nouveau outrageousness of the Michelin building, Terence placed an austerely elegant, glass-fronted modern building. Having restored the fine Victorian industrial architecture of the Butler's Wharf building, he attempted to give contrast by creating a modernist steel-and-glass office block as its neighbour. (The planners knew better, and insisted on a faux-Victorian red-brick look: the crassness of their decision is now there for all to see.)

The living area of Terence's penthouse at Butler's Wharf was a perfect paradigm for his catholic but contradictory aesthetic. At the top of a graciously curving limestone staircase was a vast space: the west side was all window, looking into a veritable jungle of exotic plants. The east side opened onto a roof terrace overlooking a romantically tiny tributary of the river Thames. In the central space, two big, comfy sofas stared at each other over a plain wooden coffee table, designed by Terence himself. There was a large rug from the thirties; statement pieces of modern design by Kukkapuro, Charles Eames and Marcel Breuer, and dramatic abstract art by Richard Smith.

But there was also a battered old Victorian armchair, whose torn upholstery was deliberately unrepaired, an old bentwood side table, a collection of walking sticks carved by his brother-in-law as therapeutic relaxation, and a miscellany of old decorative objects, all testimony to Terence's love of flea markets. The room was a visual tour de force as well as living evidence of Terence's uncanny ability to create a coherent visual impact from an eclectic mix of objects.

At one memorable meeting with a lady property developer who was contemplating a deal with Conran, the woman in question got up from the table in the middle of the meeting, ignoring the discussion, walked slowly round the room, admiring its contents, and then proclaimed: 'I want some of this.'

She had, along with all of her generation, been hypnotised by the Conran gift for *mise en scène*.

Terence's passion for mixing old and new, spare and splendid, was a particularly powerful force in the early years of Habitat. A generation of young, thinking people were setting up home in the sixties. Their parents' lives had been overshadowed by the horrors of the Second World War and the deprivations which followed: but this new generation wanted to leave that behind and create their own new order. They wanted to express themselves with a look that was utterly fresh – but they didn't have that much money to do it with. Thanks to Habitat, they could buy good modern furniture inexpensively. The Conran look gave them permission to mix that with old pieces they had pinched from their parents, along with antique knick-knacks they'd found in junk shops.

Terence is admired for his keen sense of the zeitgeist, for knowing where taste is headed. But in the Habitat years, he wasn't just understanding the zeitgeist, he was creating it.

The mixing of old and new, the simple and the flamboyant, are aesthetically enriching examples of the contradictions in the Terence temperament. But, beyond his aesthetic, there are many more puzzling contradictions.

Terence was an extraordinarily generous host: at dinner, fine wines flowed in abundance, the food would be extravagant as well as delicious, and no meal ended without a large bottle of Marc de Bourgogne or Vieille Prune being offered. When he hosted a party, the food and drink would be equally splendid, and after the feast for the stomach there was often a feast for the eyes, in the form of an extraordinary firework display which consumed more money in twenty minutes than most of us earn in a year.

Yet Terence was unfailingly careful (enemies would say 'mean') over small amounts. He once calculated that each time the lift was used in his office at Butler's Wharf, the cost of the journey was 54p. He started to grumble about this, so the staff were well aware of the calculation.

Sebastian Conran was then working in the same office, running the Conran design business. It's been alleged that he circulated a mischievous email saying that, in future, staff would be expected to pay 54p for each lift journey they took. Because of the awkward amount, the receptionist would keep a supply of change, so anyone could get the exact 54p before they stepped into the lift. While this story may well be apocryphal, the very fact that it was invented in the first place is a remarkable testament to Terence's reputation as a man with a passion to look after the pennies.

I remember visiting him at Barton Court when he was courting me to be his chief executive. As soon as I arrived, he excitedly showed me the brochure for a BMW M6 – then a very glamorous new sports coupé. 'What do you think?' he asked. (We shared a boyish interest in cars.) I made admiring noises. 'The local dealer has a demonstration model,' Terence continued, 'and my Porsche is getting a bit long in the tooth. I thought you'd like it. I'm definitely going for it. Of course, I need to have a bit of a haggle with them over the price.' He looked genuinely excited at the prospect of his new toy.

A week later, I was back at Barton Court to continue our flirtation. 'Did you get the BMW?' I asked. 'No,' said Terence, looking genuinely downcast. 'I wanted a few hundred quid off, but he wouldn't budge.' I was astonished: Terence clearly wanted the car and, to him, two or three hundred pounds was loose change down the back of the sofa. But then I realised that while Terence was capable of extravagance on an epic scale, his obsession with money meant that he couldn't buy a car, or anything else, without getting a deal: the amount was irrelevant, it was the principle of making a saving that mattered.

Terence was similarly astringent over his driver. Having a chauffeur is, for the lucky few, one of life's great luxuries. No more searching hopelessly for a taxi in the rain, no more struggling to find a parking meter only to discover you don't have the change to put in it, no more driving home nervously after three glasses of wine with dinner. It's a privilege only enjoyed by plutocrats, but a great privilege nonetheless.

However, when Terence went out for dinner (and he probably dined out more often than he dined in), he got his driver to take him to the restaurant – and then he sent him home. So at the end of the dinner, when all his rich compatriots slid comfortably into the backs of their Mercedes, Terence was left standing in the drizzle trying to find a cab. Why? Because it saved a couple of hours' overtime, that's why. That may actually have saved little more than the taxi fare, but to Terence the gesture was important.

Yet Terence could display great generosity of spirit. One day he was at a meeting of the Royal College of Art, where he was provost. As he left the meeting, he was ambushed by a wild-eyed young student who wanted his advice. Terence brushed him aside, but then paused and gave him his business card.

'I'm busy now, but call me at the office and fix a time to talk properly,' he said to the bemused student.

The student took him up on his offer. He met Terence and explained that he felt his talent was being frustrated and he needed some new stimulus and leadership.

'I assume – as you're a student – that you live in some rather disgusting flat,' said Terence. 'I think you'd better come and live at my house in the country for a while, so you can concentrate on your work, and I can keep an eye on you.'

The pushy young student could barely believe what he was hearing. But he quickly accepted. The eventual result was an extraordinary design for a gazebo in Terence's garden. It was made of sinuous laths of wood, folding round each other, forming a kind of elongated wooden tepee.

It was a structure of great beauty. At least it was, until Terence's friend, engineer-designer-tycoon James Dyson, paid him a visit. The downdraught from Dyson's helicopter made the once-beautiful gazebo disintegrate in moments.

It was, eventually, lovingly rebuilt. In the meantime, the young student had found the springboard for the career that he had craved, and he started to get noticed. His name was Thomas Heatherwick, and he is now an internationally celebrated designer and architect of true originality.

Terence showed a similar generosity of spirit when he wanted to recruit me as his chief executive in 2006. I was reluctant to commit myself to the job, as I had decided to do a master's degree in photography, a passion of mine.

'Do both,' said Terence. 'Be my chief executive, and take time off for your degree.'

'It would mean taking one full day a week off,' I replied.

'That's fine, just do it,' said Terence.

It was a remarkable offer: not many chairmen would tolerate a chief executive who didn't work a proper five-day week.

Yet when I was in the job, I was surprised when Terence asked to see me, and said. 'I see you've been drinking Earl Grey tea,' mouthing the words 'Earl Grey' as if they had some sinister quality and were not normally to be used in polite society.

'That's right. I like Earl Grey.'

'Aren't the teabags rather expensive?' (Again, mannered emphasis on 'expensive'.)

'I've no idea, but I doubt it.'

'The rest of the staff seem very happy with PG Tips. Times are hard – don't you think you should be setting a more frugal example?'

The ludicrous truth dawned on me: the great man was genuinely agitated that his CEO had an extravagant taste in teabags. I managed to change the subject, and sidestep the great teabag issue.

But the discussion was not over. Whenever Terence felt grumpy towards me, the question of teabag extravagance would be raised again. Occasionally, he cancelled the contract with the company's catering suppliers, which would then be reinstated by my PA.

When in a more benign mood, Terence would suggest lunch. The office was close to Butler's Wharf by Tower Bridge, where there were several Conran restaurants. My favourite was the Blueprint Café, which had a stunning view, the simplest ambience, and the best chef. But Terence would normally prefer the much grander Pont de la Tour. On arrival, he would spend thoughtful time with the wine list, and would then choose an expensive bottle of white burgundy to go with the starter and an equally expensive bottle of red burgundy to go with the main course. With work to be done in the afternoon, this was too much for just two people. So after spending maybe £200 on two bottles of fine wine, both would be left unfinished. Terence and I would then return to the office. Shortly afterwards, Terence would start berating me about my costly taste in teabags all over again.

Terence chose to be a paternalistic employer. Sometimes he would come in to work with a huge trug of apples, freshly fallen from the trees at Barton Court, which would be left in the office reception for the staff to help themselves to as many as they could eat.

Barton Court did more than provide apples. Every summer, Terence would host a cricket match there, for the staff and their families. The quality of the cricket was never up to much, but the quality of the lunch Terence provided was magnificent: huge pies, generous slabs of cheese, cooked hams, giant bowls of fruit, and as much wine as you dared to drink.

Similarly, Terence frequently hosted the office Christmas party in his penthouse by Butler's Wharf, and allowed a hundred hard-drinking revellers into his home without a qualm. Apparently, when asked to sign off a friendly email to the staff inviting them to the party, Terence asked: 'Remind me – is it on a Thursday?'

'Yes, it is.'

'Why not a Friday?' Terence parried.

'Because some people, including you, like to go away for the weekend,' was the answer.

'Fine,' said Terence.

Then he added: 'Just put a sentence at the end saying that I personally will be at the office door at nine a.m. the day after the party, and anyone who is even one minute late will be sacked on the spot.'

So much for the spirit of Christmas.

Terence was always a driven and determined operator who seemed to have no time for sentiment. But he did prove me wrong once. I told him that I was taking a few days' holiday to visit the photography festival in Arles. This was not a discussion I anticipated with much joy, as Terence (who greatly preferred work to holidays himself) couldn't understand why the rest of us wanted an occasional break. In much the same way that he regarded a legitimate expenses claim as theft of the company's money, he considered a holiday to be theft of the company's time. But in this instance, he reacted slowly and thoughtfully. 'I think you'll be near my old house,' he said. And indeed Brunelys, Terence's gracious South of France country home which he had sold a few years earlier, was only a few kilometres from Arles. 'I'd like you to take a gift to my old housekeeper,' he announced. He was obviously surprisingly fond of the lady, who had looked after Brunelys and who had gone on to do the same job for the new owners. That was certainly not the kind of emotion Terence would normally show, but in this case he was concerned to make sure the gift (Terence's latest book, as I recall) was beautifully wrapped, and then reminded me about my delivery obligations several times. It was perplexing to see Terence attach so much importance to a gift to a kind old retainer whom he would never see again.

In the event, we found Brunelys (no thanks to Terence's highly misleading directions) and introduced ourselves to the new owners, a South African couple who wintered in Cape Town and summered in Provence. The housekeeper was found, given her gift, and she seemed duly touched. I reported my satisfactory delivery – and the housekeeper's satisfactory response – to Terence on my return. He grunted (his usual acknowledgement) but I sensed the episode had real significance to a man who normally abjured sentiment.

Our trip to Brunelys brought another surprise: the look of the house itself. We had assumed that the new owners would want to put their own stamp on it. But every detail radiated Terence's taste. 'You haven't changed much, have you?' I said. 'Of course not,' they replied, 'We have deliberately left everything exactly as it was.' They had bought not just the house, but all of the kitchen fittings, cutlery, crockery, ornaments, even books. It was a testament to Terence's charisma that a prosperous couple, with minds of their own, rather than putting their own stamp on the home they had bought, had instead preserved it as a shrine to the God of Design.

I have kept just one small souvenir from my years with Terence, and it is a brilliant microcosmic summary of the Conran contradictions. It's a brown card luggage label, which Terence had used as a gift tag on a present for me.

I'd moved house in December, and was excited by my new home. Terence sent me a splendid house-warming present: a bottle of Château Latour, just about the finest wine that money can buy. Round the neck of this superb bottle was the luggage label with a message from Terence and his fourth wife Vicki in Terence's instantly recognisable hand:

'Roger, this is a house-warming present & also for Christmas – I hope it may be one of the finest bottles of wine you have ever drunk. It's been in my cellar for over 60 years. Happy Christmas, Terence and Vicki.

PS Needs to be room temperature and decanted.'

On the edge of the label, at a jaunty angle, Terence had added as an afterthought: '£1,600 … Trade!'

It was a magnificently generous present, without doubt. And when we drank it, it lived up to Terence's promise. Yet Terence couldn't resist clarifying that this was both a house-warming *and* Christmas present: he wasn't going to be stuck with another gift for me. As for the claim that it had been in his cellar for sixty years, this was belied by the year shown on the bottle: a great vintage from the 1990s. It was a privilege to drink one of the world's great wines, and it had been in a cellar for over twenty years. But with Terence, there was always the need to exaggerate, to mythologise. So a twenty-year-old bottle became a sixty-year-old bottle.

I would hope that Terence realised I was worldly enough to know that a bottle of Château Latour is, by any standards, costly. Yet he was eager to emphasise his own generosity by quoting the price: '£1,600 … Trade!'

I'm slightly ashamed to say that I rang a wine merchant and asked him if he had a Château Latour of that year. He did: it was priced at £500. Again, the need to exaggerate was inescapable.

But while it's easy to mock the overstatement of age and value, it was a gift of great style and generosity. No one else ever gave me a bottle of premier cru claret for a house-warming present.

In his business dealings, Terence could be aggressive, even ruthless. Yet he avoided confrontation. If a difficult discussion was needed, he would find someone else to handle it for him.

Perhaps the most puzzling – yet potentially revealing – contradiction in Terence's character was the conflict between his very social lifestyle and an underlying desire for solitude.

Terence knew everybody that it was important to know. Guests at his lavish parties included Lord Rose, former boss of Marks & Spencer; Sir Charles Dunstone, billionaire head of Carphone Warehouse; Lord Heseltine, former deputy prime minister; Lord Foster, the celebrated architect; and more. They were all pleased to be there: Terence entertained with true style, his charisma was magnetic, and the great and good like to mingle with each other.

At weekends, Terence often had house guests: always people with something interesting to say about the worlds of commerce and creativity. During the week, he was a prodigious networker: virtually every evening he attended a gallery opening, a book launch, a dinner, some kind of social event. His son Jasper said of him: 'Terence would go to the opening of an envelope.'

Yet this tireless social animal often cut a solitary figure. At a big party in the Conran Shop, a glittering spread of fashionable guests drank champagne and gossiped enthusiastically – but Terence did not join in. Instead, he wandered thoughtfully round the shop displays, with his sister Priscilla (then an influential figure in the Conran Shop management) by his side. Notebook in hand, she jotted down Terence's *aperçus* about how the shop could be made better, while he seemed utterly oblivious to his own party. This distancing of himself from his guests did not seem to be born of absent-mindedness. Rather it appeared to be a deliberate act of withdrawal, a kind of self-imposed exile. He was a man who relished and cultivated an extraordinarily wide range of contacts, both interesting and influential. Yet he seemed most himself when he was hermetically self-contained, in contact with others but not connected to them.

Terence's extraordinary gift for interior design, for arranging the relationship of objects to one another, might have been linked to a discomfort in dealing with relationships to people.

But perhaps the most startling contradiction in Terence's complex persona was between the world he created for others and the world he inhabited himself.

The world he created for others was essentially joyful. Habitat was simple and inexpensive – but it was also optimistic, vibrant, fun. It inspired its customers with a new sense of excitement about how they could live in their own homes. Similarly, all his restaurants radiate a sense of *joie de vivre*. As you walk down the stairs at Quaglino's, you are captured by a mood of excitement. As you sit down in one of the comfortable chairs in Bibendum and look up at Monsieur Bibendum, larger than life, leaping energetically across the splendid stained-glass windows, you feel a mood of self-indulgent anticipation.

Yet Terence himself was more often seen to be scowling than smiling. He could show warmth and charm, but his default mode was that of a curmudgeon. He seemed to be endlessly dissatisfied with what he was doing, with the people around him, with life itself.

He was a man with a gift for making life joyful for others, but he seemed incurably disappointed by life himself.

A guest at Barton Court, one late September weekend, was standing in the garden with Terence, and commented how beautiful the trees looked as they changed to the rich colours of autumn.

'Autumn just looks sad to me,' was Terence's melancholic reply.

The endless dissatisfaction in his soul sometimes seemed close to despair, yet it may be that genius and despair are inevitably linked. Perhaps it is that sense of unending frustration with the imperfections of life that drives great people to do great things. Terence exhibited a continuing vibration that nothing – and nobody – is ever quite good enough.

Of all Terence's contradictions, the clash between the joyless curmudgeon and the joyful creator seems to be particularly puzzling. But it is likely that his unstoppable dissatisfaction was, in truth, the underlying driver to do things better, to improve, to create, to find a new solution.

After all, who would try to find a better way if the existing path was good enough?

14

Down, But Not Out

R.M.

Perhaps the true test of a great man is not how he creates success but how he responds to failure.

Terence would score well on this criterion.

The collapse of Storehouse in the early nineties was the brutal end of Terence's audacious and grandiose – possibly even megalomaniac – ambition to put his stamp across the British high street. The collapse destroyed not only what he wanted to do, however, but also what he had already done. Habitat had changed his life and our lives too, but it had now been taken away from him, ignominiously sold to IKEA. Where could he turn?

Terence was – the demise of Storehouse notwithstanding – still a very rich man, still a celebrity, and still busy. He had the Conran Shop and Bibendum restaurant to occupy his mind. He had enough money to keep him in Hoyo de Monterrey cigars and good burgundy for the rest of his days. And he was in his late fifties, a time when most of us are thinking about slowing down, not speeding up.

But Terence was not like most of us. In the gloomy shadow of the Storehouse failure, he generated a new ambition. London would have a new kind of restaurant.

Terence's love affair with restaurants had started when he was a very young man, and is inseparable from his love affair with France.

As a teenager, he had worked as a lowly *plongeur* in a Paris restaurant. But for the quarter of a century from its birth, Terence's mind was focused, first and foremost, on Habitat. Neal Street and Bibendum were both astonishing achievements, and testament to Terence's ability to make a number of different and remarkable things happen at the same time, but it was Habitat that occupied centre stage. And when Storehouse unravelled, he became an emperor without an empire.

In the aftershock of such a humiliating debacle, one might have expected Terence to retreat to his mansion in Berkshire, in order to take stock of his cellar. That would have been to underestimate Terence's Homeric determination. If he had been deposed as the king of retail, he would reinvent himself as the king of restaurants.

He was already transforming the once-derelict Butler's Wharf building at Tower Bridge into luxurious apartments with startling views of the river. He would create a restaurant there too. He was surrounded by doubters, all telling him that no one would go to Butler's Wharf: it was the wrong side of the river, a rundown area, not in the City, not in Docklands, not anywhere.

Terence ignored them. His ideas were always charged with an obsessive belief that people will travel to an unfashionable area if you give them a good enough temptation. Thus unfashionable will become fashionable. He was often proved right. And so it was with Butler's Wharf.

His first famous restaurant there, close by Tower Bridge, which opened in 1992, was the appropriately named Le Pont de la Tour. Elegantly designed, right on the river's edge, with a sense of sophisticated calm and fine French cooking, Le Pont de la Tour became a kind of Bibendum-on-Thames. It had a similar elegance, a similar menu, and while Bibendum was blessed by its architecture, Pont was blessed by its views of the river.

Terence's belief that he could make it a destination was quickly vindicated. Suddenly Londoners could eat classic French food, in serene modern surroundings, with a gracious view. The inconvenience of travelling across London to get there became part of the experience. Indeed, when the new prime minister, Tony Blair, wanted to entertain the new American president, Bill Clinton, he decided that Pont would be a more modish setting than some stuffy official residence in St James's or Downing Street.

In the event, the evening got off to a slow start – just as the presidential cavalcade reached Tower Bridge, the bridge opened to let some antique sailing vessel through. This kept the president, and several anxiously perplexed American security men, waiting for twenty minutes before the two leaders could meet to enjoy the menu and the wine list. But the point was made: if Pont was good enough for the Prime Minister of Great Britain and the President of the USA, it was good enough for the rest of us.

The new restaurant was a big success. But more than that, the combination of an unexpected location with a remarkable view, of classic cuisine with a modern feel, gave Pont a very distinctive personality. It was creating the template for a new kind of restaurant.

Yet Pont was more than just one restaurant. There was a brasserie area where you could eat in surroundings that were as stylish as – but much simpler than – the luxury of the main restaurant. There was a wine shop, where you could buy the same elegant wines that the restaurant offered. There was even a delicatessen, where you could buy rare olive oils, the best-quality smoked salmon, or just a lovingly made sandwich of pastrami on wholemeal bread, for a snack lunch. Terence had invented the 'gastrodome', a place where there was a cluster of different experiences, but all centred round the theme of eating well, and in style.

'Gastrodome' is invented coinage, but it instantly conveys the concept of somewhere which offers a rich spread of gastronomic experience – a Xanadu of epicurean delights. It illustrates Terence's instinct for a powerful monetary idea, regardless of etymology. And the term has fathered the now ubiquitous 'gastropub'.

Inspired by the success of Pont, Terence launched a tsunami of new restaurants. Next door to Le Pont de la Tour, he opened the Butler's Wharf Chop House, as resolutely English as Pont was resolutely French. Two hundred yards east, if neither English nor French appealed, he opened Cantina del Ponte, an inexpensive Italian restaurant. Next door to that he opened the Blueprint Café, a restaurant with a simpler aesthetic than Pont and – thanks to its first-floor riverside site – astonishing views of the Thames from Tower Bridge down to Canary Wharf.

In Chelsea, he managed to acquire the building which had once been the garage where Bluebird – the legendary car designed to win the world's land-speed record – was built. This was transformed into another gastrodome. Upstairs was the Bluebird brasserie, with a generous bar; downstairs a simple café, and an outdoor terrace café; next door a club where members could eat, drink and be merry, surrounded by a remarkable collection of memorabilia of the record-breaking Bluebird car. Even fashionable Chelsea had not seen anything quite like this before.

Leaping across London to the City, Terence opened Coq d'Argent, on the top floor of a James Stirling building overlooking the Bank of England. Tragically, the gracious roof garden became a jumping-off point (literally) for bankers whose fortunes had failed. There were a handful of suicides before a fence was built. In spite of this macabre misuse, Coq d'Argent prospered, and became one of the most profitable of Terence's restaurants.

Close by Coq d'Argent, he opened both Sauterelle (a French restaurant) and the Grand Café (which was just that) in the magnificent Royal Exchange building. Then, right by St Paul's Cathedral, he opened a sibling to the Chop House at Butler's Wharf, the Paternoster Chop House.

Having conquered the City, the next step was Canary Wharf, where he opened Plateau, the first truly good restaurant in what had been a gastronomic desert.

Terence just couldn't stop. He opened Almeida, a French restaurant, opposite the Islington theatre of the same name. He opened Sartoria, a sophisticated Italian restaurant in Savile Row, in the heart of Mayfair.

In Marylebone he converted a beautiful old stable building into a new Conran Shop with an elegant restaurant beside it. He named the restaurant the Orrery, thereby reviving the name he had given to one of his embryonic ventures thirty years earlier.

Where next? Why not Soho? He acquired a massive site in Wardour Street, the spine of Soho, and built not one but two restaurants, Mezzo and Floridita. Since Floridita took its inspiration from Cuba, he opened a cigar bar next door.

In the middle of this rush of successes, Terence even found time for one failure. He had long hankered after creating a chain of simple bistros. These bistros would be called Zinc, a tribute to the material used for the bar in the Gauloise-perfumed French cafés of our nostalgic imagination (and even sometimes of reality).

The first Zinc was to be in Heddon Street, a quiet enclave just off Regent Street. This was to be the prototype for more that would follow in the big provincial cities.

I remember visiting it soon after it opened. As an unswerving disciple of the Terence cult, I was expecting to love it. But in the event, I failed to do so. It had a disappointing blandness about it. Every other Terence restaurant had a kind of visual electricity: there was always a frisson of excitement as you entered. Whether it was the stunning view of the river from the Blueprint Café or the noisy buzz of Floridita, you stepped into an ambience with a special vibration. However simple in concept, Terence's restaurants always had a vivid overlay of glamour.

And they were successful.

Zinc – because it was intended to be cheaper, more accessible, replicable – never quite captured that Conran glamour. Remarkably, Terence had created something unremarkable. It was too understated; and it did not prosper.

In Terence's contradictory character, we see a passion and a gift for creating the remarkable: yet at the same time he was driven by the urge to democratise his ideas. But once the exceptional becomes universally available, it can no longer be exceptional. His desire to launch a chain of more accessible bistros exposed the inevitable fault line in this conflict between the special and the universal.

This was one of the very few of Terence's ventures which did not catch the public imagination. Zinc eventually faded away. Perhaps Terence was mortal after all.

One setback did not restrain him. Terence determined that mere restaurants alone were not enough: there should be a hotel too. He found a dreary one in a dull part of London. The Great Eastern in Liverpool Street was one of those hotels, once grand, now neglected, left over from the glory days of rail travel. The building was long past its prime. Yet again, Terence's gift for finding new life for old buildings came into play. He could see that the hollow shell of the Great Eastern could – with his personal magic – become great again.

But the opportunity didn't lie just with the architecture: there was also the location.

Terence had an extraordinary sense of the zeitgeist, a supernaturally shrewd instinct for where things are headed. And the location of the Great Eastern was right in the middle of the City, the staid and conservative banking district, a part of London which died daily at 6 p.m. prompt.

Terence could see that the City had been dull, conformist, joyless – a place you worked in, and then commuted home from. But he could also see that this had been changed utterly by Thatcher's Britain: driven by her extraordinary blend of arrogance and determination, the national mood had swung from a fatalistic, shared self-doubt towards an individualistic rush for wealth. No wonder the most celebrated TV character of the time was a satirical invention called Loads-a-Money. At the heart of this gold rush was the City. Thatcher's sweeping changes (her supporters called them 'reforms', others were less kind) had their biggest impact in the square mile where everything financial happened.

The City was in a state of rapid metamorphosis from stolidly dull to suddenly dynamic. London was becoming the world centre for banking, for insurance, for anything that made money out of money. The City was no longer a grey, nine-to-five temple of the puritan work ethic: it had exploded into a rainbow-hued twenty-four-hour-a-day theatre of capitalist greed. It was London's beating heart, yet it had no decent hotels.

Terence found the money to buy the Great Eastern, and set about transforming it. One of his design trademarks was the ability to fuse old and new to astonishing effect, and the Great Eastern was a perfect opportunity to put that gift to work. It soon looked a grand hotel again, but with a distinctive modern touch. As you entered, you felt you were in a special place, which in turn made you feel a special person. And with Terence in charge, of course, there was a cornucopia of new restaurants: elegant dining, chic café, fresh fish, Japanese. Yet again, Terence had transformed a place into an experience.

The revitalised City suddenly had a revitalised hotel, and where people make money, they like to spend money. It was a huge success.

The man was unstoppable, and owning London was not enough for him. In New York he opened Guastavino's, a restaurant in a huge and dramatic building close to the East River. The publicity was huge, the popular acclaim less so. And, perhaps the bravest move of all, he took on the French at their own game and opened Alcazar, a restaurant in the heart of Paris, on the site of an old transvestite club. As a sentimental nod to its transgendered past, Terence insisted that Alcazar have a cigarette girl who was, on close inspection, a bit less of a girl than you might imagine. That was a typical Terence touch: something different, glamorous, even slightly decadent.

Some of the French did not take kindly to an Englishman coming to Paris to compete head on with their own great restaurateurs. One of the big newspapers ran a furious article, savaging the notion of an upstart *rosbif* invading their turf. (We should not be surprised at their chauvinism: after all, Monsieur Chauvin was a Frenchman.) To Terence's surprise and delight, the outraged journalist later recanted, when he experienced for himself how good Alcazar was.

It was all an incredible achievement of raw energy and great vision. From a standing start in 1992 when Le Pont de la Tour was born, within seven years Terence had opened twenty-five new restaurants in London, as well as a grandly restored hotel, and restaurants in New York and in Paris.

All of them (or nearly all of them) radiated a sense of style we had not seen before.

But the paragon of Terence's extraordinary vision was Quaglino's, just off Jermyn Street, the very epicentre of smart London. It had all the classic Conran ingredients – a neglected old building now lovingly restored; modern furniture and fittings in an old space; a menu which owed much to French traditions; the buzz of a Parisian brasserie. But Quaglino's had something much more than this. It was vast. You entered at ground-floor level and descended, via a spectacular marble-and-brass staircase, into a colossal arena of glamour. The theatrical lights, the abundant, architectural flowers, the pillars adorned with murals, the sheer scale – everything contributed to a feeling of dream-like excitement. No other restaurant was so big; no other restaurant was so sexy.

And it was a hit. What made it so was not the food (never bad, but also never the high point) or the crowd who went. Paradoxically, Terence's restaurants always seemed to attract more than their fair share of outsiders looking in. No, what made it special was the look Terence had created. You walked down those stairs into a secret and exciting world.

It was the restaurant you'd take your mistress to, not your wife. Indeed, the bar was often peopled, among others, by high-priced *belles de nuit*. Terence rather encouraged this, thinking it added a spark to the atmosphere. (When Terence handed control to his right-hand man, the escorts were promptly removed. Sales went down, not up, as a consequence.)

Other restaurants could give you grouse in season or a fillet steak, but Quaglino's gave you glamour.

Terence had single-handedly redefined what the idea of eating out meant to the British public. Of course, there had been fashionable restaurants before. There had been a slew of stylish trattorias in the seventies, and then the iconic Langan's Brasserie had its own brand of raffish chic. But Terence took all this to an entirely new level: his restaurants had style, they had space, they had excitement. This was no longer restaurant-as-dining-room, this was restaurant-as-theatre. Indeed, as you glided down the grand staircase of Quaglino's, you might think this was not even restaurant-as-theatre, but restaurant-as-grand-opera.

Thanks to Terence, dining out was no longer a meal, it was an experience.

To create that experience, Terence had demonstrated a remarkable transformative gift. He had seen the hidden beauty behind a neglected façade at Butler's Wharf, at Bluebird, and at Bibendum. He had imagined that an echoing, windowless basement could become the vitality of Quaglino's. Terence had an extraordinary vision of how a space could be brought to life, and all of his restaurants radiated a sense of style and personality that beguiled London.

But Terence's imaginative gift was only half the story: he had an equally great gift for publicity. He managed to get his restaurants talked about, to become a part of the social fabric. A fine example of how he did this can be found in the apparently inconsequential issue of ashtrays. Hard though it is to imagine now, smoking in restaurants was allowed, even popular, when Terence was creating his restaurants. He was an enthusiastic cigar smoker, working his way through a good handful of Havana's finest every day. So he liked to be sure that there was always an ashtray close at hand, and he assumed his customers felt the same. But, being Terence, they had to be more than standard ashtrays; they had to be part of the experience. So each restaurant had its own individual ashtray, wittily designed for that particular place.

Sartoria was Terence's elegant Italian restaurant in Savile Row, the home of London's bespoke tailoring tradition. So the Sartoria ashtray mimicked a tailor's measuring tape. Bluebird in Chelsea had been the home of the Bluebird land-speed record car, so the ashtrays at Bluebird carried a fin that echoed the fin on the original car. Of course, Bibendum inevitably had a miniature Monsieur Bibendum perched cheerfully on the edge of his ashtray. But the *primus inter pares* of the Conran ashtrays was the one designed (by Terence, according to Terence; by his son Sebastian, according to Sebastian) for Quaglino's. A plain circular shape was cut through with a sinuous swirl, creating a letter 'Q' of elegance and simplicity. It caught people's imagination. And it fitted a coat pocket or a handbag remarkably well. Stealing a Quaglino's ashtray became a popular middle-class London activity. After all, at Terence's prices, he could afford to lose a few ashtrays. And when you displayed it at home, you showed your friends that you had dined in London's most fashionable restaurant.

Terence realised that he had stumbled on a wonderful PR opportunity. Publicly he grumbled about this shameless theft, and he put the ashtray on the menu, so you could buy your own legitimately if you wanted it that badly. Terence claimed that the price of the ashtray was pitched so that the money earned from genuine sales would cover the money lost on thefts. It was a publicity masterstroke. Nervous diners bought their ashtray, while more defiant diners carried on stealing in even greater numbers. There was much debate as to whether it was better to be a buyer (honourable, but a tad dull) or a stealer (less honest, but more raffish). Either way, you left Quaglino's with that memento in your pocket, soon to have pride of place in your home. There it would be continuing evidence of your membership of London's smart set. And a continuing advertisement for the restaurant.

When Quaglino's had been going for a few years and was in danger of losing its initial excitement, Terence deliberately resuscitated the ashtray controversy. He announced an 'ashtray amnesty', and offered a free glass of champagne to anyone who returned their stolen goods. Of course, the ashtray story was – again – all over the newspapers. Allegedly 1,500 people gave their stolen ashtrays back. But ten times that number would have read about it. That was what Quaglino's was for: it was not just a place to dine, it was a place to talk about.

From the very first, Terence had made Quaglino's newsworthy. When the restaurant opened, Terence proudly – but realistically – proclaimed that he expected the service to be frightful for the first few weeks, until systems had settled down and staff had found their way. So he offered all food at half price for the restaurant's first fortnight. This apparent modesty created electrifying publicity: no restaurateur had ever boasted about bad service before, nor had they offered a huge discount for it. Everyone flocked to Quaglino's in that first two weeks, to enjoy the price cut and to explore whether the service was quite as bad as Terence had predicted. The new restaurant was packed. And if Terence lost a bit of money on food, he more than made up for it in fame. Plenty of new restaurants do that today, but Terence got there first.

Terence's knack for getting publicity was no happy accident. It was something he worked at assiduously. Unlike many powerful people, who can be surprisingly fearful of the press, Terence was endlessly available to journalists. He welcomed them, he flattered them, he was winningly indiscreet with them. He ensured that he was always photographed relaxing in a generous armchair, cigar in one hand, wine glass in the other. This all cultivated the concept of Terence as brand, Terence the bon viveur made flesh, the impresario of stylish living.

It was no surprise, therefore, that when Elton John held a grand dinner to raise money to fight AIDS, the restaurant he chose for this flamboyant event was, of course, Quaglino's. Yet again, Terence was centre stage.

Terence had, in a few short years, created a veritable suzerainty of remarkable restaurants in London, with a grand hotel, and restaurants in New York and Paris thrown in for good measure. And these were much more than ordinary restaurants: they were places which redefined the vitality of eating out, which were famous, which made their customers feel famous. Conran restaurants oozed a modish sense of style: you felt good about yourself just being there, before you'd even looked at the menu. Traditionally, great restaurants fed your stomach, but Terence had created a new kind of great restaurant which fed your stomach, and your ego.

After the bitter disappointment of Storehouse, and the loss of Habitat, Terence's resilience, his drive, his ability to apply his flair and vision to a new arena, were utterly astonishing. That article in *The Times* from February 1989, proclaiming that 'Conran's reputation as a master of style and arbiter of fashion has suffered irreparably', now looked very ill-judged. Terence, renaissance-man-cum-restaurateur, had found both revenge and redemption.

As an agent of social change, Terence had already inspired us to rethink the way we furnish our homes. Now he had reinvented the way we eat.

Yet Terence was ever a complex and contradictory character. His passion to create and innovate was matched by a corrosive inability to stay focused on a project once it had become established. What he had done in restaurants was breathtaking in its speed, in its style, its scale, its ambition, above all in its originality. But he failed to nurture his own creations. The restaurants that had validated him as a giant of innovation and a catalyst of social change started to bore him.

Disillusionment was next on the menu.

15

Ennui Sets In

R.M.

A recurring theme in the tale of Terence is the way in which his extraordinary passion for the next big thing was matched – with startling symmetry – by a lack of passion for the last big thing. A brilliant innovator, he put relentless energy into new ideas. Yet, once they became successful, he was often guilty of enjoying them only briefly before a certain ennui set in.

Terence had started the nineties as the man who had failed publicly, and humiliatingly, at Storehouse. But by the turn of the millennium, Terence was the man whose restaurants dominated the life of London. Within a decade he had transformed the way we eat out. He created a new kind of restaurant where, as well as dinner, you enjoyed a vibrant sense of style and occasion. Every one of these restaurants was different and distinctive, though they all shared a certain Conran charisma. They were an extraordinary achievement: fashionable, original, and highly successful. Yet Terence was reluctant to linger with his triumph. As ever, yesterday was over, and the only excitement lay with tomorrow. The great man wanted to move on.

Being Terence, of course, he still had an appetite for restaurants – but only if it was a new project, a fresh challenge. In 2003, he found a site in Shoreditch which met every Conran criterion. It was an old printing works, now derelict, but with the potential for an imaginative restoration. It was in an area which had been neglected but was now beginning to turn: Terence would make it a destination. It was big enough to house more than just a restaurant: there could be a boutique hotel too, a simple cafe, and maybe a rooftop restaurant. Terence, now in his seventies, tore into the new project with the enthusiasm and energy of a teenager.

But the existing restaurant empire had lost its fascination. You might conjecture that a man who had four marriages, and a track record of relationships with business partners ending badly, exhibited an unwillingness to nurture. But whatever the underlying psychology, Terence wanted to develop the Shoreditch project and put the old restaurants behind him. But how?

He talked with his business partner Des, and an idea began to form.

Des Gunewardena might seem an unlikely partner for Terence. While Terence was stocky in build and brusque in manner, Des is suave, charming, lean, personable. Originally Sri Lankan, he first made his mark in British business as an accountant at Ernst and Young, and then in finance at Heron International. But while Des may be different from Terence in style and expertise, the two men had one crucial characteristic in common: in an intriguing echo of Terence's earlier relationship with Roger Seelig, both men were fiercely ambitious.

Des joined Terence in 1991, as Chief Executive of the Conran Group. It was a potent attraction of opposites. Terence looked after the ideas, Des looked after the money. And 1991 was the year that Terence's restaurant explosion really started to happen. For the next decade, the empire surged forward, with Terence constantly in the public eye. But behind the scenes, it was Des who was quietly making sure that the right property deals were done, that the cash was managed, and the profits came rolling in.

Terence was the captain on the bridge, inspiring all with his vision: but it was Des in the engine-room below who did so much to make that vision a palpable reality.

One of their achievements was the success of the Great Eastern Hotel. They built an extraordinary group of restaurants, but Terence had already done much in that business. Hotels were virgin territory for them, yet they had a great success there too. Even the giants of the hotel trade were forced to admire what the Great Eastern had become: stylish, distinctive, the first seriously good hotel in walking distance of the banks who were making London the world's financial powerhouse. And it made good profits.

'If you can't beat them, buy them' seems to be the motto of many large corporations. True to form, the giant Hyatt group made a bid for the Great Eastern in 2005. By early 2006, the deal was done: Hyatt were the new owners and had paid Terence over £150 million for the privilege. Terence's profit has been estimated at over £50 million.

Suddenly, he had a big, new pile of money in the bank. And he didn't have to worry about managing the Great Eastern. That was last week's toy. He could start looking for a new adventure.

And if the last adventure – selling the hotel – had made a massive windfall, maybe the next adventure should be to sell the restaurants, and reap another harvest.

But who could Terence trust with the restaurants? After all, his first great legacy was Habitat, and that had collapsed miserably once he lost control – even with IKEA, whom Terence admired, in charge. Restaurants were his second legacy: they must not be allowed to suffer the same fate.

The answer was simple: it would be Des, the man who had been at Terence's side as the restaurant empire was created, the man who understood the deals and the money, and one of the few people Terence really trusted.

Of course, this was – quite literally – the opportunity of a lifetime for Des. Nudging fifty, he had spent a decade and a half helping Terence to create an astonishing spread of restaurants across London and beyond. And these restaurants did more than make money: they were fashionable, they were exciting, and they changed our idea of what an evening out could be. Terence had – with Des close behind him – achieved fame and fortune all over again.

Des was an astute and effective number two, but Terence could be a capricious and domineering taskmaster. And Des liked the limelight too: being a highly paid employee, slightly in the background, is not the same as being centre stage while amassing millions. Des was not the kind of man to enjoy playing second fiddle for ever. If he bought the restaurants, he could show the world what he could do. And make his own fortune into the bargain.

But it wouldn't just help Des, it would help Terence too. He would pocket a tempting capital gain from the sale of the business, and his restive nature could move on to the new project in Shoreditch, leaving others to worry about the old restaurants.

Everybody would win.

Well, in theory, everybody would win: but theory doesn't always translate into practice as easily as we would like.

Terence liked a deal where he could eat his cake, and still have it afterwards. So, while he wanted the profit from the restaurant sale and he was happy for his trusted lieutenant to take over, he was still reluctant to let go. How could that circle be squared?

But if Terence had a gift for handling space, Des has a gift for handling deals. He created an ingenious structure whereby Conran Holdings continued to own a significant shareholding in the new restaurant business, but Des had a worthwhile shareholding too – and he was both Chairman and Chief Executive. So Des had complete control and a stake in the business, yet Terence made a profit from the sale of the old business, but continued to have an interest in the new one. It did seem as if Terence and Des had found a way to defy gravity.

The deal was done at the end of 2006. Conran restaurants had been sold, and Des took charge with his business partner, David Loewi, beside him.

Des and David used their first names as an inspiration to name their new company 'D&D'. Terence didn't like the new name. He complained that it sounded like a couple of East End scrap metal dealers. Des and David studiously ignored him. It was a portent: Terence experienced for the first time – though not the last – that when you allow someone else to inherit the throne, they will make the decisions, even if you still own a large chunk of the business.

Ironically, whatever name Des and David gave the company, the punters still thought of them as Conran restaurants. So Terence found himself in the bizarre position of having all of the reputational risk but none of the real control.

Regardless of any misgivings Terence might have had, Des surged forward with a plan for spectacular expansion. He opened Skylon in London, next to the National Theatre. He bought three fashionable London restaurants (Kensington Place, Launceston Place and The Avenue) from a rival. He opened a smart hotel within a minute's walk from his earlier success at the Great Eastern. He opened new restaurants outside London – including one in the exotic city of Istanbul and one in the less exotic city of Leeds. He was unstoppable.

Meanwhile, Terence was expanding too. His development in Shoreditch opened, under the name Boundary. It was the first stylish hotel in that rapidly changing area of the capital. Guests could not only enjoy the rooms – each one designed by a different designer – but eat in an elegant French restaurant in the basement, snack in a chic café on the ground floor or have a simple grill in a restaurant on the roof.

The ink was barely dry on the Boundary menus when Terence opened yet another French restaurant, named Lutyens as a nod to the building's architect, in Fleet Street.

In theory, Terence and Des were still partners: Terence owned a big stake in the business that Des ran. But in practice, they were clearly becoming competitors. Eventually, both men recognised that truth. Accordingly, they agreed that Des (and a bank) would buy out

Terence's stake in what was now D&D. At last, they had become rivals, not partners.

One might assume that the rivalry was destined to be an amicable one. After all, they had worked together and had been friends for twenty years. And the success of each man owed much to the gifts of the other.

It didn't work out that way.

Des was still on the board of Conran Holdings, Terence's main company. But once Terence had sold his remaining stock in D&D, it seemed logical to him that Des should stand down from the Conran board. Des had little choice but to accept.

However, Des was a shareholder in Conran, and when he left the board he was asked to sell back his shares. That too was perfectly logical: but how much were Des's shares worth?

Des, a shrewd financier, estimated the value of his stake at £3 million. Since he owned 7.5%, that would make the total business worth £40 million. It didn't seem unreasonable.

Terence had very different ideas. He pointed out that the company's rules for valuing shares were based on a multiple of recent year's profits. Applying this formula (which had, ironically, been designed by Des) he offered Des the startlingly modest sum of £1,254.

Des was horrified. £1,254 wouldn't even buy a sofa from The Conran Shop. It didn't seem a fair reward for two decades of hard work. Nor did it seem fair recognition for the crucial part Des had played in building Terence's fortune.

Des discussed this with Terence. The discussion became a row. And then the row became a court case. Des sued Terence to get what he saw as a fair deal.

The case lurched from arcane points of company law to more comprehensible and human issues. In one exchange, Terence was asked whether he had ever fallen out with Des. Terence replied, to laughter from the court, 'Well, I've never punched him.'

But while the case had such entertaining moments for the rest of us, it must have been painful for both protagonists. In the end, the judge ruled in Terence's favour, saying that he found Terence to be a more credible witness than Des.

So Terence won, and kept his £3million. Whether he kept his friendship with Des is less clear.

How very different it must have seemed to Terence nineteen years earlier, on 14 February 1993. He had celebrated Valentine's night by opening Quaglino's with a glittering party that filled that vast space with the great and glamorous of London society. This was the place to be. It was a new kind of restaurant for a London that was discovering a new kind of prosperity. And Terence was the ringmaster.

The gloom of Storehouse's collapse was forgotten. Terence was already famous for reinventing great buildings: now he was reinventing himself. Once he was the king of retail; now he was the king of restaurants, and Quaglino's was the jewel in the crown.

Nineteen years later, the jewel that was once a diamond had become a rhinestone. With success, Terence had lost interest. With D&D, he had lost control. Now D&D was lost too.

16

The Thing That Never Was

R.M.

Meanwhile, the Neal Street Restaurant, which had been one of Terence's early successes, was facing extinction. Terence had for many years entrusted the running of the restaurant to Antonio Carluccio, husband of his sister Priscilla. In 1989, Carluccio became the owner. He changed little: the décor became a little softer, which slightly undermined the original idea, and the food became more Italian. But the similarities outweighed the differences, and it remained a fine restaurant.

The restaurant's location in Covent Garden, which had been positively edgy when Terence opened in Neal Street, had become fashionable, then prosperous, and then tourist-ridden. As the charm went down, so the rents went up. And when the Neal Street lease expired, the landlords saw an opportunity for a lucrative new property development.

The restaurant was an inevitable casualty. Carluccio was on his way to becoming a celebrated TV chef as well as the progenitor of the Italian restaurant chain that bears his name. But by 2007, the distinctive, modern elegance of the Neal Street Restaurant was about to turn into a memory.

With perfect irony, the Neal Street Restaurant closed its doors on 17 March 2007, only a few months after Des Gunewardena had taken over Conran restaurants.

Don't imagine that, shorn of his beloved restaurants, Terence had little to do. His interests still covered the glamorous Conran Shops (a kind of Habitat for oligarchs), Conran & Partners (an architectural practice) and Studio Conran (a design business led by Sebastian, Terence's eldest son). Bibendum remained a showpiece, although its lustre was fading. There was Benchmark, a company which made very beautiful bespoke wooden furniture, and more.

But none of these were *new*. And to Terence, the next project was always intrinsically more exciting than the last.

So his energies were increasingly focused on his new development in Shoreditch. But that was not running to plan. Converting an old printing works into an elegant hotel and three restaurants was proving to be a much more complex structural task than anyone had expected. And 'more complex' quickly translated into 'more expensive'.

Terence was becoming increasingly irate about the cost overruns at Boundary, as the hotel was going to be called. It was even rumoured that he threatened to sue the architects, whom he blamed for underestimating the scale of the task at the outset. The only problem with this plan was that the architects were Conran & Partners, largely owned by Terence's own business. 'Conran sues Conran' would have been a provocative newspaper headline, but not very helpful to the Conran architects' new business drive.

But eventually, the structural problems at the Shoreditch site were overcome, the arguments about who should pay for what receded, and the Boundary hotel officially opened on New Year's Eve 2008. The design of every bedroom was different, each one created in the style of a famous designer. Terence himself designed one of the suites. As you would expect of Terence, it combined luxury and simplicity: there is a white leather Karuselli chair (Terence's personal favourite) facing a specially designed white leather sofa. But there is also a striking sculpture – a large but simple piece of broken tree branch that Terence had rescued after a storm had damaged trees in his country home. It was a characteristically Conran contrast: you could sit in a chair that cost thousands and stare at a sculpture that was debris salvaged from a storm.

Boundary had every Terence trademark. It was an old building, transformed. It pioneered the gentrification of a once-seedy area. True, Shoreditch was already on the turn, with quirky boutiques and young, creative businesses, but Terence was the first to give the area a very smart hotel. And it was more than a hotel: there was a stylish French restaurant, a rooftop restaurant, an English café, a small shop, a bakery. It was another Conran gastrodome.[*]

Shoreditch had come of age, and Terence had surprised London yet again. Would he now take a well-earned break? That, of course, was not Terence's style. He was already hard at work on his next project – an elegant restaurant in Fleet Street. The building had been the home of Reuters, the news agency, and its architect was the celebrated Edwin Lutyens, the man who, in the days of the Raj, had indelibly stamped the face of Britishness on the great Indian city of Delhi. Terence's restaurants are often named with a nod to their origins – Bluebird and Bibendum being two good examples. Clearly, the new place must be named after its famed architect, and so 'Lutyens' was born.

Whereas the restaurant at Boundary had a glamorous, nightclub flavour, Lutyens's style is more one of restrained quality. It is, after all, immediately opposite the offices of that powerhouse of money, Goldman Sachs, so you would expect nothing less.

Lutyens's most dramatic visual statement was a massive painting by the erotic British pop artist, Allen Jones. It dominated the wall at the head of the staircase. Terence decided that this space needed an

---

[*] This awkward term now needs explaining. A self-consciously clever coinage, it was typically Terence in that it attracted attention, but was also a bit wrong. Neither a classicist nor a pedant, he was hinting at the Greek 'hippodrome' to suggest a grandeur perhaps beyond the reality of a small cluster of riverside restaurants. But this pretentious invention always occurred without the 'r'. No-one had the temerity to correct him and so it remained: ambitious but not quite correct.

Allen Jones, so he set about persuading the great artist to accept the commission. He set a typically Terence budget – which is to say a lot less than Jones would normally expect. Jones politely said no. But Terence never gives up without a fight. Eventually a deal was struck, and the result is a truly fine work of art, which made the journey from the bar to the loo a cultural experience as well as a necessary one.

Lutyens was one of Terence's most polished restaurants. The quality of the food and the grace of the room invited comparison with Le Pont de la Tour or Bibendum. But Lutyens lacked the excitement of the other two, and their sense of entering a special world. It felt like a carbon copy of a great original: perhaps Terence was starting to repeat himself.

Lutyens opened in 2009 – the year of Terence's seventy-eighth birthday, and an astonishing testament to his undimmed energy. It would have been more than enough for most people. But while Terence was excited by Boundary and by Lutyens, there was still a void in his ambitions. They were both good restaurants, but he wanted more. He wanted something with *scale*.

Terence was a man intoxicated by scale. His magnificent penthouse at Butler's Wharf was grandly generous in its proportions. His country house had once been a school. The glamour of Quaglino's owes much to its sheer vastness. The concept of Storehouse, albeit unsuccessful in execution, was huge in its ambition. When he threw a big party, the wine was usually served in magnums. He liked their sense of bigness, of generosity. It's a good metaphor for how Terence thought about other things. Scale excited him. Terence's sense of theatre was motivated by the idea of a big performance, on a big stage. And yet again, the appetite of this insatiable visionary was hungry for a *big* idea.

As so often, the idea grew from an empty building. Most of the buildings that inspired Terence are architecturally distinctive: this one certainly was not. It was huge, but it was also hugely dull.

It was a disused postal sorting office, hidden in a cultural limbo between dismal Holborn to the east and vibrant Soho to the west. The British Museum was a few hundred yards to the north and Covent Garden a few hundred yards to the south. Even though it couldn't have been more central, the immediate hinterland was dreary. Yet, Terence could see how vital the space might be, if reimagined with a big new idea. And if a big idea needs a big space, the disused sorting office had endless space. It was as big as a giant department store. Which, in a sense, was what Terence wanted to create. But being Terence's, it would not conform to the traditions of department stores: it would offer something new, something different.

His plan was stunningly original. There would be two floors of retail. But it would not be conventional retail. One of the floors would be devoted solely to British brands. So you might see Burberry alongside Church's shoes, then Hackett, followed by Barbour, and then a shop selling malt whisky.

The other floor would be devoted to young designers: people with fresh ideas who wouldn't normally get exposure to a big market. They couldn't afford to pay a high rent – here they wouldn't have to. They would get the space without a lease or a deposit. Instead of conventional rent, they would pay a share of their turnover. If that was big enough to justify them staying, they were welcome to stay. If it wasn't, they'd had their chance, so they'd have to leave and make way for another designer.

It was a splendidly Darwinian concept. This was the survival of the fittest for design talent. The designers whose work commanded sales would stay and prosper. The others would go, leaving a vacuum to be filled by the next talent. Eventually all of the space would be filled by new young designers whose work was commercial as well as creative.

The rest of the building would house offices, some smart apartments designed by Conran, a basement nightclub, and – obviously – lots of restaurants. All of this would be in addition to an utterly new kind of shopping. Terence had succeeded before with a gastrodome. But this concept was far, far, bigger: it would be an everythingdome.

For a man approaching eighty, with nothing left to prove, in a viciously hostile economic climate, this was a plan of breathtaking ambition.

The idea was there, the site was there, the retail and restaurant expertise was there . . . and if anyone could make the impossible possible, Terence could.

This brave and unusual idea only needed the right name. Terence and Vicki were in the car talking about it one day. Vicki said: 'It used to be a sorting office – that's what it should be called. The Sorting Office.'

So an original plan now had an original name. And The Sorting Office consumed a huge amount of Terence's energy and imagination.

Ambitious ideas are hard to realise, but Terence's ability to make things happen against the odds was impressive. Everyone had told him that the dereliction that was Butler's Wharf could never be transformed. He had proved them wrong, as the massive prices now being paid for flats in the Butler's Wharf building demonstrate. He had launched Habitat – then an utterly different kind of shop – while still in his early thirties. And he had created dozens of celebrated restaurants all over the world.

But his passion for the Sorting Office was mounting just as the global economy was collapsing. This exciting, but costly, new scheme had to swim against a ferociously strong tide of fiscal conservatism.

The owners of the sorting office building were reluctant to respond to Terence, even though the building was empty. The kind of price he could justify in a nervous market was not the kind of price they would accept. In frustration, Terence started to search London for an alternative site – preferably with a more accommodating landlord.

He found one: just off Oxford Street, with Soho to the south and ad-land Charlotte Street to the north. It was just as good a location.

It was similarly big. And, unbelievably, it was also a disused sorting office: surely that was an omen? The idea could continue in a new home, and so could the name.

Regrettably, there was one other similarity between the two sites – a landlord who wanted more money than Terence was willing to give. Negotiations ran into a brick wall. Between 2008 and 2012, Terence dedicated endless days and an intensity of passion to this great project.

The financial climate was not on his side but time was not on his side either. His ability to carry all before him had been eroded by age. His mind was as quick and incisive as it had ever been, but his body creaked. Afflicted by a bad back after a car accident in India many years earlier, Terence moved with visible discomfort. Simple things, like getting out of a chair or into a car, were clearly an effort for him. Investors would realise that it could take five years or more to complete such a far-reaching project. By then Terence would be well into his mid-eighties – if he was with us at all. They would have known that the project was nothing without Terence. On top of that, the financial anxiety of the time made any idea seem dangerous to investors. A truly big idea seemed doubly dangerous.

None of us, including Terence, will ever know what the Sorting Office might have become. It could have been startling. The idea itself was astonishingly brave. The conjunction of shops selling great established British brands with shops promoting provocative new designers, interwoven with restaurants, a club, and more, was potentially a thrilling cocktail. It could have become as celebrated a London landmark as Harrods is today.

But it was not to be.

For once, Terence's astonishing ability to make things happen had been thwarted by a nervous economy and the injustice of old age. There was a certain sadness in watching a man who had been used to carrying all before him now failing to make his dream a reality. The Sorting Office had become the thing that never was.

17

'Age Shall Not Wither...'

R.M.

In Shakespeare's play, Mark Antony says of Cleopatra: 'Age cannot wither her, nor custom stale her infinite variety.' It's a thrillingly romantic sentiment. But sadly it is also a dream, a falsehood. Age shall wither all of us, whether we like it or not. And Terence failed to like it more than most of us.

There are many admired Conran characteristics – design flair, innovation, creativity and so on. But it was the sheer energy and drive, the extraordinary brute productivity of Terence's temperament, which gave meaning to his creative gift. Without that, Terence would simply have been someone who had imaginative ideas. But it was the ability to translate those ideas into action, the ability to make things happen, which was such a potent part of Terence's gift. That talent depended to some considerable degree on raw physical energy. And as Terence aged, so that physical energy dimmed.

As he moved from his seventies to his eighties, Terence, more precisely Terence's body, was inevitably less able to cope with the massive demands that his own ambition placed on it. He was endlessly eager to jump on aeroplanes to rush all over the world, attending events, chasing opportunities, putting his own personal stamp on affairs. But he was no longer strong enough to do that with impunity. One sensed that his staff and his family appeared to be engaged in a constant, though guarded, struggle to slow him down. They feared that if he took on too much, his already fragile health might let him down. He could do damage to himself, and perhaps to his reputation too.

Terence did not take kindly to being inhibited in any way, and tried to carry on as he always had. Sometimes this worked, sometimes it didn't. On a visit to the Milan Design Fair, he missed his flight home for the embarrassingly simple reason that he got stuck in the bath in his hotel room, and could not get out unaided, nor could he reach the telephone. After a very long wait for the great man, someone was sent to his room and his entrapment was revealed. Terence was prised from his bath, but his dignity was left behind.

Terence's determination was never to be underestimated. He was convinced, as he aged, that through sheer willpower he could carry on as before. Others around him were less confident. They were worried about him travelling: but they were also worried, back home, about the Conran Shop.

The Conran Shop had many significances in Terence's life and achievement. With Habitat gone and most of the restaurants too, it was the cornerstone of his diminished empire. It was the one business which carried the Conran name on the door. It was the flagship of Terence's personal taste and style.

After its 1987 move to Michelin House opposite and consequential great enlargement, the Conran Shop had rapidly become more than just a splendid place to shop; it was also the unofficial Saturday morning club of London's wealthy chatterati. Media money, design world money, European money all commingled, eager to be seen as much as to see. Like his restaurants, the Conran Shop had become *an event*. And so it remained, for at least a decade. But gradually the world moved on, and the Conran Shop didn't. It failed to innovate, to keep ahead of the game. Come the millennium, it started to lose its sparkle, and then its customers. Thus it followed a path marked out by all of Terence's businesses: great promise followed, symmetrically, by great disappointment. In 2005 Terence was infuriated by the suggestion that Peter Jones and the whole John Lewis Partnership, a *bête noire* of his since his fifties training, were usurping the Conran Shop in the matter of selling smart merchandise to discriminating and affluent consumers. This thought was stimulated by the sight of an Eames chair in Peter Jones' Sloane Square window.

The *Evening Standard* also reported that the Conran Shop on Conduit Street and its Paris branch had shut. The last part was not entirely accurate, but was perhaps indicative of a mood in the reporter and no one seemingly bothered to double-check.

The Conran Shop once occupied privileged space on shopping's high ground. Its descent from exclusive, special and fascinating to acceptable but unexciting tracked Terence's later career. While once it demonstrated enthusiasm and originality, it became complacent, as the man who invented design no longer patrolled the floors, frightening and motivating staff by turns. As competitors caught up, it lost credibility and logic.

To those who admired Terence's vision, a regular visit to the temple that was the Conran Shop was almost religious in its importance. And the sacrament of spending while there – be it £9,000 on a sofa or £9 on a pack of Christmas cards – was equally important. But the congregation was gradually dwindling. The shop was not making the money it did in its heyday. There was a feeling that the Conran Shop, which had once been great, was now merely good. It needed revitalisation.

The family, whose future fortune was partly linked to the success of the shop, started to be concerned. There was growing consensus that new ideas were needed, and therefore new leadership was needed too. In principle, Terence agreed with that. But in practice, he found it near to impossible to cut himself off from the business which so perfectly echoed his own vision.

Terence's five children had all demonstrated the Conran genetic flair for design and entrepreneurship. His two eldest sons, Sebastian and Jasper, both ran successful design businesses in their own right. But whereas Sebastian was a highly intelligent designer, it was his younger brother, Jasper, who had translated design skill into a massive personal fortune. Originally a dress designer, he moved into the high street with a vengeance when he signed a deal with Debenhams, the department-store chain, to provide Jasper Conran designs for a seemingly endless range of products. You could get Jasper-designed women's clothes, Jasper-designed men's clothes, Jasper-designed crockery, Jasper-designed almost-everything. It had made him a very, very rich man. At weekends, he commuted by Bentley from his grand Bayswater apartment to not one but two stately homes in the country.

His success, rooted in undoubted commercial acumen and a ruthless streak, made him the obvious candidate to follow Terence as the guru behind the Conran Shop.

Even Terence agreed.

And why wouldn't he? The son had inherited the father's energy, and had demonstrated an ability to combine creative flair with commercial nous. And keeping a Conran at the helm seemed instinctively right, as well as safeguarding the heritage of the brand. So in 2012, Jasper took over as head of the Conran Shop.

Almost instantly, the shop started to look very different. It was more dramatic, more glamorous. And more expensive. Everyone noticed that the Conran Shop had recaptured its sparkle, albeit at a price. You could visit and see piles of Terence's didactic book *Plain Simple Useful* in front of mountains of meretricious but costly knick-knacks manufactured in the People's Republic of China. To those prepared to see a connection, Terence's consistency looked like a lost cause. But as a great historian once said, consistency is a puerile temptation.

Jasper's accession brought with it the beginnings of Terence's retirement. If Jasper was in charge at the Conran Shop, then, by definition, Terence was not. He found it monstrously hard to let go. Most of us might hope to retire long before we're seventy-nine, and we'd be delighted to do it on Terence's 'pension'. But Terence wasn't most people. He defined himself through his work; it's what kept him going.

Terence used his home as his office. In truth, he was unable to see the distinction. The rest of us value some separation between home and office: they're different places for different purposes. But not Terence. Barton Court was where he lived, but was also where he conducted much of his business – the celebrated Habitat marketing committee meetings being but one example. At weekends, he would entertain guests: but these encounters were often as much commercial as social in purpose.

For many years Terence had a penthouse in the Conran office building near Tower Bridge, which served both as a London home for Vicki and himself and as his weekday office. Eventually Vicki, fed up with her breakfast being interrupted by yet another meeting, persuaded Terence to buy a separate London home in an elegant mews near Sloane Street. Inevitably, soon this too became used for working meetings. The physical overlap between work and home in Terence's routine was a clear metaphor for how he saw his life: living is working, working is living. If retirement was a word that featured in Terence's personal dictionary, its definition was a grim one.

Of course, there was still work to do – Boundary, Lutyens, Bibendum, all needed looking after, as did the Conran design businesses. And the Design Museum was hunting for a new and larger home. But all of these activities had been delegated to good managers, so on a day-to-day basis there was not that much to do. Carrying his name and much of his passion too, the Conran Shop was different.

Intellectually, Terence accepted the change. Emotionally, he was bereft.

The temptation to interfere in the life of the shop was almost irresistible. When Terence gave in to that temptation, Jasper fought back with a ferocity that his father would – in other circumstances – have admired. But to battle with one's own son only added to the pain of ageing.

It soon became apparent that to have Jasper in charge of the shops and Terence in charge of everything else was not a formula that could last. There was only room for one person in the driving seat. In 2013, there was a revolution: Jasper was in charge of everything. Terence no longer had his magnificent penthouse office at Butler's Wharf, no longer had his loyal chauffeur, no longer had his pride.

It was almost certainly the right decision for the future of the family business. But it was not the right decision for Terence's personal well-being. Terence did not do relaxation. He acted it, wine glass and cigar in hand, for the camera, to build the myth of the brand, but it was not the real Terence. The real Terence hated holidays (he got bored instantly) and loved work. It was the fuel that powered his engine. And retirement was a holiday without end, a holiday with no prospect of returning to beloved work.

As Jasper took over the reins, so Terence slumped back in Barton Court in a mood of great sadness. He had a vibrant wife, five children, more grandchildren, great wealth and a great reputation. But he did not have the one thing he craved more than any other – a sense of purpose.

This was a man who had shaped our lives. He had widened our horizons over the way we furnished our homes, the way we ate when we went out, the whole spirit in which we lived our lives. Yet his own horizons seemed to be narrowing all the time. He had always defined himself through work and through his ability to create. And that ability was now being remorselessly undermined by the cruelty of old age.

18

Conran as Competitor

R.M.

If you saw Terence from afar, it was easy to admire his achievements – not just as a designer but as an engineer of social change. But if you worked closely with him, as both Stephen and I have, you could study the personality that drove those achievements.

One of the characteristics which shines through with a ferocious consistency is the sense that he was endlessly in competition with everyone. And it was a competition he had to win.

This was often as apparent in the trivial as in the significant, and I had an insight into Terence's unstoppable competitiveness over everything, large or small, on a business trip to Paris in the early days of Habitat.

Habitat needed a new advertising agency in Paris, so it was decreed that I would go with Terence and John Stephenson to Paris for the day, to check out the most likely candidate.

I met the two at Heathrow early on a Friday morning. They made an unlikely pairing. John Stephenson was Terence's right hand in business, specialising in marketing and advertising. He was tall, slender, elegant. He cut a dash, and he dressed the part. Terence, by contrast, was stocky and jowly, even as a relatively young man. While John wore clothes with a George Clooney-like sense of ease, Terence managed to make a Savile Row suit look as if he'd found it in a charity shop.

When I arrived, John and Terence were waiting together – Cary Grant and Just William.

We all got on the plane; I was sandwiched between them. They each put their briefcase on their lap and opened it. John's was an expensive attaché case, by Gucci (of course). Inside was a copy of *Time* magazine, a black Dieter Rams-designed calculator, a leather-bound notebook, and a matching Mont Blanc pen-and-pencil set. The contents of his case somehow endorsed his stylish and perhaps overly mannered sense of self.

I then looked across to Terence. His briefcase was a raffia affair, cheaply made in China for the Conran Shop. It had a kind of bohemian chic, and it looked as if it would just about last the journey. He opened it to reveal a box of twenty-five Romeo y Julieta cigars, his passport, and nothing else.

Terence leant across to me. 'John and I were both married to the same woman, you know,' he confided. Before I could tell him that I did know, he continued: 'Not at the same time, rather obviously.' I laughed politely.

He then explained to me with an almost gynaecological level of detail that he had fathered two children with Shirley, while John had fathered none. The clear implication was that – in the fecundity stakes – Terence had triumphed where John had failed.

The remark, expressed in language that was unprintably coarse, seemed strangely shocking. I realised that Terence was in competition with John – his friend and partner – over everything. Whether it was who had the cooler briefcase, or who had the greater procreative potency, life was a battle.

But it wasn't just a battle with John Stephenson; it was a battle with everyone.

On another occasion, I mentioned to Terence that I had been invited to a party at the country home of his one-time partner, Rodney Fitch. 'You should go,' said Terence, 'just to see the house. It's magnificent . . . huge.'

There was a pause, then he added with a voice quaking with force: 'But it's not as big as mine.'

Such anecdotes may seem trivial, and in a sense they are, but they are indicative of a deep truth in the Terence temperament. Everything was a battle, and every battle must be won. Of course, successful people are competitive by nature, but in Terence's case that competitive fire came with an edge that bordered on hostility. It could be extremely uncomfortable to live with.

Certainly Jasper, his chosen heir, seemed to find it testing. His New Year resolution in 2016 appeared to be to win back his independence of spirit from a highly controlling father.

It was revealed in *The Times* of 16 January 2016 that Jasper – who had not long before been appointed as the head of the Conran business – had resigned. So a smooth dynastic succession in the Conran court seemed to be unravelling.

Jasper's unexpected departure appeared to have been provoked by an interview which Terence had given to the *Evening Standard*, implying that the son was unwilling to take guidance from the father. In the interview, Terence had said that Jasper 'never, or hardly ever, talks to me'. He added: 'I kept on saying I've got the experience and the knowledge. I know things you don't. I know how to design furniture.'

In spite of Terence's remarks, this was not really a competition about design. Clearly this was about control. And when you compete for control with a strong personality like Jasper (a force-field in his own right) he may punish you by isolating you. As Terence had now discovered.

With his original business empire taken from him, many of his more recent achievements sold, and cut adrift by one of his sons, old age offered Terence a bleak and empty prospect.

Lunch, an Interlude

S.B.

I knew Terence for nearly forty years and, while his interest in food was undisputed, it is a matter of curious note that he never once told me a single recipe, nor cooked anything at home other than a roast chicken. Although it was always an extremely good roast chicken. But we had many lunches out, mostly very enjoyable, although some less so than others. It was really quite hard to get Terence's attention when he was studying a menu or a wine list.

Lunch was the theatre where some of our small dramas played. It was at Enzo Apicella's Meridiana in Chelsea that we had the conversation confirming the Boilerhouse Project and the Design Museum, the legacy project that would immortalise Terence and make design part of popular culture. There was some beauty here: Apicella was the Neapolitan journalist who had designed many of the Italian restaurants which broadened London's gastronomic horizons in the sixties. Pizza Express was one of them. Alas, I cannot remember what we ate at Meridiana.

A dinner at Chez Victor on Wardour Street was the first occasion I had ever shared two bottles of wine over a single meal. And then, unwisely, followed Terence's Porsche in my Ford Capri down the Mall at improvident speeds. When we met after one of several periods of not talking, it was in a restaurant. That was the then new Fifth Floor at Harvey Nichols, so it must have been 2002. He had phoned to say: 'All my friends are dying, let's make it up.' We ate an astonishing *tête de veau*, which made the febrile ladies lunching at the next table gasp.

In 2005 we made a three-day trip to Paris to do nothing other than eat. I took Terence to La Ferrandaise, an eccentric veal restaurant in the rue de Vaugirard, where cows are fundamental to the decorative conceit. He rather approved.

We made a nostalgic trip to La Méditerranée on Place de l'Odéon, the restaurant where he had, according to his telling, been a *plongeur*. We ate twice at Chez Georges, and the French interior designer Andrée Putman joined us for dinner in Les Ambassadeurs in the Crillon. There were mid-morning strong drinks in the Café Marly in The Louvre. A driver in a Renault Vel Satis, a strikingly ugly car, took us everywhere. I have a good appetite and a strong constitution, but the regime was daunting. In those days, Terence's appetite never seemed to flag. For my part, I needed to lie down in the Hôtel Montalembert at unusual times of day.

And in 2005, we were ready for another project. Terence wanted a new edition of *The Conran Directory of Design*, which I said we should call *Intelligence Made Visible*, adapting something Le Corbusier had once said by way of a definition of this elusive subject. This was eventually published in 2007 and appeared in translation in Europe and the Far East, providing many further opportunities for lunch, both to prepare and to reflect.

One day at Boundary, Terence's restaurant in Shoreditch, I actually took notes. They went something like this. 'The food connection runs deep: one of Terence's very first clients was, after all, Walter Baxter, the butcher who created the Chanterelle restaurant. What does he like to eat? A perfectly roasted chicken. What does he not like to eat? Anything complicated. His worst dish ever created is probably the late Charlie Trotter's red-wine-braised artichokes with eggplant confit and jerk goat.'

I got to the restaurant first because it is my habit to prepare the ground: it was my lunch so I wanted to make sure the wine was organised. And affordable. And that we had Table 64, his favourite. Last time we had been there Terence had ordered a Domaine de la Romanée-Conti Romanée-Saint-Vivant. It wasn't on the list, but would have been about £2,500. This time I asked the sommelier for something delicious, but cheap. He told me it had already been organised.

A figure appeared, preceded as ever by the residual smell of fine Havana. Terence always intuited that moving slowly conferred gravitas, so he always moved slowly. Latterly there was a bit more of a shuffle, but I got a cheery, 'Hello, Mr Bayley,' and a cock-eyed smile. The sommelier arrived with a Bourgogne Aligoté, the cadet grape of Burgundy, and I reflected that '*cru bourgeois*' might one day be the subtitle of my own autobiography. I explained to Terence that we were about to drink a good, but cheap, wine. The ordinary thing extraordinarily well done – an often-repeated definition of excellence in design in our many conversations. He told the sommelier: 'Give him five-pence worth.'

We soon started to talk about a new book we were planning on luxury and how it might be defined in a rapidly changing, possibly even rapidly deteriorating, world. This provided an agenda, something I have always found useful. I talked a lot. Sometimes Terence was silent. What, I asked topically, do you think of Pierre-Yves Rochon's newly refurbished Savoy Hotel? 'Simply terrible,' he said, tutting in exasperation with eyes half closed.

I didn't pursue more explanation because I knew exactly what he thought. Refurbishing the Savoy had presented the opportunity of making new, not retreading the past. This was an opportunity that the owners – in slavish thrall to a misunderstanding of history and design – had bodged. 'Luxury,' Terence said, looking up from the menu with the infinitely pained emphasis of a tragically disappointed schoolmaster, 'is not fucking decoration.'

So we were not planning a lunch at the Savoy. At this point Terence was more interested in the menu than me. He had for some time been tormenting Boundary's chef over the perfect recipe for *bisque* (plenty of roasted lobster shells ground to powder is part of the process). *Bisque* was ordered and the torment continued. Other options included half a dozen natives, Jerusalem artichoke and salsify salad, pink fir apples and an *onglet aux échalotes*. Perhaps some pan-fried foie gras.

Next arrival at the table was a big bottle of Faugères Domaine Leon Barral, a wonderfully jammy southwestern red that tasted of sunshine and sex. Here was a cue for that excellent Conran apophthegm. 'A magnum,' Terence said, 'turns even *vin ordinaire* into a luxury.'

My return of serve was to say that sorting out ideas of luxury was, in fact, a way of restating the principles of design, which had in recent years got rather lost in a muddle of pseudo-art, preening charlatans and crass consumerism. 'Yes,' Terence said, wagging a well-wagged finger. 'Edit! Edit! Edit!' He added: 'Less really is more.' It was part of Terence's singular talent that in quoting Mies van der Rohe's most tired and trite observation, he could make it sound like the discovery of the human genome sequence.

In 2015 I took Terence to lunch at Hunan in Pimlico, to many people London's very best Chinese restaurant. I had something to explain. Amazingly, despite having lived near here for many years and Chelsea being his back yard, he did not know it. I told him I was writing a book about him. Glumly he said: 'You must, dear Stephen, you must.' He was preoccupied and not much interested in Mr Chang's peppered squid and bak choi. By the time we were ready to leave, his driver had not arrived. Terence did not have a mobile phone. I called him a minicab.

That was the last time we were on civil terms. At least, it was lunch.

PART 5

THE DESIGN MUSEUM

19

The Boilerhouse, the World's First Pop-Up Museum

S.B.

If Terence had an idea of exactly what he wanted the Boilerhouse to be, he certainly did not articulate it in any great detail. Instead, he let others decide in his name. Thus, in its way, it was similar to Habitat or any of his other projects. Others were allowed, or required, to execute his will. Sometimes this demanded unusual clairvoyant powers. Sometimes, when it worked, this liberality produced exceptional results.

For my part, sitting at my new electronic Olivetti ET121 typewriter in that white proto-minimalist room in 1982, I wanted the Boilerhouse Project to work like a magazine in three dimensions. Which is to say, a form of journalism. Terence did nothing to stop me. He liked journalism. Well researched, if at all possible, but topical and provocative too. And, after a period of intense immersion in an exhibition idea, it was forgotten and never considered again. Like Terence, my own concentration can be strong, but is temporary. Meanwhile, our ambivalent status of being within, but not entirely of, the V&A was extraordinarily valuable and gave extra point and thrust to whatever we did.

There is nothing radical about putting a vacuum cleaner on display in Selfridges or even in a private gallery, or, being Jeff Koons, to say that it is art, but in the august and patrician V&A, with all its pieties, pomp and imperial values, to do such a thing was to excite all sorts of comment about the general theory of value and the frontiers of art and design, at least as determined in the eighties. This was exactly our purpose and this we did with relish.

We were to occupy a space in a grand old museum still organised on nineteenth-century taxonomic principles. For example, no one in the V&A took any interest in cars since no one could decide whether a car was 'Sculpture' or 'Metalwork', so no department wanted to take responsibility for collecting one.

My own ability to concentrate intensely and then frivolously move on was, I realise now, a reflection of Terence's own fragile and fidgety consciousness. The Boilerhouse programme – with a mixture of chutzpah, research, guile, lifting, borrowing, theft and whimsy – was intended to draft a broader definition of design, but, as it became ever more popular, had the subsidiary effect of giving Terence ownership of a newly enlarged and intellectually credible design fief.

It was not quite intended as such, at least not consciously, but it was one of the most successful ever promotional exercises of its type. Comparable, I suppose, to Elsie de Wolfe's achievement with Henry Frick: introducing new American money to old French furniture. But this was introducing new English money to Italian and Japanese design. A million Habitat shares, a simple piece of paper, secured Terence's reputation not merely as a designer, but as an enlightened patron of design itself.

At once, the Boilerhouse achieved for Terence a position of authority in the world of museums that he had already enjoyed in retail. The dullards of the RDI and the Design Council were made to look flat-footed. Just as Habitat refreshed the high street, so the Boilerhouse Project refreshed the V&A and helped make 'design' the popular everyday topic it is today. That, at least, was the plan.

The exhibition programme was, additionally, intended to combine up-to-date scholarly research in design history with unashamed commercial sensibility, irreverent stimulus and flagrant violation of claustrophobic museum norms of propriety. In this I was very much influenced by Lisa Taylor, the very grand Mrs Bertrand Taylor III of New York's Cooper Hewitt Museum. In the seventies Lisa had done splendid agitprop shows, not excluding events on the subway where frazzled commuters were taught the principles of design. This was the sort of engagement we were looking for.

On the whole, the Boilerhouse programme was very successful indeed. While he was inspirational, I cannot recall Terence actually making a single practical contribution to its evolution after he suggested the word 'Project' – he was, happily, too busy making the money that kept us going. The exception was an introduction to Philip Garner, a California exotic who in 1984 had produced a novelty book called *Better Living Catalog*. This had been brought to Terence's attention by Suzy Slesin, *High-Tech* author and at the time a big influence on his thinking. Garner was a West Coast Heath Robinson, and his book was a miniature Rube Goldberg take on Stewart Brand's epochal *The Last Whole Earth Catalog* of 1969, but with joke pictures instead of survival goods, and photographs of curious things Garner had 'designed'. We turned this into an exhibition, with Garner scouring London rubbish dumps (they were not called recycling centres in those days) and fabricating strange things in our basement.

One such included a fireplace made out of the bonnet of a Renault 4 which, in the days before Health and Safety concerns became pervasive, we installed in the stairwell. I thought it was very funny, but design prudes – the sorts of people who felt Terence too 'commercial' – thought it frivolous. Personally, I feel frivolity has its place. Besides, only serious people can appreciate silliness.

Garner used to carry with him everywhere an Austin Maxi workshop manual, whose exploded diagram of the gear-change mechanism with its mad loops of cable made him howl with laughter and slap his knees every time he saw it. Last time I heard, Garner had returned to California and taken a course of hormone injections so as to grow female breasts. Initially, this was not a gender reassignment stratagem, more an act of existential curiosity, although Philip has now become Pippa.

More often, Terence's interventions in the Boilerhouse programme were restricted to titanic rages after the event, focused, usually, on my assumed vanity or evident incompetence, sometimes both. The brief rages were accompanied by longer-term criticism, veiled and unveiled threats, continuous refusal to engage in subtle debate, occasional more-in-sorrow-than-anger moans, and majestic refusal to give encouragement, let alone praise. This was combined with bullying messages and a generalised and often emotionally violent end-of-my-tether attitude which I was, at the time, brazen enough to regard as a challenge to be savoured and overcome. We got on well.

More positively, so preoccupied was Terence with business, I was effectively left entirely on my own. Our own trustees had little to say, certainly nothing to say against Terence, and while Roy Strong had, in theory, the power to veto Boilerhouse activity, he was emotionally located somewhere between a lofty disdain to descend to our level and a keen enjoyment of the cheerful hullabaloo we generated, helpful to his political cause in the perpetual scrap between the V&A and the government. Thus, he said nothing.

'Art and Industry' was the first exhibition and opened at the beginning of 1982 with a huge party. Here, a Saab 92 became the first car ever shown in the V&A. In the exhibition, we explained how aircraft interiors were designed – with no reference to Terence's 1951 flying boat, but lots of documentary material from Frank Del Giudice of New York's Walter Dorwin Teague Associates, who was responsible for early Boeing interiors and thus framed the world's concept of flight.

We resurrected the Saab designer Sixten Sason and gave Eliot Noyes, the American who had reorganised IBM and Mobil on Bauhaus principles, creating our current concept of 'corporate identity', his due. Harley Earl, General Motors' wizard of kitsch, of whom we had glorious video footage on the first Boeing 707 passenger flight eating a banana, was a star. So too was Raymond Loewy. It was an eclectic view of how mass-market design had evolved in the twentieth century. There was serious documentation and Alan Irvine designed an installation of exquisite tact and elegance.

In 1982, however, design was poorly understood, if it was understood at all. Despite the fact that our aim was to be populist, and despite the fact that Fiona MacCarthy had been writing witty and erudite design columns for the paper for twenty years, a different reviewer in the *Guardian* mysteriously felt that the Boilerhouse 'might have been calculated to distance the public'.

The *Observer* came out in comradely solidarity and agreed with its sister paper: 'The work of the industrial designer would be sinister if it were not also mildly ridiculous . . . The Boilerhouse is a strange nether region where the homage paid to goods and gods is wreathed around with dubious assumptions.' With perhaps a little intentional ambivalence, the *Financial Times* said: 'Terence Conran's new Boilerhouse gallery of industrial design continues to carry a startling message.' It did not specify whether this message was startlingly good or startlingly bad. But at least a message had been identified.

We held a monographic exhibition on Sony when the Japanese company had an equivalent status to that of Apple today. No one had ever done such a thing in a museum: elevating a cassette player to the prestige of Giambologna was a shock to many systems. The Sony show gave rise to many exquisite encounters, the best of which was the day its founder, Akio – Mr Transistor – Morita demonstrated his Mavica to a beaming and giggling ex-Prime Minister Ted Heath in my office. The acronym stood for Magnetic Video Camera and this was the original digital photo device. We were, truly, able to say: 'You saw it here first.' Alas, Terence was not at the Morita–Heath meeting.

There was an exhibition about Dieter Rams, Germany's greatest product designer and chief influence on Apple's Jonathan Ive. The great graphic designer Otl Aicher worked on a show about cars and accused me, not with any pleasure, of turning him into a 'pop artist' when I put small red dots on some of his austere black-and-white captions.

The Boilerhouse also held an exhibition called 'The Car Programme', about the design of the then-revolutionary Ford Sierra. A crane lifted successors to the Cortina (the 'Dagenham Dustbin') into the Boilerhouse, perilously above some sculpture galleries housing Renaissance and baroque masterpieces. Six million pounds' worth of insurance was required for the morning, lest a clay model of the Cortina replacement crashed through the skylights upon a statue of a dryad, a penitent or an orgasmic saint.

This all continued in a hectic, carnival atmosphere. I gave bottles of whisky to uniformed staff to encourage helpfulness. I had a key to the front door of the V&A: in those days security was relaxed and access to a silent museum at night remains a keen memory of pleasure. However, there were problems.

The conservative 'Keepers' of the V&A, a feudal institution, comprising a band of medieval barons, with their own territories, beneath the powerless titular king, Sir Roy, were both horrified and fascinated at the liberality and popularity of the Boilerhouse. Views on Terence were equivocal: clearly a person of importance, he was also not quite proper and certainly no scholar.

They despised the commercial consciousness of the Boilerhouse and at the same time envied the money that made it possible. They were jealous of its success, but lacked the funds, nerve or energy to replicate it. These people are called 'Keepers' because that is their closed and protective mentality. But since I needed access for exhibits through those baronial fiefs, and since this access could easily be refused, I mollified as many as I could by a long sequence of lunches in my office, where I served identical dishes of smoked salmon, rye bread and some half-decent white burgundy. Terence licensed such things: design is about living well in every sense and, indeed, with all the senses.

These same Keepers had intense curiosity about my Conran lifestyle, mingled with intellectualised loathing of it. But with voyeuristic distaste, no one ever refused an invitation. Although one memorably angry and absurd Keeper (who pronounced 'ceramic' with a hard 'c'), greedily ate his lunch, then banged the table, told me we had 'traduced a fine tradition of a great museum' with all this modern industrial rubbish and sniffed his way, chin aloft, out of my office smelling of Chablis. I knew we had won a point.

The same office saw many other memorable encounters, richly redolent of Terence's world and the antic mood of the eighties. Nigel Broackes of Trafalgar House, a gung-ho City *commandant*, shuffled in one day and took one of the cigars my father had given me for my birthday. You could smoke in offices in those days. Raine Spencer, Princess Diana's stepmother, called in to ask me to ask Terence if she could have a discount in her local Habitat. That made Terence laugh. The Formula One designer Gordon Murray gave me the male mould of the nose cone of his Brabham grand prix car for display in my office. My tiled white box soon became surprisingly cluttered because Issey Miyake also gave me a neoprene model of a nude Grace Jones taken from the life which I artfully arranged on the floor.

The wife of postmodern architect Michael Graves did callisthenics on this same floor, on the Bauhaus rug found for me by Terence's sister, Priscilla, refusing a glass of Perrier because it contained salt which gives you cancer. There was enormous publicity, but also criticism. Terence liked the good news, but not the bad. Normally, I am tolerant of negative comment, thinking it far superior to being ignored, but I made an exception for the egregious Waldemar Januszczak. I don't mind lying, but I detest inaccuracies, and I found some in his early accounts of the Boilerhouse. The faintest of praise was his chosen voice. But really, misinformation from an art critic did not much bother me, especially when the Boilerhouse enjoyed all the spectacular fun of being the first place outside Milan to host the then-astonishing Memphis, the name of a group, with references to Egypt and Elvis, who wanted to campaign for anti-design. Or, at least, a version of design that troubled institutions and mocked lazy nostrums.

Memphis's leader was the great Ettore Sottsass, Junior. No one had better credentials as a designer hero: he was one of the great figures in Italy's post-war era. But Memphis was a merry jape, at once ironic and insolent . . . and very easily copied by less adroit designers. So there was later some mild regret at having introduced it to the public.

After long and apparently nugatory negotiations in Milan, with no documents to support important decisions, I knew the show would go ahead only when a V&A security guard called me at four o'clock one morning and said a large truck with Italian plates was blocking Exhibition Road and the voluble driver was speaking a very fast foreign language in which only my own name was recognisable. The Memphis consignment had arrived. Terence hated the ironic posturings of Memphis, which so carelessly undermined several truths he held dear.

The Boilerhouse was both a symptom and a cause of the new, popular design awareness in the eighties. At one time or another, most of the world's outstanding designers passed through my office, paid their respects, donated ideas, drank a little wine. When no other museum in the world had such a lively programme of activities, nor any similar media interest nor popular following, the Boilerhouse created a human nexus of astonishing value. It seemed to me, completely persuaded by the virtuous-circle logic that had inspired it, that the Boilerhouse was a real resource of potential value to Terence's business.

Why not use these astonishing creative contacts to collaborate on projects for Habitat or Mothercare? Put them on show and test them on the public! This seemed to me to be absolutely in the spirit of the enterprise and respectful too of Henry Cole's original intention of using a museum to raise popular taste and inspire or rebuke manufacturers. If Terence thought this too, he never said such a thing. To a surprising degree, he ignored the potential of what had been created for him. Instead, he limited his intervention to lacerating post-hoc criticism of any activity that did not match narrow criteria of what is and what is not 'design'.

Only by the most elastic measures could Terence be said to have been broad-minded, culturally speaking. His inability to handle complex or subtle ideas was nowhere more evident than in his reaction to certain exhibitions. We organised one called 'Handtools'. I commissioned a new friend of mine to design it. He created an astonishing installation of dramatic black wedges laid out like the plan of a hand. Vitrines were embodied in the wedges and visitors had to stoop to see what was on display at the thin end of each wedge.

Never mind that this new friend and young designer was the talented John Pawson (and this was just his third job, after interiors for Bruce Chatwin and Doris Saatchi), Terence went into a volcanic rage at the sight of it. He swore, he shouted, questioned my sanity and probity. It was always difficult, if stimulating, when he was angry, but I was not perturbed in this case as Issey Miyake, Mario Bellini and Richard Rogers all told me that 'Handtools' was one of the best exhibitions they had ever seen. Later Terence liked to look back on 'Handtools' and fondly recall how, through vision and commitment, 'young Pawson' had been given his start. An older Pawson designed the interior of the second-generation Design Museum in Kensington.

But one particular exhibition specially enraged Terence. This was because it was a major offence to his own taste; and because it attracted so much criticism, he was exposed for the first time in his life to someone saying: 'No, Terence.' As the decade wore on and his business unwound, this was an expression he would hear more often, but hearing it for the first time was a rude shock. Terence had only a modest ability to tolerate criticism . . . even to understand it. His reaction to criticism of the exhibition called 'Post-Modern Colour' was revealing.

'Post-Modern Colour' was one of several exhibitions I had had to take on because Boilerhouse funds were so exiguous. The Boilerhouse never actually had anything like enough money to afford its programme, so scraping, begging and borrowing, extemporising and winging it, were part of my job. Presented with the chance to display a collection of furniture that Formica had commissioned in its new ColorCore product which, unlike laminate, had colour running all the way through it, I decided to recast it as 'Post-Modern Colour', so as to give the display some character, integrity and purpose. But, evidently, nothing like enough.

Press comment was unusually hostile. The response of Colin Amery in the *Financial Times* was deeply revealing of the contemporary mood. Amery was mandarin and aloof and disdainful, but witty and mischievous too. An architectural arbiter, he had advised the Sainsbury family on the choice of Robert Venturi, author of *Complexity and Contradiction in Architecture* (1966), for the new National Gallery extension. Venturi's book is the genesis of postmodernism, so the playful, pastel, shape-making, attention-getting, referential aspects of our furniture were not unfamiliar ground.

Still, Amery sniffed that the great achievement of Formica was to make wood look like plastic, an expression of abuse in his High Anglican vocabulary. He continued: 'Stephen Bayley . . . has isolated these crazy designs in his white-tiled gallery so that they look like drunken guests who have stayed long after the party is over. Postmodern design, if it wants to be taken seriously, has got to recover from art of the 1960s. The Boilerhouse has done us all a great service. This show is a warning that designers who become slaves of the latest silly trends will just inspire laughter – and the laughter is becoming more ribald than sympathetic.' Actually, I see now that this was quite fair.

But it did not inspire laughter in the patron of the Boilerhouse. Terence would, if they met in private, have had no time for the waspish Colin Amery and his camp High Church affectations, but when appearing in the pink 'un he took him very seriously indeed. Perhaps because he did not see it, Terence missed Amery's irony. Sometimes, he missed quite a lot, that one eye being quite selective. I received a letter, positively humming with vehemence, complaining that I had allowed the Boilerhouse to become a showplace of the latest silly trends, a condemnation I thought feeble given the silliness of the decade. Terence, who had never troubled to question this exhibition idea when invited to do so, threateningly added that I was a sore embarrassment to everyone, myself included.

Terence was not wrong. 'Post-Modern Colour' contained some very odd and not very intelligent designs. One piece was by the artist-craftsman John Makepeace, whose work I did not much like, but that wasn't the point. Other designs were either straining for effect or poorly thought out, occasionally both in the same piece. But I felt it was nonetheless of interest to young students and designers. Besides, it had cost us almost nothing.

You could imagine, above the noise of air being sucked in over clenched teeth, Terence mumbling that the Boilerhouse was becoming a place of ridicule (not even nearly true) and that my seriousness and judgement were to be questioned (no doubt about that, but there were few dissenters to the fact that the Boilerhouse was, with no thanks to Terence other than his cheque book, a place that changed the public's perception of design).

Terence was very literal and very linear. Like many educated in art school, he could not appreciate the independent value of criticism, could not accept that you can be interested in something while not necessarily liking or admiring it. To Terence, good and bad were absolutes, and resident not in the lofty world of ideas, but in the more earthbound world of products.

I replied: 'I was saddened, but not surprised, by your letter about the *FT*'s review of "Post-Modern Colour". You must try to distinguish between fact and opinion. I like the furniture on display perhaps as little as you do, but that does not prevent me from thinking that it is important to give people the chance to see it and make up their own minds. Colin Amery was not, for once, being facetious when he said we were doing the public a service by displaying "silly trends". Remember: Henry Cole started the Museum of Practical Art with his "Chamber of Horrors". We are an educational body and I take it as a fundamental principle of educational philosophy that it is just as easy to learn from the "bad" as from the "good". Perhaps even more importantly, if the Boilerhouse is to have any credibility as an independent voice promoting an awareness of design, I think it is essential that our exhibitions should not merely be vehicles to express your taste (or mine, for that matter). At least, not all the time. Personally, I find it curious that you think furniture designed by, for instance, the head of design at Georgia Tech, Robert Venturi, Stanley Tigerman, Eva Jiřičná and Rodney Kinsman is lacking in "seriousness", but there you are.'

The Boilerhouse now, without further creative intervention from Terence, continued its programme of popular exhibitions. We exhibited, at another budget crisis, an international survey of retail graphics for an expense of a mere £5,000, through the device of sending people to New York, Paris and Tokyo with instructions to collect carrier bags from all the shops on certain streets and hanging them from wires suspended from the Magnagrid ceiling. It was called 'The Bag'. And it was very popular, but I cannot recall Terence saying: 'Well done.'

The last major Boilerhouse exhibition was in 1986 for the centenary of Coca-Cola. In this Terence took no interest. Yet 'Coke! Designing a Megabrand' became a phenomenon, at one point helping the Boilerhouse to claim attendances superior to those of the whole V&A. In 1986, discussing a 'megabrand' in a national museum whose pride included a superlative collection of Constable landscapes seemed a shocking travesty, exactly as intended, but it led the way to the V&A's later populist exhibitions, which turned Kylie Minogue's knickers and David Bowie's trousers into objects of aesthetic and intellectual scrutiny. Design is, after all, concerned with the aesthetic value of everyday things. Terence was eventually to remind people how radical and popular 'Coke!' was.

At first, Roy had seen the Boilerhouse as an intellectual investment, giving him additional credibility at no personal cost other than the alienation of Keepers who had alienated him anyway. He also saw it as a refuge from these same Keepers: often he would descend to my shiny white basement to gossip very amusingly about his exasperation with them.

Once he descended to discuss his exasperation with Terence, at the time a trustee of the museum. At a trustees' meeting, a medieval illustrated psalter, or some such, had been presented for consideration as a purchase. Roy expressed his horror that Terence had actually picked up the sacred object, rubbed its texture and sniffed it. He asked me how I could work for a man of such clumsily robust instincts. Here was a perfect illustration of the methods of too-similar, but very different, aesthetes. If a museum professional handled a museum piece, it would only ever be when wearing cotton gloves. To Roy, Terence's approach was tactile and careless. To Terence, touching and sniffing was a means of connecting directly with the sensual and real aspects of the psalter's design.

At one stage, Roy Strong, restless with the agitation caused by demands that the V&A should have its own twentieth-century collection on proper display, let it be understood that this same collection might find a more suitable home in the future Design Museum, which I had essayed in Oslo in 1979. Never mind that Roy had perhaps not discussed this sensational offer with the relevant members of his staff, it made very good sense to us. Even if it meant the new Design Museum would be almost a satellite of the V&A, this was an association which the Boilerhouse had proven valuable.

But at some point, for what reasons I cannot say, Roy cooled. As the end of our government licence to occupy the old Boilerhouse Yard approached in 1986, we attempted to renew it so as to enjoy success a little longer and to buy more time for fund-raising and planning our future Design Museum. But, perhaps piqued by its popularity, Roy resisted any extension of the tenancy and the Boilerhouse Project closed in summer 1986. By most measures, it was London's most successful gallery of the eighties and turned Terence from being a Chelsea shopkeeper to the undisputed symbol of authority in that strange territory he had invented.

Barton Court was Terence's home for fifty years. Its indisputable grandeur was offset by requiring visitors to enter by the kitchen door, as if servants. He enjoyed a connoisseur's delight that the Kennet river passing through the grounds was a unique home to the greenback species of fish. *(Photograph by Snowdon/Trunk Archive)*

(above) The purchase of the old-established Heal's furniture business in 1983 seemed to confirm Terence as a master retail strategist: a business and a design colossus. *Look on my desk, ye mighty, and despair.* *(Bill Lovelace/ANL/Shutterstock)*

(left) In 1970, the old Covent Garden was on the cusp and the opening of the Neal Street Restaurant soon established its new reputation as a smart bohemian destination. For a decade, Neal Street was London's optimum modern restaurant: a perfect statement of Terence's taste. David Hockney illustrated the menu. The Conran design studios were upstairs: it was a small colony of idealists. *(Simon Turner/Alamy Stock Photo)*

Monsieur Bibendum was Michelin's corpulent and convivial hominid, designed to give character to boring tyres. When he acquired the Michelin Building, Terence was happy to absorb the hedonistic and inflated tyre salesman into his own iconography. *Nunc est Bibendum!* Now is the time to drink. *(Fernando Blanco/EPA/Shutterstock)*

The Oyster Bar at Bibendum was Terence's vision of absolute felicity: an eternal lunch of langoustines and champagne with glamorous people. A *plateau des fruits de mer* did for Terence what religion did for ordinary people: exaltation. *(Victor Watts/Shutterstock)*

This Francophiliac phantasmagoria in Chelsea was conceived as advertising for the Clermont-Ferrand tyre company. Terence co-opted a site opposite the original Habitat for his own purposes. In 1987, it was repurposed as a shop and a restaurant, confirming Terence as a patron of all things French. Two years later there was Terence's *dégringolade* and he was, at least symbolically, marched out of the City. *(Ianni Dimitrov Pictures/Alamy Stock Photo)*

Quaglino's, the St James's establishment, was opened in 1929 and closed in 1977. In the early nineties, Terence's restaurant commander-in-chief Joel Kissin found the site and, by 1993, when the new Quags opened, it was perhaps Terence's greatest *coup du théâtre*. Acidly, the critic Fiona MacCarthy said it was 'a deprived child's dream of sophisticated living'. *(Photograph by Geoff Howard, Camera Press London)*

In 1979, a new 'design museum' for London was announced at an academic conference in Oslo. *(Author collection)*

Saturday – Nov. 10

9.00 Jørgen Schou-Christensen:
      The Saxbo Ceramic Industry

10.00 Marika Hausen: The Finnish
       Society of Arts and Design
       and their Design Commitment
       since 1945

11.00 Stephen Bayley: The Need for
       British Design Museum

Terence Conran and Stephen Bayley on the roof of the Design Museum circa 1988, each in David Chambers (double-breasted) suits: period costume. Like Big Bang, the Design Museum was a result of eighties euphoria, although financial deregulation had not yet affected the distant City skyline. *(Christine Voge)*

Ten years later, it was a reality. An abandoned banana warehouse near Tower Bridge had become Bauhaus-on-Thames. This startling building enhanced Terence's reputation for wizardly transformations. The big head in the foreground is by Terence's friend, Eduardo Paolozzi. *(Peter Durant Photographer/Alamy Stock Photo)*

The 'Handtools' exhibition of 1984 was visually startling. It certainly startled Terence who disliked it very much. The designer was John Pawson and it was only his third commission. Pawson went on to become one of Britain's best-known design celebrities and architect of the second-generation Design Museum. *(John Pawson)*

In 2016, the Design Museum relocated to Kensington's old Commonwealth Institute, eviscerated for the purpose by John Pawson. Its impressive emptiness has been interpreted as a symbol. Where, some visitors ask, is the museum? And a museum of exactly what? *(Photo © BOEGLY + GRAZIA)*

A very young Terence in 1953 on display in one of his first popular designs: the conical basketware chairs sold in his Piccadilly Arcade rental. The frames he welded himself. The freshness and modernity astonish: stores at the time were selling brown furniture under dull yellow light. *(Ray Williams/Estate of Ray Williams)*

Presentation was always very carefully considered for photogenic effect. But there is also a proprietorial element: are these chairs artfully hung off the wall Gio Ponti, Vico Magistretti or Terence Conran? *(Popperfoto/Getty Images)*

Later in life, Terence fetishized Yrjö Kukkapuro's Karuselli chair of 1964, described ten years later by the *New York Times* as 'the most comfortable chair in the world'. Terence met Kukkapuro in Finland when drunk. *(Jonathan Player/Shutterstock)*

20

The Design Museum,
a High-Concept Shop

S.B.

Only two people ever knew what the Design Museum was meant to be. And one of them is now dead. Latterly, the other one has had no formal contact with it. This may be why it has existed in a state of almost continuous muddle since 1989. But I can explain.

There was no philosophy for the Design Museum, but there was a set of convictions. Plus an intuitive belief that if you exhibit excellence, the public will admire it and seek it out. And, of course, there was a didactic element as well. If there is a single thing that Terence and I unequivocally agreed upon, it was that you could learn by looking. And to appreciate how something is made is to understand it. That, and a belief that anything that is made betrays the convictions and principles of the people who made it. Every object tells a story, you could say.

Terence has often listed his ideas of excellence in design: the Citroën 2CV and the Citroën DS19, for example. The distinction between the two is amply illustrative of his eclectic, sometimes inconsistent, taste; elemental functional chic on the one hand, *grande luxe* on the other.

Additionally, he had often celebrated the café chairs of Thonet, and Charles Eames's furniture, as well as late Rothko paintings. Terence had also said he would like to be able to put his name to the Guggenheim

Museum, the Ronchamp chapel and the Seagram Building. Who, frankly, would not? But Frank Lloyd Wright, Le Corbusier and Mies van der Rohe got their names there first. Surreptitiously, I suspect Terence was making a claim to some sort of kindred authorship. Whatever, this subject matter had all been carefully laid out in 1985's *Conran Directory of Design*, a fair shot at a popular encyclopaedia, compiled in the days before Google or Wikipedia.

I researched and wrote it all the hard way, but Terence insisted that I only be credited with 'Edited by'. Essentially, it told the story of the aesthetically significant products of industrial culture. 'Classics', if you like, but as Sainte-Beuve knew, a classic is something both universal and permanent. The Design Museum was built to enable study of these classics, a corpus of work with its own traditions, disciplines and propaganda and art – less comparable with, say, the baroque or the rococo.

In this way, perhaps even more so than Habitat, the Design Museum was to be the permanent monument to Terence's view of the world and its priorities. That's to say, educating the public in the 'importance of design', the better to make informed judgement while out shopping. Indeed, to make the best of their lives. And it must be committed to making the most of contemporary possibilities, rather than out-of-focus antiquarian longings.

Just as Terence was always worried about sadness, he was equally worried about living in the past. He said: 'I think a civilised society is one that has the confidence to live in the present, to learn from history rather than repeat it.' Unfashionable to say it now, but the idea of 'design' in the Design Museum was an essentially moral one. Better design, we felt, might create a better world. And moreover, design must always have an aesthetic aspect.

Between 1986 and 1989 I managed the creation of the Design Museum building from grim, indeed sad, offices clawed out of an old warehouse in the shadow of Tower Bridge. The site was within the Butler's Wharf development, an ambitious mixed-use project of deluxe apartments and restaurants, with the Design Museum as the 'planning gain'.

The spine of Butler's Wharf was an evocative urban canyon called Shad Thames, often used as a film location when a macabre Dickensian atmosphere was called for. Latterly, before falling into near ruin, the buildings had been used as performance spaces and studios by squatting artists.

A compact riverside building was a suitable starting point for the Design Museum. Incredible to say so now, but in the mid-eighties this area just a Tower Bridge away from the City was run-down and neglected. At this time, the only building to punctuate the City skyline as seen from Butler's Wharf was Richard Seifert's NatWest Building. It was a wretched and bereft area, but full of promise for those with eyes to envisage. The person who helped us find the site was Max Gordon.

In 1981 Max Gordon, aged fifty, had opened his own office, intent on serving the art 'world', although in this context 'world', as in 'design world', cf. 'caravan world', must be construed to mean an exclusive clique, not a global community. At that moment, this world was about to leap the species barrier. No longer the exclusive province of anguished artists, critics and connoisseurs, art was about to become a new financial asset class, the ultimate luxury commodity.

Gordon's clients included the art dealers Anthony d'Offay, Annely Juda and Nigel Greenwood. When 'genius' became 'brand', Gordon was there to design its container.

In 1983 he was commissioned to convert a disused St John's Wood paint factory into the Saatchi Gallery. Stripped-back, white-painted and defiantly, if politely, industrial, this slightly absurd vanity project in bourgeois Boundary Road became the Santiago de Compostela of new art. It was a destination and a shrine. Thus Gordon was, directly or indirectly, the architect responsible for two of London's most influential galleries of the eighties.

I do not think Terence came on any of the early site visits, although, with Alistair McAlpine, he was a major investor in the development. The building we proposed to creatively reuse had been built in the fifties as a warehouse, originally for bananas, latterly for Korean War army surplus. It had a tough concrete frame, low floor-to-ceiling heights, and made no concessions whatsoever to charm or delight. I was incontinently excited at the prospect of occupying it.

But first we had to design the Design Museum, an amusingly self-reflective task. It seems astonishing now to say that Terence played no part in this. That's as in *no part whatsoever*. Instead, the detailed process began with Stuart Mosscrop, architect of the Miesian Milton Keynes Central Shopping Building, and the structural engineer Frank Newby of Felix Samuely. Gloriously and appropriately, Newby had worked, aged twenty-five, on the Skylon at the 1951 Festival of Britain, and had interned with Charles Eames in California. I felt this was a good team.

We went away for a few days to Justin de Blank's Shipdham Place hotel in Norfolk. I remember driving, very proudly, in my aerodynamic silver Audi 100 and being so preoccupied with the business in hand that I had a small collision near Swaffham. Justin de Blank we met earlier. He was an architect who had worked both in advertising and in the design business, most notably for Terence in Hanway Place, where a brittle mutual respect was established, although not a lot of love lost.

He also had, Terence's Soup Kitchen notwithstanding, some claim to being the founder of the modern London bistro and, when Justin de Blank's Hygienic Bakery was opened in Walton Street in 1983, to being in at the very beginning of London's real food retail revolution, in its artisan mode. The *Telegraph*'s obituary of Justin called him a 'society grocer' and the urbane, sceptical de Blank would not have been displeased. His Shipdham Place was a gloriously shambolic country-house hotel, run with great patrician style and a slightly cross demeanour by Justin, and with cheerful brio by his wife, Melanie.

In rural Norfolk, Mosscrop, Newby and I spread huge rolls of white drafting paper on a hotel floor, gripped our Magic Markers, ordered some good red burgundy (de Blank always wore masterpiece shoes and was, happily, an Olympian wine snob) and agreed the general arrangements of the world's first museum of mass-produced design. What we agreed was to remove some of the banana warehouse's concrete slab floors, build on the roof, render it all white and, all in all, create what many commentators later described as 'Bauhaus on Thames'.

Driving back to London with a slight Gevrey-Chambertin hangover, I realised all that needed to be done was to find the money to build and run it: Terence was offering a lot, but not quite enough. My job was to make it happen, like the sort of competent contract manager Terence so contumaciously despised. I was prepared to try anything, even royal approval. True, Terence was all but a republican, and I had noisily criticised Prince Charles's *retardataire* architectural views, but even visionaries sometimes embrace realism.

In 1988, Major Christopher Lavender, Equerry to HRH the Prince of Wales, wrote to Terence on Buckingham Palace paper, confirming a meeting at St James's Palace at 10.30 on 21 July. 'The aim of this meeting will be for you to discuss the Conran Foundation's plan to build a new museum of design at Butler's Wharf.' Terence felt able to subjugate his republican instincts in the interests of a royal trophy which might encourage our fund-raising campaign.

We went along with a model of Mosscrop's concept, a startlingly white and angular building that might, in hindsight, have been designed for the sole purpose of annoying and alienating Prince Charles, then at the very height of his anxiety about the way modern architecture was despoiling the world of gables, turrets, bargeboards, vermiculated rustication, stained glass and pargeting that he preferred.

I was told that the meeting was to be 'informal', although HRH had busy note-takers standing behind him. Presenting the model,

I spoke, as convincingly as I could, about how the Design Museum would help prove our point that a greater national awareness of design would be good for both the economy and the culture, thus bringing universal benefits.

Outside, a violent thunderstorm was overhead with drenching rain. I was momentarily distracted as I had left my convertible in the yard with the hood down. I was snapped out of my brief reverie by HRH who, looking infinitely pained, wheezed, winced and simply said: 'Mr Bayley, why does it have a flat roof?' Of course, there was an answer, but the circumstances were not appropriate to offer it.

We heard no more, so the prime minister, Margaret Thatcher, was recruited as royal surrogate. Again, Terence felt able to subjugate his socialism against the presentational advantages of the Iron Lady's backing. (We both conveniently and hypocritically overlooked the fact that Mrs Thatcher's anti-industrial policies had ruinously undermined what remained of British manufacturing, thus removing the last shreds of empty canvas on which our national school of designers might go to work.)

Accordingly, on 7 March 1989, Mrs Thatcher hosted a dinner for us at Downing Street. I asked Simon Hopkinson of Bibendum to suggest a menu and to cook. I had found Simon at Hilaire some years before and, by a roundabout route, had introduced him to Terence, making one of the best patron-chef combinations of contemporary London.

Very good, but the prime minister's private secretary explained that Mrs Thatcher was not inclined to fuss about food and was prepared to eat anything, provided only that it did not contain bones or shells or cartilage. So the famous wild rabbit cooked over Provençal olive wood and a plate of fresh clams in their shells were not options.

The objection here was that dealing with edible matter requiring mastication would have a retarding effect on the progressive thrust of polemical conversation that was Mrs Thatcher's rationale for sitting down to any dinner. The same private secretary asked me to bring an envelope with £120 in cash to pay the washing-up staff, evidently employed off the books in the grey economy.

Once again, I presented a model of the Design Museum to an audience comprising twenty or so *extremely* senior people in British business. Terence let me do all the talking. They were more or less uninterested, but in those days no one refused an invitation from Mrs T, or, indeed, Sir T. I made my pitch about the significance of design. Or, at least, had made most of my pitch when I was interrupted by a hard object clinking on a glass and I heard the prime minister say: 'Have you finished?"

It must have been very evident that I had not, but Mrs Thatcher continued magnificently undeterred. Fixing me with a terrifying stare she then said: 'You [there was horrible emphasis on this personal pronoun] must not call this a museum!' She added, rather defiantly, I felt: 'Museums are things of the past.'

At this point I made a serious mistake in the course of what had otherwise been a fairly continuous upward career trajectory. My plan was to say: 'But, Prime Minister, although we acknowledge its unfortunate antiquarian associations, Sir Terence and I have discussed the matter and we feel the archaic term "museum" is justified as it brings a neglected subject into the area of culture which, as we are competing for funds with the Royal Opera House, is exactly where we wish to position ourselves.'

Alas, I got only as far as saying: 'But, Prime Minister . . .' when Mrs T shot me an evil gorgon stare and said rather coldly: 'Don't "but" me, young man.' There was an embarrassed shuffle in the audience and no more was said that evening. (We raised no money, but Gerald Ronson sent a cheque for £100 the following day.) As we were descending the grand staircase of Number 10, a figure in a cape came running up the stairs two at a time. I had never met him before, but he said very amiably: 'Hello, old boy.' The PM said: 'Denis, where have you been?" to which he replied: 'I've been to a golf club reunion, sweetie.'

The next day, several guests called me to say how very sexy they had found her.

Terence was curiously unperturbed by the failure of the Downing Street dinner to raise any money, although he was well aware that his donation was capable of meeting only the capital costs of the Design Museum, leaving the future budget for any activities, including employing people, unfunded. In fact, he was never very active in using his then-uncontaminated lustre and huge influence to get us much beyond the opening ceremony. While he was preoccupied by making it, Terence was often too fastidious to talk about money.

There were exceptions. I remember a particularly vicious bout of fury when I explained that I could not give John Sainsbury a sales tour of Butler's Wharf as I was going on holiday. It may have made it worse for Terence that I was going to France and leaving him with the famously difficult Sainsbury.

Terence had always felt that the supermarkets were more professional than Habitat, so there was an added edge to this encounter. Never mind that he had neglected to tell me about the Sainsbury visitation until the day before, and never mind that it was naive to expect one ambitious retailer to make a significant charitable donation to a *vanitas* memorial of another ambitious retailer. But I think Terence's regard for himself and for the project eluded rational analysis.

Most of my own time in the three years between the closing of the Boilerhouse and the eventual opening of the Design Museum was spent talking up the project wherever anyone would listen, while planning the programme of exhibits and activities. In the latter, Terence took not much interest, possibly because he trusted me. In the matter of the former, I was regularly castigated for spending too much time out at lunch. Of course, this was a rite that Terence had actually taught me to acknowledge, even worship, and besides, it was the competitive arena where fund-raising pitches were made.

One such pitch was to Kenneth Clarke, then at the Department of Trade and Industry. Such was our confidence, we had actually done a financial exercise in which the Foundation assumed all the roles, as well as the budget, but none of the staff, of the DTI-funded Design Council. In a rare moment of diplomacy, I opened the conversation by saying to Clarke: 'I don't want to say a word against the Design Council . . .' Clarke immediately responded: 'Why ever not?' Eventually, it was decided that, while the Design Council was felt to be pretty much useless, there were no votes in making three hundred public servants redundant.

Instead, the Design Museum received a £650,000 grant from the ministry. This seemed to me quite good value for a lunch spent out of my office, especially as the venue and catering had been provided by Walter Hayes, Ford's legendary PR boss, in the company's gorgeous Grafton Street offices, bought as a resort for the Ford Motor Company's clandestine commercial business as well as Henry Ford II's clandestine romantic business.

Described by Mr Ford as the only man who could 'overspend an unlimited budget', Hayes had put Grafton Street, with its fabulous Barbarella-era interiors by Chester Jones, indefinitely at our disposal. Terence was unimpressed; it was not something he appreciated or understood. Possibly because it was not something he had done himself.

In this manner, the Design Museum evolved in the late eighties. The Butler's Wharf building was on time and on schedule, getting ever whiter and squarer by the day, providing a luminous signal of what we were aiming to achieve.

It was a cause to which no reasonable person could deny his allegiance and the excitement and energy were palpable. So too were the jealousy and resentment. But more than ever, I felt strong spasms of missionary zeal and, even as Terence nagged and rebuked and chivvied and threatened, I felt empowered as a true representative of the Conran spirit. The purposes of the Design Museum were vast and all-embracing. It was a symbol of national revival, no less. I never tired of writing or being interviewed about this for newspapers and magazines, building credibility and anticipation the while.

And Terence never stopped being cross at my writing or lunching, even when it was directed at his own future aggrandisement. I'd be excoriated for spending time in restaurants with, say, Fiat. But that time eventually led to Fiat underwriting the costs of running the Design Museum for its first five years with a handsome donation of £500,000. Impossible, of course, to prove that a bit of *sprezzatura* over lunch at Bibendum had given rise to this generous gesture, but I felt confident I knew what I was doing.

And I knew what I had done. Apple set up a cluster of Macs for us, demonstrating the new hypertext system, a primitive browser, but advanced for its day. We all thought this was a bit of a coup, but Terence, who could not even type, let alone compute, took no interest. Ever the practical man, he was inclined to see fund-raising as piss and wind. Still, none of us doubted it was going to happen. And none of us understood the anguish Terence was suffering that year.

So the Design Museum opened in August 1989, the culmination, we can now see, of every aspect of Terence's career. It was modern, it was bold, it represented an improving idea, it was a rebuke to convention and complacency and, of course, all of the work realising it was done by others.

At the opening party there were fireworks and we ate, with a view of the glowering and newly liberated City in the background, Lorna Wing's miniature fish and chips in cones made of the *Financial Times*. I danced with Akihiko Amanuma, one of the team from Sony in Tokyo who created the original and epochal Walkman. I think I may even have danced with Terence, but my memory is not very clear on that particular point. The next day, badly hungover, I stood on the balcony overlooking the Thames and ruefully wondered: 'What on earth have we done, but build a high-concept shop?'

Because Roy Strong had not been able to deliver his idea that we could take on the V&A's twentieth-century possessions, the Design Museum's own permanent collection was only modest and hurriedly assembled, using *The Conran Directory of Design* as its guide. Still, I was undeterred by this, as I felt the real purpose of the new building was to provide a permanent home for the journalism-in-three-dimensions that had been so successful in the Boilerhouse.

The opening exhibition was called 'Commerce and Culture', intending, I told myself, to reveal the complex interrelations between the two which formed the intellectual basis of Terence's world-view. Actually, at this stage, it had become my world-view too.

It was a terrible exhibition: I did not do a good job of explaining a subtle, but over-complicated, brief to the designers, and they did not do a good job of articulating interesting ideas. It was clumsy, cluttered and too busy, although it did give rise to a good book, one of the first to be published by 4th Estate. Terence, never at the best of times able to deal with abstract ideas, absolutely hated it. So too did Peter Fuller, editor of *Modern Painters*, a Marxist critic turned radical rightist and a spokesman for 'traditional' values.

An apostate of the modern world, he expressed dismay in a long review in the *Sunday Telegraph*. Fuller spoke of his 'grave forebodings' about the whole enterprise. A champion of shabby painters, he was sour that the government had given the Design Museum £650,000 at a time when it was cutting back on art education; this might not have endeared him to our project. 'I imagine,' Fuller wrote, 'that both Mrs Thatcher and the corporate sponsors will be pleased with what they have got for their money.' In Fuller's outlook, mere association with such untouchables as 'Thatcher' or wicked commercial 'sponsors' was damning.

What Fuller found was the old banana warehouse divided into three parts. The upstairs 'permanent collection' was one of the first major installations, impeccably realised, by the architects Stanton

Williams, who have since made beautiful museums something of a house speciality. Beautiful too were the full-size wooden models I had commissioned of Le Corbusier's *Voiture Minimum* and Gerrit Rietveld's *De Stijl* motorbike. I was astonished that Terence never paid these any attention.

The rest of the display was thin – a few pens, some kitchen machines. As noted, this might have been very much more substantial had the V&A's then homeless design collection been rehoused in this westernmost part of Docklands. This daring stratagem might have released Roy Strong from various administrative torments in South Kensington. But the clarity, logic and boldness of this idea were not enough for it to survive the hostile reality of *Museumpolitik*.

Additionally, there was a 'Review' section, which Fuller said – intending, I think, to be funny and taking inspiration from the reliably unfunny Waldemar Januszczak – 'advertises the latest lines in washing machines and cocktail cabinets'. It did no such thing, although if I had known that a washing machine and cocktail cabinet would have enraged Fuller, I would have been certain to include them. It was conservative old prigs we had set out to violate. But Fuller reserved his real wrath for 'Commerce and Culture' in the space intended to revive the spirit of the Boilerhouse.

The motif of 'Commerce and Culture' was Milton Glaser's notion: 'Why don't we discard the word "art" and replace it with the word "work"?' which seemed to me then, and still does now, a helpful stimulus to debate. Fuller, pained by this modernism, moaned: 'After all, what's the difference between a Fra Angelico Madonna and a packet of Mothercare extra-large nappies?' There was an answer, but, like Prince Charles, he did not want to hear it.

When in September *Design Week* – now defunct, but at the time an often-read trade rag – said that there was 'something unappealingly suburban' about 'Commerce and Culture', Terence was irked. After all, the escape from suburbia was the story of his life. A photocopy of this offending review was sent to me by Terence with nothing but a large red exclamation mark. I should have read the signs. There really were quite a lot of them. Peter Fuller had said: 'If this is indeed the Museum of the Twenty-First Century – God help us all.' Cheap and ungenerous. But maybe he had a point.

It is a gruesome irony that 1989, when the Design Museum opened, was a year of spectacular triumph and humiliating failure for Terence. Until 1989, Terence had never had any criticism. Now he had lots.

What's more, his retail revolution would soon be over.

On 3 May 1990, with his own holding estimated at £30 million, reduced from £120 million, Terence resigned as chairman of Storehouse. The plan had been to retire on his sixtieth birthday eighteen months later. But the emotional pressure was too great. He was replaced by an accountant, the sort of people who Terence saw as treating creativity as a cost and not an investment. 'At last people will stop referring to it as Sir Terence Conran's beleaguered Storehouse Group,' he sighed.

He bought the Conran Shop out of the failing group for £3.52 million and sold the Conran Design Group to the Paris-based agency RSCG (Roux Séguéla Cayzac Godard), where he became joint president. He also bought the rights to the Conran name. Alas, he might have lost the Conran touch. Perhaps no amount of money could buy it back.

Symbolically, Terence had left his fine office in the Heal's building – theatre of the spectacularly misconceived eighties' deals – and moved to Butler's Wharf. He was contemplating the ruins of his business at the same moment that he was admiring his new monument to design.

Through the Design Museum, he had promoted himself to national curator of the subject he invented, but simultaneously he was the stand-out individual who had failed to persuade the doggedly philistine City of the importance of creativity in business.

He offered himself to the City and the City said no, thanks very much. This was an ultimate insult with the angles and vectors of a Greek myth. In 1989, Terence had experienced a shocking repudiation of his beliefs: a designer was replaced by a despised bean-counter. Yet he also experienced perhaps his greatest triumph: a whole museum devoted to his own concept of design. The tensions here might have made a less manically driven individual incline towards despair.

Maybe the tensions did exactly that. At about this time, one day our cars passed in slow traffic in Pimlico. In those days he still drove himself and he was in his big twelve-cylinder navy-blue BMW 7 Series. He did not notice me. But I could not fail to notice him: he looked utterly bereft and mournfully preoccupied, staring straight ahead at a future he was trying to understand.

At least I was no longer a part of that future. Soon after the opening of the Design Museum, I went for three weeks' holiday in Italy. After ten years of quite hard effort, I saw this as a bit of *meritato riposo*, but Terence saw it as arrogant negligence, a sort of calculated insult, a suicide note. He was never a formal holiday person, even as he enjoyed the pleasures of abroad. And talking of signs and symbols, the Italian holiday had been at Ponte Rosso, the resort south of Rome where, according to myth, the bad fairy Circe was a long-term resident.

On return I was asked to a meeting in Terence's Butler's Wharf office. This was unusual as, ever since Neal Street, when I used to bring a good bottle of wine as an entry ticket to his attention, Terence and I had arranged to see each other without the intervention of secretaries. I duly arrived and found an uncomfortable-looking Terence with the chairman of the trustees.

At this point, paraphrases and telescoping are necessary. This chairman of the trustees, a Midlands industrial designer for whom I had not much affection or respect, a decent man, but not an adventurous intellectual, had been imposed on me by Terence as, it was hoped, a moderating influence. This, despite the fact that Terence very well knew my immoderacy had been the driver of a successful collaboration.

The chairman said: 'This is all very well, Stephen. You have done very well. But are you now going to settle down, stop going on television and become a proper museum director?' It was a Dreyfus-like moment. The chairman was, I think, encouraged to say this by Terence who, while grudgingly admiring, had been fatigued by my enjoying myself too much. And, as he saw it, enjoying myself too much at his expense.

And for a while, I was eclipsing him in press comment. It was almost mythological.

Essentially, my reply to the chairman, recalling his own sub-zero contribution to the whole project, was robust. And then I walked out. For the first time in my life, before the days of internet porn, I bought a girlie magazine and a bar of chocolate and went outside to sit on a waterside capstan and contemplate what I had done. Perhaps a little too hastily, Alan Parker of Brunswick PR was asked to write a press release about my resignation.

While Terence was mercilessly critical of my vanity, frivolity, contempt for detail, arrogance, nerve, tactlessness, conceit and general difficultness, I was nonetheless his creation and he saw in me many of the qualities, bad and good, that others had recognised in him.

After this resignation, which surprised him as much as it surprised me, I saw a genuinely kindly and concerned man, who might even have been shocked that a tactic intended to scare me by proxy had caused me, in an existential funk of ultimate cussedness, to abandon what he had himself, one summer's day on the banks of the Kennet and Avon canal, required me to see as a 'lifetime's commitment'.

He asked me: 'Are you really sure you want to leave?' I was not sure at all, but the people who start businesses, perhaps, shouldn't run them. In essence, the Design Museum could now be all his, even if he did not know what exactly to do with it. Keith Hobbs had observed:

'One thing I do know about this man is: I cannot rely on him for my future. I knew I couldn't trust him with my life. It would all go wrong and I'd get binned.'

Hobbs had walked. And so did I. I binned myself. Or rather, Terence watched complacently while I was put in an impossible situation. Still, I think he was glad of the result, if a little perturbed by it. So, in compensation, he suggested we form a business called Conran and Bayley – to do exactly what, we never decided, although the joint-venture file grew to be an inch thick.

That October I went to Nagoya to give a talk for a good fee. At the time, Terence and I were sharing an office. When I got back, he asked how it went and if I had been paid, always a sensitive question. I said indeed I had. He then said I must give the money to the Design Museum, since it was the credibility of the institution I had created with his money that validated me. Terence was forever concerned that people were stealing from him, while freely taking his own inspiration from wherever he might find it. I said I would do no such thing, but would put the money into our own venture. Or give it to charity.

This led really quite quickly to another flounce by me, to recrimination, abuse and threats from him. Terence suggested he would prevent me from working since this would be selling knowledge that I had acquired at his expense (conveniently ignoring the fact that I arrived with a great deal of knowledge and had put it at his disposal for several years without payment).

He also wanted me to repay all the fees I had received from television and journalism over the years, again on the basis that I had been exploiting his time and resources while flagrantly enriching myself and inflaming my ego at a cost to him. And here was a reflection of the larger truth about our relationship. Terence felt the Design Museum was his idea and got me to organise it. I thought the Design Museum was my idea and got Terence to pay for it. We were both half right.

Anyway, this, I believed, was not a fair interpretation of the give-and-take in our relationship. I had been a tireless champion of Terence's causes, defending him like no other. I had abandoned a vaguely promising academic career to make a 'lifetime's commitment' to the Design Museum, only to have the conditions of that commitment removed at the first obstacle. Terence may have felt exploited. I certainly felt betrayed.

And the stand-off was only resolved when the lawyer Victor Mishcon, a specialist in pre-emptive litigation, wrote Terence a letter on my behalf. As Lord Mishcon suggested he should, Terence ceased and desisted, but we did not talk again for years.

While it is inelegant to talk ill of one's successors, the Design Museum never fully achieved what was intended for it, existing in an untidy sequence of cash and credibility crises, ill managed by lacklustre directors, all of whom either did not understand or decided to ignore its rationale. In 1991 *The Times* reported that expenditure was being cut from £2 million to £1.5 million and corporate membership was declining during the recession. The paper said: 'Sir Terence continues to support the museum, despite the serious financial difficulties of his Butler's Wharf development.' At this point, Terence was saying he had given the Design Museum £12 million.

By 2004 Terence was himself becoming alienated from the Design Museum because of the behaviour of Alice Rawsthorn, its fourth director in five years and the first actually to have a sense of direction, although not a direction I would personally want to have taken. Nor was this a direction Terence much cared for. Rawsthorn it was who proposed the Constance Spry exhibition about flower arranging, a very bold test of the meaning of design.

21

Constance Spry,
the Fallout from Flowers

S.B.

In 2004, the idea of 'design' was travelling on vectors that Terence was unable or unwilling to follow. Late that year, the uncertain direction and muddled management of the Design Museum became a hilarious public spectacle: a spat with cut flowers between James Dyson, the billionaire bagless-cleaner genius, and Alice Rawsthorn, a critic and journalist, now its director. Dyson was, at the time, an exasperated chairman of the museum's board of trustees. Rawsthorn was its headstrong director.

The cut flowers belonged to Constance Spry, the florist whose work Rawsthorn featured in an exhibition. On her behalf, this exhibition was partly an act of defiance against a male board and partly a serious attempt to enlarge the popular perception of 'design'. Spry made a good controversy, and would have been a clever choice for someone actually seeking a showdown.

So far from the Central School, let alone the Bauhaus, Spry had been headmistress of the Homerton and South Hackney Day Continuation School before she became a society flower-arranger. Her displays included adventurous combinations of pussy willow and kale and her shop Flower Decoration became a media sensation of its day. On its last site on Mayfair's South Audley Street, there is now an English Heritage blue plaque. Spry's biographer claimed for her an inspiring lesbian romance with a floral painter. One of Spry's colleagues invented Coronation Chicken.

An exhibition about Constance Spry seems a perfectly legitimate extension of 'design', but conservatives were worried and the technocratic Dyson was outraged. He said the show was ruining the museum's reputation and 'betraying its purpose'. Dyson's preference was for technical 'problem solving', optimising pressure-relief valves, for example, perhaps failing to recognise that flower-arranging has methodological problems all its own. Not to mention an aesthetic established in many different cultures.

Terence's old friend, the furniture designer Rodney Kinsman, told the papers that he thought the Design Museum was a victim of the 'fickle finger of fashion and big sponsors'. Eventually, Dyson melodramatically resigned in protest at what he regarded as frivolity. He composed a list of complaints, an incriminatory dossier, which he handed to Terence. And which Terence then handed to me. 'Do you want to come back?' he asked rather wearily.

It is an astonishing document. And the fact that Dyson fumed in his Malmesbury HQ while compiling it was surely evidence of a malaise in the Design Museum's native culture. A well-managed organisation would never allow such a public conflict to occur. But Rawsthorn was not stupid. Headstrong and charmless, maybe, but the assumption must be that she was orchestrating a power struggle. Championing Constance Spry was a blatant attempt to assert her authority as a critic, based on a well-received 1994 biography of Yves Saint-Laurent.

Terence, while sometimes bullying, rather disliked explicit conflict. And was left perplexed by the dispute, not least because Dyson had heroic stature and was a rare example of a successful native designer-engineer-entrepreneur. And here he was, dismayed by the conduct of an organisation intended to sanctify Terence's understanding of design. Additionally, Dyson also had very deep pockets and philanthropic instincts. The Design Museum lost not just a chairman, but an urgently needed additional sponsor.

There was a sense of crisis at the Design Museum. An institution founded with optimism and a clear vision was riven with dispute of a fractious and unintelligent sort. Terence himself was despairing; he seemed to have lost control of the vessel of his dreams. There was a madwoman on the bridge and, worse, a madwoman with no apparent respect for Terence, his achievements and his view of the world.

'Under its current curational steer, of which [Terence] and eleven other trustees have no say, the museum is betraying the proper ideas of its founder,' Dyson wrote in a statement. The critique perplexed Terence and perhaps made him feel even more isolated from his own museum. Rawsthorn attempted to mollify him by impertinently offering him the role of 'president'. This he refused to consider while the museum was still in crisis. He contemplated his own resignation. In the end, Rawsthorn suddenly left the Design Museum in February 2006. There were no floral tributes. Her lengthy website bio today contains no reference to her period as director.

In 2008 it was decided, for no very good reason, but ambition and vanity might have been involved, to move the Design Museum to a new location in a creatively reused Commonwealth Institute on the quiet end of Kensington High Street, a building as forlorn and neglected as the old banana warehouse in Butler's Wharf had once been. This was the year of the financial crash, and the timing could not have been more maladroit.

But the move suggested 'design' was a dynamic subject that might again be seen as a catalyst in bringing something hitherto dead to life. The Commonwealth Institute was moribund and the building itself a wreck: it had a little more structural sense or design integrity than a temporary stand at a fair. But Kensington High Street was a dull and predictable shopping boulevard, and the opportunity to make a splash tempting.

Critics said the move to this location might unhelpfully confirm that design was only a version of shopping. Worse, in 2008 no one could have predicted how online would marginalise traditional retail, turning the western end of Kensington High Street into a wretched accumulation of pound stores, charity shops, and tacky sellers of party goods and tourist trinkets.

Moreover, the impetus for this move seems to have been more founded in opportunism than in pedagogical principle or museological logic, since the old Design Museum was popular and well able to meet its functional needs. There was also a perfect logic to its style and existence: it was fully expressive of the historical moment that created it. So, we can now see, was the new Design Museum revealing of the circumstances that gave rise to it . . . but not in a good way. Still, Terence had the wit to observe that the Commonwealth Institute's hyperbolic paraboloid roof was a nice contrast to the flat one Prince Charles had earlier disdained.

At least the architectural profile of the new Design Museum hinted at the more complex realities of the twenty-first century. Today, the huge US discount chain Target claims to be selling 'design' irrespective of the merits of the actual product, surely testing any lingering weight of meaning in the term. In a more innocent era, the original Design Museum was built to meet philosophically clear and practically simple needs.

The original Design Museum was intended to treat 'design' as a coherent subject, one with a beginning and an end almost as clear as, say, the baroque or rococo. It understood that 'design' had a tradition, a discipline and an aesthetic. It had key artefacts, true believers, articulate spokesmen and a popular, inquisitive public.

It was an unashamedly modernistic project, as the lucid geometry of the building suggested. We knew with absolute clarity what we wanted. Design deserved to be taken seriously, so a traditional museum was built for it.

Clean lines and clear objectives were our original motto. People would be given cultural and intellectual justification for wanting that elusive better salad bowl and a tubular-steel cantilevered chair. High purpose would transcend the mere cupidity of the high street. And, additionally, visitors might be inspired to curiosity about how salad bowls and chairs might be further improved in the future.

With a nice mixture of patrician arrogance and genuine concern, ignoring the wince-making elitism of it all, ever since Habitat, Terence had believed that if you educate the public to expect better merchandise they would demand it. And we would be on a commercial and cultural journey that would go round and round for ever in virtuous circles. It was an analogue idea in a world about to become digital.

Of course, there is a Platonic perfection in a perfect circle. And this argument had been perfectly circular, curiously so given the unapologetic thrust into the future. Terence's unspoken, but clearly understood, brief to me had been: promote design on my behalf; persuade the public, if you like, that I invented 'design'; then people will buy more stuff from me and you will have ever more money to promote design.

It was an idiosyncratic adventure in commerce and culture and very much in tune with eighties rhythms. This is why Mrs Thatcher (she, no aesthete and he, no friend of hers) had little difficulty in filling the gap left by the Prince of Wales and opening the 1989 original. At the opening, Mrs Thatcher nagged me that there should have been a Jaguar on display, but I bit my tongue and didn't say it was her own industrial policies that had driven proud Jaguar to the brink. Still, design was good for business. So, a design museum was a good thing. It was that simple. At least for Mrs T.

But the world has become more sophisticated since 1989 and museums, instead of leading public taste, now follow it. Or lose sight of it entirely.

The Design Department of the Museum of Modern Art in New York, MoMA, as it is always known, was among the very first art museums to devote space to design exhibitions and to build a collection of artefacts, an inspiration to my own early thinking about the Boilerhouse Project and the Design Museum.

In 1978 when I first visited MoMA's gift shop, it was stocked with inspiring modernist originals, a Bauhaus chess set or a Dieter Rams calculator. The museum itself had a fine Pininfarina-designed Cisitalia, the 1947 car that established what was to be Gran Turismo automobile. You could find Dieter Rams in sight of a Picasso, as it should be. In 2008, however, MoMA's gift shop was selling meretricious novelties, exactly the sort of frivolous junk that Charles Eames once said made him feel sick. If there was irony in MoMA's method, it was not apparent.

More recently, MoMA has completely reorganised its display of paintings. The galleries are no longer arranged with Eurocentric-style labels, but by decades. And the hanging is now more inclusive, with art from what was once patronisingly known as 'the Third World', as well as the Dead White European Men who mostly constitute the established history of painting and sculpture. This has had the effect of further isolating and alienating MoMA's design collections, which now seem a historically specific exercise in blinkered curatorship, not an appeal to universal values.

The new Design Museum faced a similar crisis, but rather lacked the intellectual wherewithal or institutional energy and style to deal with it. The location is only the first curiosity. The original Thames-side site in Michael Heseltine's 'Docklands', a quaint period designation, was intended to stimulate interest in a then-neglected area, an advertisement of 'design' as an agent of beneficial change.

But the new location confirms those cynical suspicions that 'design' was only ever a specialised branch of faceless, globalised shopping, a melancholy aspect of contemporary life which Kensington High Street once demonstrated with depressing authority, if no longer. Maybe Peckham or Hackney, Tottenham or Moss Side would have offered more challenging sites? These, surely, were places where 'design' could bring demonstrable and welcome change. But developers in Peckham, Hackney, Tottenham and Moss Side were not offering similar inducements, similar *cynical* inducements, to those that lured the unwise Design Museum to W8.

Because it was a listed building, the developer of the Commonwealth Institute site was required to retain the original, eccentric building, even if it was redundant and in poor condition. And the 'planning gain' of having a 'museum' would, in the way of these things, result in certain easements on more commercial development. These have, in fact, resulted in the flat-footed Design Museum being rather betrayed. Such an irony, as themes of betrayal were ever-present in Terence's world-view.

Its signature hyperbolic paraboloid is now invisible from the street behind a cliff-face of bombastic apartments created for non-existent, non-dom itinerant shoppers by OMA, the Rotterdam architectural practice whose principal, Rem Koolhaas, has often stated his interest in ugliness, both in food and in buildings. Additionally, Koolhaas was for a long time an eloquent spokesman for the cause of making all cities identical.

And perhaps John Pawson was too respectful of the original. His new interior of oak and air has his characteristic calm beauty, good manners and restraint, but serves the gods of circulation better than the gods of display. Here is a masterpiece atrium, if not a masterpiece museum. Mies van der Rohe spoke of *'beinahe nichts'* (nearly nothing), and here it is. Pawson is an original talent, but it was curious to commission a designer who has often said he is more interested in disposal than acquisition to create a building which should be full of diverting objects and images. Its vast emptiness strikes every visitor and maybe there is a metaphor here: a handsome vessel with no cargo and no direction. Was this vacuum really to be Terence's monument?

The new Design Museum opened on 24 November 2016, two years late, an event sponsored by Swarovski and Vogue. If expensive jewellery and a magazine dedicated to the spurious dynamics of fashion tell us anything, we must listen to what they are saying. These were surely markers of an institution whose destiny was to be a venue for the crappier sort of corporate entertaining.

As he spoke at the opening, Terence was by every account lachrymose. Hesitant too. His soft-spoken delivery was not enhanced by a faulty sound-system. People feared he was only going to stop whispering by some sort of intervention. He had to be helped off the stage.

One guest noted: 'I had mixed feelings about attending the "new" Design Museum's opening. Intrigue about its new base, sadness recalling the heady days of its launch in 1989. Passing a roped-off area for paps to snap photo-worthy guests, inside there was absolutely no sense of design, no design statement, nothing. 'Are there any things in this museum?' someone asked. The Design Museum has morphed into a tiered lobby. A space less for stuff and more for shindigs. A more hardy design crowd loitered round the edges of a rather sad impromptu dance floor, despite the best DJing efforts of Jarvis Cocker and Bella Freud. Instead of reaching a crescendo, the party deflated like an old balloon. I couldn't help comparing this with the glorious July day in 1989 . . . the positive media anticipation and excitement across London . . . Margaret Thatcher arriving by boat . . . the celebration continuing all day and long into the night.'

Subsequent press comment did not often rise above moderate rapture. In the *Financial Times* Edwin Heathcote deplored the descent of a great museum idea 'from radical public vision to private trophy'. One online comment described 'a tragic culmination of the endeavours of Tel-boy: essentially, a giant bourgeois gift shop'. Another thought it an unfunny 'joke'. Anonymised online comment tends to be spiteful, but there were few dissenters from this line of criticism.

The distinguished architectural critic Rowan Moore wrote in the *Observer* that John Pawson might have been a better choice for designer of the luxury flats which obscure the hyperbolic doings from the street, leaving the new Design Museum to the more exuberant Rem Koolhaas: 'For both seem to be playing out of position, trying to work with a situation with which they don't feel comfortable.'

In the *Guardian*, Oliver Wainwright described, without much enthusiasm, 'boxy levels of oak veneer . . . a mid-range business hotel shoe-horned beneath the great concrete kite'. But the fiercest criticism came from John Jerbis in *Icon*, who described the Design Museum as 'a sharp reminder of the narcissism of starchitects and the expansionism of design advocates'. He disliked 'an overbearing bulk that both contradicts and conceals much of the roof's famed curves', adding, 'This is not how museums should be made, nor how buildings be preserved.'

As he was no longer talking to me, I don't know whether Terence felt this was £54 million well spent.

Perhaps the Design Museum, as Mrs Thatcher suggested, really was a thing of the past. Certainly, the new one stands as a monument to lost promise. When a visitor steps inside and asks, 'Where's the museum?', it's confirmation of the essential emptiness of the idea, or, at least, the flaws in its execution.

It's also evidence of our increasingly dematerialised world. Soon there will be an app that allows you to point a device at an object and everything you need to know about it will pop up on the screen. André Malraux, the French Minister of Culture, used to talk whimsically about a 'museum without walls': soon, it will be with us. If we had had apps in the eighties, Terence and I might not have built a solid concrete museum to accommodate a collection of objects we did not possess.

Terence felt no poignancy at the passing of the old Design Museum, even if it remains a better monument to his own taste than the new one. The old Design Museum was an idea of the late twentieth century. Or perhaps it was really, to be honest, more an idea of the 1980s, which were like Habitat's sixties, but with more money and better technology.

Agreed, the music was worse, but everything else was – at least for a moment – faster, brighter and more expensive. This was a world that was gorgeously contoured with a very high finish. It was as a showcase of a laboratory for the higher consumerism that the first Design Museum was conceived. It was Terence's monument. The new one belongs to others, but, tragically, they do not have a clue what to do with it.

Perhaps every age gets the Design Museum it deserves. When Mrs Thatcher wagged a finger and said, 'You must not call it a museum! Museums are things of the past!', I do sometimes wonder to what extent she was entirely wrong. We created the first Design Museum by following speedy, shiny vectors towards brittle certainties about the importance of 'design' to industry. Those certainties seem less clear now.

If you look at a list of today's great US corporations, only three are in manufacturing. The old belief that 'design' can transform industries is under severe test. Those very industries are under severe test themselves. The old Design Museum used to champion, for example, IBM, Saab, Wedgwood, General Motors, Sony and Braun. Alas, great design could not save them from humbling commercial marginalisation or oblivion.

Moreover, globalisation, consumer fatigue, and new manufacturing or communications technologies have undermined all the old Euro-centric ideas about form-and-function, truth-to-materials. Of course, charm and beauty and usefulness will always be attractive in products, as in people, but the new Design Museum cannot articulate what it stands for.

When Terence and I opened the first Design Museum, people, myself included, felt both delighted and perturbed at the strange result of more than a decade's work. Critics said it did not look so very different from a sophisticated department store.

And I wondered at what stage in the history of a subject someone creates a museum to cater for it. Ethnographic museums appeared when exploration was at its adventurous peak. New York's Museum of Modern Art was established in the thirties when abstract painting was a bold transgression. Thereafter, modern art became atrophied and institutionalised. And London's Design Museum, the first in the world? There's a debate to be had here.

Terence was pleased that the Design Museum had an afterlife as an idea, but it made a very poor job of presenting a world he no longer understood. Which is to say that Terence no longer understood the world, although exactly the same could be said of many distinguished gentlemen in their mid-eighties.

Yet he took an uncritical pleasure from the monument, even if it was hidden behind a greedy sprawl of ham-fisted overdevelopment which he deplored. Ever the practical man, and not one for acid self-analysis, Terence made grandiose, and increasingly vague, claims for the new Design Museum without ever quite realising, £54 million – or was it £75 million? – later, that it was no longer really his. The Design Museum's problem is that it is nobody's.

And it was unhappy. In the period before the 2016 opening, trustee meetings were occasionally held in the Museum of Garden History near Lambeth Palace. That museum's director said he had rarely seen a more grim and concerned-looking set of grandees. Leaving one meeting, Terence damaged his wheelchair against the tomb of the plant-collector John Tradescant. For those seeking a portent, here was one: Tradescant's 'Ark' was a famous cabinet of curios, the prototype of every museum in the land.

From the start, the second-generation Design Museum was over-extended, overstaffed and underdeveloped. Success depended on paying customers reaching attendance figures which are impossible, given the building's commitment to emptiness. It has been unable to generate excitement about any exhibitions developed in-house: the only popular shows have been bought in from Germany, France and Italy. It is creatively and intellectually bereft.

The genial and very well-liked chef Rowley Leigh did not last six months in the museum's restaurant, a grim space like a municipal canteen. It closed soon after his departure. Leigh was too polite to explain or complain. In late 2016, Peter Mandelson was appointed chairman of the trustees, a certain betrayal of founding principles. In 2020, with the museum financially precarious, Deyan Sudjic, who had driven the Commonwealth Institute development, 'stepped down'.

Terence had no more to say. Although others spoke of financial mismanagement and a woeful lack of creative direction.

Conclusion

Lived Forward, Misunderstood Backwards

S.B.

In the end, who could ever work for so contrary and conflicted an individual as Terence? A man who was genial, energetic and inspirational one minute, belligerent, bovine and sometimes just plain nasty the next.

A man who would present himself as an outspoken champion of principle, only spontaneously and without reflection to reverse that position when it was to his advantage.

For example, when Claude Bosi won two Michelin stars for Bibendum, Terence was thrilled by the longed-for (and, in his opinion, delayed) accolade, even though Bosi's gastronomic rococo was, and he declared this at the time, the exact opposite to his own preferences in food. Indeed, a witness to Bosi's audition at the Bibendum kitchen recalls a sense of comic dismay over some of the elaborate sample dishes. There were fingers down throats and dramatic gagging gestures. *Faites simple* did not have a chance against *faites compliqué* when preferment was involved.

For another example, Terence nodding through Peter Mandelson as chairman of the Design Museum. Mandelson, who some find a comically sinister, slippery opportunist, had been the murky Robin to Tony Blair's brighter Batman. Mandelson, no matter how tacky he seems, never appeared to me to have evinced any appreciation in the life of the mind nor the adventures of the eye. If, that is, you ignore his decision on one farcical occasion to be art-directed into a photographic portrait sitting, pharaonically, in an Eames chair.

I first met Mandelson in the Cabinet Office and he had some genteel tea set and, if memory serves, with his pinkie extended as he sipped Earl Grey, told me: 'I am very interested in design, you know.' To my mind, this harlequin was only accepted because there was, as Design Museum financials looked dire, some slight hope of his dwindling political influence being able to help, sponsor-wise. While some people have seen in Mandelson a conniving egoist, no-one has seen an inspirational aesthete or idealist. Yet Terence acquiesced.

Who could countenance working for a man like Terence, a man of such fluid principle, of such fluctuating beliefs, of such day-glo opportunism, of such sun-dried narcissism, guilt-less hypocrisy and *Hallelujah Chorus* egomania? A man whose enormous appetite for celebrity consumed every trivial moral obstacle in its path.

The answer is an awful lot of people, although the best did not last long. The fall-out from Terence's megalomaniac tantrums and orchestrated betrayals was always substantial. Only the meek inherited long-term positions in his various enterprises because the strong always walked out. Or were pushed. In either case, they slammed the door. The brave inherited redundancy.

But a strange loyalty persists even among those who slammed that door. This is because when Terence's good angels were at home, which was by no means all the time, his personal appeal was so strong, the need for his approval by acolytes (myself included) so ineluctable and the causes he articulated so attractive, that no reasonable person could deny his or her fealty. And good memories often erase the bad, even if bad fairies have an ineffable homing instinct.

For example, one of Terence's long-term employees (who asked not to be identified here) had over the years seen him shout out managers until they cried, exercise borderline insane economies (such as charging staff to use the lift), refuse customary politeness, insult the weak and suck up to the strong . . . and yet she demurred when asked to comment, citing a fear of appearing 'treacherous'.

At his most potent, Terence had the qualities of a cult leader. And even people who disavow the cult that once bound and blinded them are often reluctant to acknowledge their errors. Perhaps because they think the cult leader will eventually return, uncorrupted and persuasive. Meanwhile, why risk apostasy?

Few did. Even those who had seen or felt the worst of Terence's behaviour, which, at its nadir, went beyond bullying into destructive abuse, were reluctant to condemn.

I know. I still replay the conversations in my head.

'Tell me, Terence, what exactly does "design" mean?'

'Well, dear Stephen, I think you know the answer. It is about *douceur de vivre*. The good life. Absolute truths, as opposed to "silly trends". Plain, simple and useful.' I can hear now the slightly camp emphasis on that last word 'useful'.

He had a mania for detail. In fact, his psychology might best be understood in terms of an uneven conflict between the restless urge to do new things and the more static, possibly more boring, imperatives of getting those things correct.

Terence once wrote a memo to Charles Campbell, first manager of the Neal Street Restaurant, which went something like this: 'I had cause to have dinner in the restaurant last night and I'd appreciate it if you could make the chips a little longer. They were too short.'

What else exactly did Terence love and admire? I know that once in Eaton Terrace, Terence's primary London home, when I correctly identified a Côtes du Rhône in a blind tasting, I was, up to a point, a made man. It was in Eaton Terrace that the noise from the pub made Terence hang out of his very expensive Belgravia window and shout: 'Be quiet! Someone's got to fucking live here, you know.' No irony was intended and none, I am certain, was understood by the noisy drinkers.

Anyway, Terence believed, I think correctly, that: 'We react against things which are coarse, bogus or puny, and are drawn to things which have guts, wit and ingenuity.' He once wore red braces with his Dougie Hayward suits and Turnbull & Asser shirts. The cornflower-blue shirts only came later. He stopped wearing the suits. Terence had very soft skin. Thin skin too, sometimes. His small feet were always in very good shoes. He wore no scent other than burnt tobacco. I never saw him with a camera, astonishing for someone so consumed by the visual part of life.

Cars were important. There was Michael Wickham's Lagonda, in which he made his legendary trip to France. The Riley – model unspecified – he used to bring home an espresso machine from Italy. There was an electric-blue Volkswagen cabrio in the early sixties and that mysterious freight-bearing Vespa for delivering furniture early on. An E-Type Jaguar for King's Road work. A lot of Porsches, including the abandoned one he was so reluctant to sell to me . . . at least until I acquired a better car of my own, when suddenly it became available at a good price. There was LTF 380X, an S-Class Benz. My wife said it stood for 'left testicle faulty'. Several 7 Series BMWs and Audi A8s. At one bizarre moment, a plush Bentley for his back (acquired second-hand in a conscience-saving bargain transaction for a miserly £15,000). Then back in an Audi. It was black. The last time we had lunch I put him in an Addison Lee Ford Galaxy. I do not think he could explain the four-stroke cycle.

But Terence really did have a very good eye. And a keen sense of thrift. Rattling the heater controls on a car his foundation had bought me, he said with what I took to be fake anger: 'I thought I told you to buy a cheap one!'

A great part of my life has been lived in between coordinates established by Terence. My honeymoon at La Colombe d'Or was in a Conran-approved venue near Nice. We came back for his fiftieth birthday, which featured many lobsters, a large tent and an unusual amount of very fine wine. For a long time I got a frisson of excitement-tinged fear when he called.

Not often, but sometimes, he did self-mockery. Michael Wickham's eight-year-old daughter once asked: 'Daddy, what's a plagiarist?' Terence cheerfully volunteered, 'I am.' That's funny. But Jonathan Meades was less charitable and got the impression that Terence might be a 'borderline swindler'.

There is a curious humility in any rare confession of weakness from Terence: his genius has its consequences, practical and human. Terence's great ideas have been littered behind him, mostly abandoned, undernourished or sold short. But they remain.

Kas said: 'Terence can make people cry. Just like Howard Hodgkin. I wonder if they make each other cry.' With genius, Terence was sometimes able to disguise self-interest as generosity. In the art market slump of the eighties, Kas was left with a lot of hard-to-sell Dick Smith paintings. Terence bought the lot . . . at a bargain price, thus helping two friends while enriching himself.

Terence could be very, even extremely, genial, but was not quick to sponsor or encourage others. When he ceded the business to his son Jasper, Terence very publicly – I mean in a newspaper interview – said his oldest son Sebastian lacked focus. What benefit might have been imagined to arise from such unnecessary criticism? There was lots of delight in Terence's career, but quite a lot of carnage too. His tightness was wholly democratic, affecting his family as well as his colleagues. Discussing Christmas presents in the *Financial Times*, Jasper said: 'My mother was a very generous person. My father was very busy; let's put it that way.'

Terence's essential interpersonal stratagem was of withholding approval, a little like a manipulative lover. And, as manipulative lovers all know, there is no more effective stratagem for winning devotion. For a figure whose public image was benign, Terence could be surprisingly cruel. Although he was, once again, democratically fair in his distribution of pain. His HR strategy closely tracked the classic profile of the psychopath. Not, of course, a *murderous* psychopath, but a deadly manipulative one: selection, grooming, encouragement, rejection.

Close associates (there were few close friends) were as likely to suffer as family. My own summary? Terence gave me the opportunity to do wonderful things, an opportunity I certainly made the very best of, but as soon as I appeared to be enjoying myself, possibly even succeeding, he became resentful. Still, I am not certain whether he was exploiting me or whether it was the other way around. He gave and he took. And you learned from him.

Then there was the oceanic megalomania. Terence had a mulish and stubborn inability to give praise or share credit. 'His assumption,' Keith Hobbs once said, 'is that no one else has knowledge, ability or skill. And that's where he is wrong.' By extension, Terence also believed no one else was worthy of the generous rewards he gave himself. He was the centre of a universe he had designed. When Caroline, his wife at the time, was seriously unwell, Terence complained [to Keith Hobbs]: 'When Caroline is ill, I have to have some dental treatment.' That sounds very funny; it was not intended as a joke, however, but as a formal complaint.

Terence gave a lot, empowering people to do things they never felt possible. But he took a lot away from them too. Many of his collaborators, colleagues, employees and friends still rue the deficit in these deposits and withdrawals in their personal account with him.

Terence's conflict with Keith Hobbs was epic, and perfectly illustrative of all his flawed business relationships. Hobbs was working for Terence between 1990 and 1994, the most expansive years for the restaurant business when the 'gastrodome' at Butler's Wharf was created.

Hobbs, a clever and combative character not inclined to take hostages in any encounter, was hugely influential here. And Hobbs had a sensible understanding of his role in a master–servant relationship. He always acknowledged that Terence was the inspiration in any project, and that it was his own responsibility to make that inspiration, often rather vague, into a feasible, working reality. The two became locked in an increasingly vituperative exchange of recriminations and threats. There were rancorous charges of interference, questions about autonomy and always, always, always questions about authorship. I me, me, mine as The Beatles song had it.

Their dispute is an archetype of all arguments about creative autonomy. When Hobbs left he took his immediate staff and various jobs with him. One of his first clients was the Chandris cruise line, for which he designed a huge 'Island Café' on a ship called *Century*. In 1996 a trade paper credited Hobbs with the design and also cited his credentials as the person responsible for designing Terence's own favourite restaurants. It is really quite difficult to imagine anything that would have incensed Terence more.

Never one for sharing fame or money or credit, Terence wrote to the Chandris brothers denying Keith Hobbs any role as a designer of his restaurants. Instead, Hobbs was a simple project manager, a description intended to demean by suggestion of its horny-handed uncreative artisanality. Instead, every Conran restaurant had been a unique and fabulous Terence autograph, a work of art by an autonomous genius. Of course, this begs several questions. Is the author of a work of art the person responsible for the conception or the execution? That is not a question Terence would want to debate.

Terence had a distinctive, which is not to say always 'attractive' method of dealing with those who worked for him. First, there was identifying the talented designer or cook or journalist or fixer who could advance the whole Terence project. Second, with witty and engaging exchanges, with flattery and promises, through a process of exploitation, professional goals were realised. Third, tired now of the novelty and perhaps threatened by the protégé's success, a row or a conflict was manufactured.

Promises were withdrawn, a future relationship would be denied and the individual was, usually, rejected. And then the whole process began again as other designers, cooks, journalists and fixers were identified, chewed up, digested, and spat out or evacuated in some other fashion. At least, that's how it felt when it happened to you. For Terence's part, he was inclined to see the third part of the process, expulsion, as a just result of treachery or incompetence. He was always right and anyone who disagreed with him was always wrong. At least, that was the attitude he adopted.

There are very few exceptions. Had he not been forced out after the post-9/11 depression at New York's Guastavino's restaurant, Joel Kissin said that he and Terence could have built the best restaurant group in the world. Rodney Fitch was bitter to the end of his life about Terence's callous treatment of him. And on 24 November 1992, the *Daily Mail* ran a story under the headline: 'Habitat tycoon in gun tragedy'. The same day, the *Daily Telegraph* had: 'Former Habitat designer dies defending doves'. Oliver Gregory, the papers reported, was presumed to have shot himself accidentally with a 12-bore shotgun while fending off a bird of prey in his Wiltshire garden.

Oliver was described as a 'millionaire designer', but, despite his handsome house, was financially straitened. Terence, perhaps disguising kindness by cruelty, believed that the person who should solve Oliver's money problems was Oliver himself. Oliver's death was a sad loss. The coroner found 'misadventure'.

Restaurant staff wanted the celebratory opening of the Pont de la Tour to be postponed as an act of respect for Oliver. Terence refused on grounds of cost.

The catalogue continues. Antonio Carluccio was admired and talked up when he was an amiable serf, but blast-frozen when he began to assume an identity of his own. Meanwhile, Keith Hobbs, the interior designer who claimed the original Quaglino's, has the distinction of being what Kissin calls 'the only person', at least since Caroline, 'who ever fucked Terence over' by reversing the process and leaving him bereft.

Few resisted this destructive process. Thomas Heatherwick (whose gazebo dedicated to cigar-smoking is weathering a little sadly in the Barton Court garden) has survived his relationship without reprisals, enjoying the transition from being a junior darling to an indulged celebrity. The reason here is perhaps that Heatherwick had such a peerless reputation of his own that Terence felt little might be achieved by hostilities.

Roger Seelig, the one-time Morgan Grenfell banker and Terence's ultimate fixer, the man-of-business, also survived. The suave Seelig, who some find oily, was charged, but not convicted, after the Guinness trial against him collapsed. But he and his Windsor knot were invulnerable, perhaps because, if there were bodies, he knew where they were buried.

One day, just before a back operation which was, it turned out, making him notably hypochondriacal and self-pitying, Terence called me. He said something very much like this: 'You know, dear Stephen, that as I get older, I am more and more aware of the mistakes I have made. I do have some regrets.' Me: 'Oh, yes? And what exactly are they?' (Thinking that, at last, Terence was going to repudiate past episodes of his sometimes insensitive treatment of others and was anxious to make amends with the discarded army of helpmeets he had left behind.) He said: 'I wish I had started using private jets earlier. I'm convinced that flying commercial has ruined my back.'

I got a postcard from hospital which pleased me greatly. It was titled 'Saucy Puss' and now has a place of honour in my personal collection, near a postcard of Courbet's *L'Origine du monde*, his spectacular muff shot now in the Musée d'Orsay (also a favourite of Terence's). The card, touchingly, says: 'Certainly the delicious gin and the postcard cheered me up in a most depressing place. They even stole my credit cards and used them to go to Liverpool! My back looks a bit like one of the trenches at the Battle of the Somme and feels about the same. Everybody tells me it will be better soon! Still, the weather is nice. Come and see us soon.'

Of course, I did.

The entire episode of the back, and this and earlier medical or dental misadventures, was amusingly illustrative of Terence's taste for fantasy and, to put it no higher, adjusting the facts so that people were impressed by him. His natural teeth were always rather poor, but when they were replaced by expensive orthodontistry, he insisted that the reason for the dental intervention was that a London black cab in which he was a passenger had driven very badly, braked hard, and caused an injury that loosened his incisors.

And, explaining away a period in hospital that might have been caused by a small stroke, he told a tale of being so enraged at the quality of food and service in Paris's Lucas Carton restaurant that he could not sleep, angrily got up in the night and slipped on his hotel room's marble floor. There was something very touching about this need to glamorise the grimmer aspects of personal life. Everything got styled.

He made only a partial recovery from the operation, but returned to his Butler's Wharf office as soon as was practicable, though in no better mood than heretofore. My last time seeing him there, I recall walking up the stairs to the fourth floor of the Conran building in Shad Thames, the Dickensian quarter where we built the Design Museum. This was always an exquisite experience, a real madeleine-of-Proust moment. The higher you got, the more pungent became the delicious aroma of Hoyo de Monterrey Epicure No. 2. Proust's anticipation of pleasure, indeed.

Of late, Terence could not – at least legally – smoke in his own studios. Or even in his own restaurants. Since he tended to work from his own apartment, this distinction is not always forensically clear:

the blurred line between work and play, home and office, was one he conveniently exploited for psychological and tax reasons as well as reasons of smoking a cigar. His bad back turned an occasional surliness into an epic grumpiness as he sat in the capital of his lost kingdom. There was melancholy too.

Terence had a mania about being cheated out of both money and time: 'Who,' he wrote in furious exasperation to a manager, 'keeps a tally of staff holidays and sickness?' He had a nightmare vision that everyone he paid was continuously going on clandestine and sybaritic holidays without his approval. People were thieving behind his back. Maybe all self-made men feel this way. Then, again, maybe not.

In this model of the world, Terence was the only true source of effort and wealth and all the rest of us were potential thieves, impudent ingrates and unrepentant cheats. The cheating motif is especially sad as larger mortal circumstances cheated him. As John Ruskin knew, the only true source of wealth is life. And that has a terminus.

The literary critic Lionel Trilling once said that leftish intellectuals worry about mortality because it denies the perfection they thought could be created on earth. Leftish designers perhaps feel the same. A nice bread board is no weapon with which to confront or even deter the Grim Reaper.

Meanwhile, there is work still to be done. Never mind the Bauhaus; if they reinvented Habitat, people would be grateful. Terence may not have cared much for poetry, but he makes me think of Ben Jonson: 'In small proportions we just beauties see; and in short measures life may perfect be.' Or, at least, that was the idea. The best short measure being the distance between lunch and dinner.

Terence was also often dismissive of other designers. At the beginning of the twenty-first century, David Collins was the most successful restaurant designer in London, with the madly popular Wolseley and Delaunay and the Blue Bar of the Berkeley Hotel to his credit. Collins's style was lush, layered, a modern baroque with an emphasis on expensive finishes and rarefied plush. His restaurants were always fabulously successful. Terence never patronised them, never even talked about them and never took Collins at all seriously.

Jeremy King is the affable proprietor of the Wolseley and the Delaunay and, once, of the Ivy. It is his pleasant habit to circuit his wildly popular restaurants and talk to his customers. Once, at lunch, he came to my table. When I mentioned Terence, Jeremy made a very histrionic and pained shaking of the head. He told me that some time ago Terence had been at a table at the Ivy with several others. He had made a gesture to Jeremy which anyone who knew Terence would immediately recognise. It was a beckoning gesture, at once matey, patronising and demanding. Jeremy did as he was bid and Terence said: 'You know, my dear Jeremy, the food here is getting *much* better.' Jeremy explained his annoyance: 'That man could compliment you and insult you in the very same sentence.'

It is actually quite difficult to compile a long list of people Terence admired, although Charles Eames, the quintessential designer, was certainly on it. And, being dead and buried in America, one at a safe historical distance. He once touchingly confessed that Eames had 'the wit, style and ingenuity I so desperately wanted to emulate'. It is almost impossible to imagine Terence saying that about anyone living.

The thing Charles Eames wanted to emulate was the London black cab. He thought it the greatest design ever. Eames had a knack for giving memorable quotes. These helped build his own reputation. This facility for publicity may have interested Terence as much as his ethics. For example, Eames once said: 'I visited a good toy store this morning . . . it was sick-making. I longed for the desert. Affluence offers the kind of freedom I am deeply suspicious of.' Eames would not have enjoyed what became of the Conran Shop, which, like the Design Museum shop, became a gift bazaar, while Habitat survives only as a sad little concession in Homebase. The Conran Shop was sold in 2020.

The Times published its obituary of Bibendum's most famous customer, Elizabeth David, on 23 May 1992. It could very well be of Terence himself. It says she was 'highly critical, but fair, giving praise rarely, for her standards were very high'. And also adds, sadly, that Mrs David was a 'solitary figure in her old age'. The consanguinity of Terence and Mrs David hardly needs emphasising.

Someone who knew Terence extremely well – and, on the whole, rather liked him, some stern tests notwithstanding – recently said to me: 'He was never really a designer, was he? He was only a stylist.' Meaning, I think, that Terence never had the true disciplines or painstaking patience required to see a project through from concept to execution. And 'stylist' has always been, in any conversation about design, a generally understood term of abuse.

Of course, Terence was a life-stylist. To counter this attack, I said to the accuser: 'I know what you mean, but maybe he designed things that were bigger than chairs. A whole belief system, for example.'

But, as though a figure in a tragic novel, Terence did not live the life he envisaged for others. Latterly, he rarely cooked, but sometimes, Vicki said, put on an apron and picked up a wooden spoon if guests were expected. In the kitchen and elsewhere, it was eventually left for others to realise his dream. Terence was, indeed, an editor more than an author. He discovered little, but had a true genius for merchandising the familiar.

And maybe he dallied a little too long with affluence and power to have kept his principles pure. I often mentioned to him Oliver Goldsmith's line that 'the greatest riches are ignorance of wealth', or Thoreau's belief that you should beware of all enterprises requiring new clothes, but I never really got a flicker of acknowledgement about my championing of austerity. Terence's simple tastes might have been a design equivalent of *arte povera*, but he never much wanted to be *l'uomo povero*.

He could be irresolute. When I, briefly its creative director, was in a position to explain that the evolving Millennium Dome project was, because of Mandelson's ignorant interference, going to be a third-rate embarrassment unless he used his influence to help me get the ear of Tony (the prime minister), I was sent yet another letter marked 'PRIVATE' in big, blue handwritten Pentel. This was during September 1998, long after I had left any formal employment with Terence, so I was rather flattered by his genuine concern.

He accused me of being 'childish' and of drawing attention to myself in my criticism of the Dome. I was also being 'stupid'. As for my criticism of the lowbrow political muddle which prevented anything worthwhile happening in Richard Rogers's Millennium tent, Terence told me that positive optimism was better than tawdry, obtuse criticism. I said there was nothing obtuse about my criticism and, if anything was tawdry, it was the Dome itself. He then explained, briefly attempting the avuncular mode, that he was concerned about my career and life prospects after trashing Tony's daring efforts to stimulate a mass hysterical outburst of national creativity. I repeated that I thought the Dome contents were going to be crap. We heard nothing from Terence after it became painfully obvious that crap it was.

Perhaps Terence's most enduring characteristic was his impassioned, visceral rather than intellectual, attachment to fine objects. But this engagement with the material world did not always bring correspondingly profound satisfaction.

I think of him sitting in a litter of the products he made famous: duvets, chicken bricks, louvred doors, conical basketware planters in black iron frames, a Paris goblet, a magnum of unlabelled wine, a single bloom in an old French milk bottle: a bit like a high-concept version of the Chelsea Oxfam. There is a comparison to be made with Albrecht Dürer's *Melencolia*, where the emblematic figure sits, brows furrowed, surrounded by abandoned or unused architectural instruments and other more mysterious symbols. Dürer perhaps intended it as a self-portrait of an artist who had lost his confidence; just before the print was made in 1514 he had written, 'What is beautiful I do not know.'

Literature also has many images of great figures contemplating momentous change in absurd conditions.

Late in his extraordinarily productive and enriching life, Terence was thwarted by Nature in the matter of finding yet another project. Decay rather than change became the prospect. Meanwhile, the old projects which made Terence's reputation atrophied. The restaurants, for example, were gruesome caricatures of eighties and nineties taste, and sadly out of touch with the practical and psychological realities of contemporary food and eating out.

The Design Museum was relatively uncontaminated, although its status and authority equivocal. But his influence here was deliberately diluted by management. In the sixty years since Terence became a designer, to many 'the' designer, the practice and meaning of design had changed. These changes he could neither understand nor tolerate. The old certainties of geometry, charm, primary colours and artisanal chic had gone.

Comfort and delight belong to an older register of experience. The dreadful and artless Royal Bank of Scotland now says it has a 'design director'. To see this as a triumph in Terence's personal campaign to get businesses to better recognise design would be to misunderstand. RBS's design director is concerned not with specifying the shape of a pretty table, but with buying enterprise social media for the bank's 100,000 employees. To Terence, that would have been an incomprehensible extension of design's meaning.

Instead of beauty and utility, we have critical design, third-world design, open-source design, collaborative design, feminist design, luxury design, mass-market kitsch, global products and (on account of all the foregoing) a very great deal of boredom experienced by consumers.

In the *New York Times* the critic A. O. Scott discussed the personality of Steve Jobs, the charismatic and, let's be honest, maniacal founder of Apple. He wrote: 'The fact that Jobs . . . in the course of his rise, has betrayed his friends, alienated his allies and mistreated his loved ones challenges some deeply cherished myths about the correlation between virtue and success.'

Clearly, an archetype is being described here. Scott continued that Jobs was both 'heroic and despicable' and that his impressive achievements also confirmed 'equally deep assumptions about the ultimate virtue of ruthlessness in the capitalist economy'. Yes. Terence was that ruthless socialist.

Like Terence, Jobs 'inspired loyalty and resentment, often from the same people', and all who attempted to judge him were left with a 'fascinating residue of ambivalence'.

Joel Kissin, never credited with his contribution to Bibendum, not least the exceptional wine list, said of Terence: 'He had many faults, but I owe him a great deal and cared deeply for him.' When Kissin made his own fortune from revamping an Upper East Side brownstone, Terence suggested a part of the capital gain should be his since the refurbishment took place while Kissin was in his employment. Kissin was never quite certain whether this was a joke.

These ambiguities are defining of the man. Love-hate, you could say. Like Jobs, Terence was 'at once democratic and totalitarian. His understanding of human desires, of consumers as well as co-workers, was both empathetic and chillingly instrumental.'

This sounds very true and very familiar, although it has to be said that Jobs left behind a better-functioning business empire than Terence's, if fewer cheerful memories of good lunches and dinners. At his death, Terence's business empire was little better than skeletal. So odd and sad to choose that image when, at its height, the corpulent and jolly Monsieur Bibendum with his cigar and brandy balloon was a workable stand-in for Terence himself.

Yet Terence's achievements were grand and benign. If the scale was modest, the importance can best be appreciated now as a sense of loss. Unquestionably, he made a huge and beneficial contribution to national life, helping us take pleasure from ordinary things.

The fact that assumptions which were daring in the sixties have become commonplace today is a remarkable victory, not a failure. The shock of the new has aged into the comfort of the familiar. If we are fortunate to live in a culture where most people – at least, those above subsistence – care about their surroundings and enjoy eating out, then that culture flourishes in a territory first mapped by Terence's shops and restaurants.

He did this without resource to theory of any sort. He was quite extraordinarily un-bookish. When Fiona MacCarthy went to interview him in 1995, the year her magisterial biography of William Morris was published, she said: 'I know instinctively he will not have got further than page twenty-two.' Yet Terence would claim inspiration from, and identity with, Morris. Each was escaping a suburban upbringing, and used their personal discontents to empower an argument about the shortcomings, artistic, practical and political, of the age they grew up in.

But, on the whole, the world has not evolved quite how Terence wanted. His assumptions about design were founded in a noble pedagogical tradition that went back to the movement for art-school reform in mid-nineteenth-century Europe. This was the movement that gave rise to the great European museums of applied art, including London's V&A and perhaps even the Design Museum itself. Terence did not know about the Bohemian Gustav Pazaurek's Museum of Art Indiscretions in Stuttgart, even if I told him about it several times. But he would agree with everything Professor Pazaurek (who died in 1935) said about design.

Of bad design, Pazaurek said: 'The absolute antithesis of artistically inspired work of quality is tasteless mass rubbish . . . it disregards all the demands of ethics, logic and aesthetics; it is indifferent to all crimes and offences against material, technique, and functional or artistic form; it knows only one commandment: the object must be cheap and yet still attempt to create at least some impression of a higher value.'

This is to say: a detestation of the bogus. Like Professor Pazaurek, Terence was a product of a system of art education evolved from teaching 'truths', which were valid at the time, but which have been overwhelmed by a more complex world. These truths were beautiful and noble, but not necessarily immortally valid.

The Bauhaus was their ultimate formulation: students learnt by doing, and the process of making was considered essential to civilised life. Simplicity is better than complexity; materials should not be disguised; superficial decoration is, almost always, to be discouraged; things should work well and look good. In short, there was a compulsion to be tidy, both practically and conceptually. And to eradicate that tasteless mass rubbish and to replace it by thoughtfulness, charm and comfort. Or, at least, that was the plan.

Withal, Terence's approach to design was to assume that there was a moral character to things, as if they were human personalities. A chair could be given moral attributes: it could be honest, good or bad, cheerful or sad. And there was a religious belief that if something worked well, it would be beautiful. (Although the belief was not held to work the other way around.)

And these ideas, through the Bauhaus diaspora, found themselves established as a set of conventions which applied to life outside the designer's studio, on the street, even. Terence adopted them. 'Design' was a way of disciplining industry, a sort of nagging aesthetic conscience, while providing a set of standards to which the consumer might aspire. 'Design' would purify society. Of course, the lore of design was understood by only a handful of adepts who held the status of druid priests in Roman Britain. But that only empowered the priesthood and inflamed its zeal.

This was all very well, but took no account of awkward truths, such as the fact that a great many ugly things work extremely well and a large number of people have a positive preference for mess and clutter. And Terence took no account of the fact that many people who cannot afford river-washed and hand-laundered linen actually find a benefit in easy-care polyester. But, for a while, it all seemed valid, attractive and possible.

This view of design also took no account of, or failed to anticipate, globalisation and the emergence of new markets which did not share European, still less Chelsea, tastes; the extinction of manufacturing industry; a new generation of consumers who renounce (or cannot afford) possessions; another new generation of consumers who positively enjoy vulgarity and certainly do not consider a perfect afternoon to be one spent with a table saw, a glass of Marc de Bourgogne, a Havana cigar, the smell of woodchips and a memory of Eric Gill.

Then there was the other fundamental founding principle of the Design Museum. Besides lessons in taste (Terence having assumed that he had acquired in this matter *le droit de donner les leçons*), the museum was also meant to be devoted to the notion of mass production. Indeed, Terence's working definition of 'design', and here I gave a little help, was intended to separate it from craft and art, and the means of separation was to be the qualification that design is an 'idea intended for mass production'. Or so I told him.

But the emerging process of additive manufacturing undermined all the old assumptions about high volume, economies of scale and uniformity. When anyone can make anything with a 3-D printer, where does that leave the idea of 'design'? It leaves it in the arena of taste.

Probably aware that the subject he invented was in a crisis, Terence and I planned a book on 'luxury' in order to re-establish some attractive vintage truths about design; luxury being a state of grace rather than a lot of expensive possessions, at least in our view. Alas, the book did not survive the Lehman burn-out, so we were unable to lecture the new world of oligarchs, sheikhs and Guangzhou bio-engineering billionaires who drink chilled Pétrus in hot tubs on the contemptible, moral, practical and aesthetic failings of their excesses.

Still, the paragraph I extracted from Terence about his attitude to luxury is one of the most complete statements of his world-view. It contains wit, snobbery, hypocrisy and good sense in equal measure. It is well-meaning, but self-indulgent and solipsistic. It is totalitarian, elitist, interesting and elegant all at the same time. Terence believed an egg is plain and beautiful while a Fabergé egg is suitable only for oligarchs. He liked to quote the billionaire Nubar Gulbenkian on the pleasures of good service: 'Just me and a damned good head waiter.'

This all speaks of good nature and uncritical self-obsession as well as robust appetites. In Terence, the angels mixed surliness and taciturnity with charm and wit. He could often appear persecuted or put-upon, even maladroit, although any anxiety you might briefly develop about his vulnerability was always quickly dispelled by a remark of impressive megalomania.

Most of all, you got the impression of suppressed emotions, or perhaps it was difficult to discern the real ones. He distrusted ostentation of any sort, particularly in manners, although he did shout a lot. The illness of others was always construed as an imposition on his own self and well-being. Sometimes, conversation was difficult. At these moments, the only way to get a response was to feed him strings of flattering comments and enquiries. His view of the universe was Saul Steinberg's view from Manhattan. The small island dominated the page; the vast continents of Asia, Africa and Europe were shown as small, insignificant, distant incidentals.

Around the time of the new Design Museum's opening, Terence sat, solitary, in his study at Barton Court, surrounded by a fug of cigar smoke. The French houses were gone. The shops were not at all what they had been. The fashionable people were dining elsewhere. There was no future to dream about, but there was a lot of history to ponder. The new Design Museum would be his mausoleum.

When I told him it should honestly be called the Conran Museum, he looked frankly disgusted. His aim was more universal, yet his aim was no longer quite so true. Less able to love people than love things, money or fame, Terence always expressed his passions in terms of products and dinners, but rather less so recently. Sixties here-and-nowism may be a poor protection from the bad weather of autumn.

The last dinner I shared with him was in the upstairs dining room of Les Deux Salons, his new restaurant evocatively close to the site of the original Soup Kitchen in London's Charing Cross. Terence had bought the business from owners who had overspent on the kitchen and were consequently financially distressed. Late in life, Terence retained a single eye for a bargain. They were probably emotionally distressed after the negotiations as well.

The interior design of Les Deux Salons comprised several layers of pastiche. Or what, in another context, Terence might have called 'bogus'. To the original interior by Martin Brudnizki, a pasticheur of genius, Terence added additional favourite Paris brasserie details of his own (assisted by one Isabelle Chatel de Brancion, whose impressive name suggests an authority in French matters).

I ordered an Anjou pigeon, whose heart and liver, barely cooked, were crushed on to a crouton. In her review of the restaurant, Terence's old friend Fay Maschler cited Richard Olney, Simon Hopkinson's mentor, and correctly explained that this conception of 'simple French food' was, paradoxically, not simple at all.

As I chewed, pigeon and blood ran down my chin. I kept on wanting to ask Terence why this pastiche interior, artfully faking Saint-German on London's Strand, did not fall within the category of 'bogus' which he so reviled. What sort of retreat from principles did it signify to *pretend* that Paris was in London? What happened to all those old inspiring ideas about authenticity and appropriateness and national identity?

But I thought it too harsh to say. Fantasies and illusions are often delightful, and who but a prig would not enjoy such indulgently comforting pastiche? So I forgot about plain, simple and useful, and just took pleasure in the moment. As ever, Terence was an inspiration. Then I looked at the walls of Les Deux Salons and saw the adored Sem's pictures of the *Musée des Erreurs*, and thought how very many beautiful contradictions were implied in the artist's title. A museum of mistakes? Well, yes. We have been here before.

Terence had lost his one good eye. In 1980, the 'best' restaurants in London might very well have been French inspired. He often said his Last Supper would be an Anglo-French classic: langoustines with mayonnaise, roast grouse with all the bits and bobs, fresh berries and jersey cream. Forty years on that menu seems as culturally remote from us as those breakfast preferences of the Incas. A sure knack of getting ahead of everyone had been replaced by a peculiar lack of curiosity.

'Design' is a word now so attenuated in meaning that an idea is being stretched to the point of snapping. What exactly was it Terence invented? It is all rather fugitive. People talk today about designing committees and situations. It's a nonce word, as nearly redundant as 'executive' or 'luxury'. Even more, we exist in a world where Terence's pellucid version of 'design' is marginalised. He owned a restaurant that's an architectural lie. It is neither a Guggenheim nor a Ronchamp.

But Terence's 'design' was never the absolute truth that he claimed, still less a science. It was Terence's personal taste. It was this taste that he monetised and sold to us as 'design'.

And while that taste was admired by many who wanted to replicate his admirable *douceur de vivre* and buy his rolling pins and salad bowls, or eat a veal chop with truffled honey fat, it was never a taste that had universal appeal, even while it was very attractive to a privileged, mediagenic and influential cadre. There is, despite the millions spent, still work to be done in educating the public. Maybe the new Design Museum will eventually rise to the challenge. Maybe it is an impossible dream. A fantasy. We will see.

I doubt that Terence, who had no interest in poetry, knew those mordant lines of W. H. Auden where he mocks the 'Shape of Things to Be', which he rhymes with 'Industry'. The poet sniggers at the idea of a cinema with 'perfect taste in seating'. He mocks 'high-grade posters'. In fact, Auden dislikes everything Terence championed.

Alas, Auden and Terence never met, but the great poet would have appreciated the curious reality and enduring legacy of an often unhappy man who, for a long while, made Britain a more cheerful place.

Epilogue 1

Autumn

R.M.

The first time I met Terence, he wasn't there.

Well, not in person at any rate. But his spirit was very definitely present. It was when I walked into the first Habitat, not long after it opened.

I'd recently left the slightly suffocating comfort of semi-detached suburban life with Mother and Father, to find my own life in London. I was nervous, inexperienced and painfully poor. I lived in a cramped bed-sitter I was ashamed to let anyone see. But I still had an optimistic sense of what could be. Older friends had their own flats: I could imagine that one day I too would have a proper place to live, with my own furniture and my own taste.

So when I heard about Habitat, I was curious. A couple of weeks later, I was nearby, so I wandered in.

A door opened for me – metaphorically as well as literally. It was a completely new idea about how we might live. That was when I first met Terence's vision: a home that was generous, modern, young, vibrant. It was intoxicating – everything I'd dreamt about, but made real.

The Conran idea was so vivid that I felt as if I'd met him personally. Nine years later I did.

I lived in a terrace house in Barnes: white painted walls, Habitat spotlights on the ceiling, a Habitat sofa and two leather chairs (designed by Terence's friend Rodney Kinsman) in the living room, the modernity relieved by some junk-shop knick-knacks. I was a faithful devotee of the Conran religion; Terence was my design God; and there was even a copy of the bible – Conran's *The House Book* – on the shelf.

I'd just been made a director of French Gold Abbott, a bright young advertising agency. One day, the phone rang: Habitat were looking for a new ad agency, and wanted to check us out. As I was known to be a design fetishist, I was asked to lead the pitch. I felt like a village curate who'd just been told by the Archangel Gabriel that the Almighty wanted to come by for a chat and a cup of tea.

A few days later, the Almighty did come by for a cup of tea. I told him enthusiastically and at length everything I loved about Habitat, and even some things I didn't. I forgot to mention anything about French Gold Abbott, or our desire to do his advertising. This omission didn't seem to put him off: he valued raw enthusiasm. We were appointed to handle Habitat advertising, and for the next five years it was my favourite project.

Terence lived up to his reputation for being demanding and difficult. But so powerful was his charisma and so great my admiration, that I was just pleased to have a part in the great man's drama.

I also handled the advertising for *The Guardian*. There was a moment of cruel conflict when Habitat took out a full-page colour ad, but the advertisement was printed poorly. Terence thought the newspaper were at fault, so they should pay. The reality was a little more complicated than that, but I instinctively took Terence's side, even though *The Guardian* were clients too. I wrote a letter to their managing director making it brutally clear that we were not going to pay.

Terence was pleased with my stance. The *Guardian* were not: they sent a letter back by messenger, sacking us.

Terence became a friend as well as a business client. One evening, I took him and his then wife Caroline to the National Theatre to see a new Tom Stoppard play, followed by dinner at the newly opened Langan's Brasserie. Quite a coup, I thought, as Langan's was already the most talked-about place in London. The next morning I saw Terence at a meeting.

'Thank you for last night,' he said. 'A wonderful evening.'

But Terence didn't like you to have the initiative for too long.

'The only thing I can imagine to be more enjoyable,' he continued, 'would be to have spent a quiet evening at home watching television.'

After five years I left French Gold Abbott to buy a stake in a new agency, Cherry Hedger Seymour. I was an owner at last, and I was desperately ambitious to win the Habitat advertising account again.

One day I heard that Habitat were looking for a new agency. I rang Terence and asked for the chance to pitch our wares. He rebuffed me, brutally. Wounded, I lost my cool and screamed abuse. The phone went down. I assumed I'd never speak to Terence again.

But he was a man who admired passion. The next day, one of his underlings came to check us out, then Terence himself, and then we were appointed to handle Habitat.

It was a short honeymoon. Terence wanted a close dialogue with our creative head, as you might expect, given Terence's own creativity. But our guy refused – don't ask me why. I suspect he was frightened.

After a bit of this, Terence sacked us.

I'd won – and lost – the client I particularly cherished. And I had my own savings invested in the agency that Terence had hired and then fired. I was mortified. And worried about my agency's reputation.

So I told *Campaign*, the adman's weekly magazine and a kind of bible for advertising gossips, that we had fired Habitat. Not the other way round. Perhaps because of Terence's mercurial reputation, *Campaign* seemed happy to believe my lie without demur, and without checking it with Conran. The story appeared on the front page two days later.

Terence protested, but the damage was done. We had got our retaliation in first.

I was regretful. I knew I'd lied. I knew Terence was right to sack us. And I knew he would be justifiably angry with me. It seemed best to give him a wide berth.

Several weeks later, I took a prospective client out to lunch. I wanted to take him somewhere impressive. I chose, recklessly perhaps, the Neal Street Restaurant. As we were finishing our meal, Terence came in with two others. I groaned inwardly: I could anticipate him throwing us out mercilessly, humiliating me in the process. My horror increased when he sat down at the very next table.

I tried desperately to behave as if he wasn't there, but there was, inevitably, a moment when our eyes met. He gave me a look which said: 'Don't worry, I'm not going to kill you.' Hugely relieved, I paid the bill, said farewell to my would-be client (no, we didn't get the business) and went back to Terence's table.

'Thank you for being merciful,' I said. 'I owe you an apology.'

Terence smiled. 'What for? For those lies you told *Campaign*? Don't worry, dear boy – exactly what I would have done in your position. Sit down, relax, have a glass of red wine, have a cigar.' And I did.

Eventually I set up my own ad agency, and we were asked to pitch for a big Storehouse project. We won it, and created a rather beautiful TV campaign, which I suspect did more good for my business than for Terence's.

For many years after that, our commercial paths did not cross, but we stayed friends, lunching regularly. Then, late in my career, Terence asked me to be his chief executive.

The previous CEO, Des Gunewardena, was to buy the restaurants from Terence, and so he needed a new person to fill the gap.

It had been a long journey from my first visit to the original Habitat, half a lifetime ago, to Terence asking me to run his businesses. During that time, I'd come to admire not just Terence's vision but his passion, his drive, his ability to make things happen.

I turned the job down.

I was enjoying being chairman of a PR company: the work was fun and the role gave me time for other things. I was working on my first book; and had started to study photography, with a place at Westminster University that autumn to do a master's degree. After a lifetime of workaholism, I was beginning to make my own rules, and I liked that. By contrast, I knew that life with Terence would be all-consuming.

I think Terence was surprised, and genuinely disappointed. I didn't want to lose a friendship, so I invited him to lunch a couple of months later.

He clearly thought I wanted to reopen the job discussion. When I didn't, he said with typical Terence frankness: 'What a shame. I thought you were going to tell me you'd changed your mind about working with me. It's a pity. We could have had fun together.'

We could have had fun together – the phrase stuck in my mind. In spite of myself, I was beguiled. I rang him two days later.

'I like the idea of fun, but I still don't think I could take the job – I've signed up to do a master's degree in photography, so I couldn't give you a five-day week,' I said.

'Do the job and the degree,' came the unhesitating reply. 'Do a five-day week in four, and do your photography.'

This time I accepted. Terence was as good as his word over the degree. Though he ostentatiously rang to pester me over something trivial whenever it was my day at university, he did allow me to lead this curious double life of student and chief executive. For that I shall always be grateful.

He was always slightly dismissive about my photography. He referred to it as 'your porn' (some of it is marginally erotic) and avoided showing any interest. Yet he was endlessly obliging in allowing me to use his home as a location, and when he thought Quaglino's needed perking up, he arranged for me to have a show of my work in the restaurant, accompanied by an extravagant party.

I've no idea whether it helped Quaglino's turnover, but it certainly enabled me to sell some pictures. And to enjoy a very good party.

Whatever I thought of my new life as Terence's chief executive, other people treated me like junior royalty. I'd done CEO jobs before, often in much larger businesses than Conran. Then I was treated as a businessman, no more, no less. But on my move to Conran, I found people behaving as if I were some kind of minor celebrity. When I told them – truthfully – that the Conran group was smaller than they imagined, they smiled knowingly, as if I was just being overly modest. Such was the potency of Conran's glamour.

And it *was* glamorous. My office was in Terence's magnificent penthouse suite on the top two floors of the elegant Conran office building close to Butler's Wharf and Tower Bridge. I had a huge room overlooking a romantic inlet to the Thames. Off it was my private bathroom, itself much larger than most people's offices. (The bathroom was so big that I used it – along with its original purpose – to store my increasing volume of giant but unsold photographs.) Most lunchtimes I would go for a short walk along the river's edge at Butler's Wharf, enjoying marvellous and perpetually changing views across the Thames.

It was hard to believe. Forty years earlier I had fallen in love with Terence's vision, when I walked into Habitat for the first time. Then, nine years on, I had met the man himself, when I pitched for his advertising work. Now I was running his businesses from this gracious space, with Terence himself sitting in the next room, the aroma of Cuban cigar smoke drifting around us both.

Things in life often turn out rather differently from what we expect, however.

We had hoped, in Terence's phrase, to 'have fun together'. But after the fall of Lehman's and then the collapse of much of the West's banking structure, followed by an unparalleled recession, 'fun' wasn't really on the agenda. In public statements, Terence would boast about how many economic recessions he'd seen and survived. But in private, we both knew that this time it was different. Recovery, if it came at all, could be a decade away. And ten years is a long wait if you are already seventy-five.

We'd assumed that we'd be working together to build the business, to hire new talent, to explore new ventures. But in this new, arctic climate, too many of our discussions were about defence rather than attack, about preservation rather than expansion, about survival not success.

Much of our seven years together was spent in a long grind of cost-cutting, with little growth to cheer us.

Now that he had sold the restaurants, Terence felt disenfranchised from his own legacy. He knew that their original excitement was fading, but he was powerless to generate change. There was a period of strange misalliances. Very briefly, he thought that an arrangement with Marks & Spencer would offer a market for his furniture designs that he had never been able to realise himself. But it was a lacklustre and half-hearted venture; very little positive came of it, although some unremarkable furniture turned up in some Marks & Spencer stores. The 'Conran' name maintained prestige and value, but Terence was spending its capital. Yet he maintained an admirably dogged loyalty to M&S management, even when it was obvious to every other observer that they did not have the will to be necessarily creative or daring. It did not end in tears; nor, however, did it end in whoops of triumph.

Of course, he still had his new ventures, Lutyens and Boundary. But they were under pressure. Boundary had overspent on building costs and would have to perform astoundingly to get that money back. Bibendum, of course, was a firmly established star in the London restaurant firmament. Yet I remember Terence coming back from a meeting there, where they had been examining the possible threat from a suddenly austere economy. The idea that even the mighty Bibendum (or 'Bib' as Terence called it) had to face the chill winds of a recession was deeply painful. His demeanour was etched with a real sadness that day.

The ageing process will eventually hit us all, but to Terence it seemed especially cruel. His back injury as a result of that car accident in India many years before had been exaggerated by a recent fall in a Paris hotel. He was in almost constant pain, and the simplest of manoeuvres, like climbing a short flight of stairs, or rising from his chair, became acts of difficulty and discomfort. His mind continued to be a powerhouse of energy and ideas (sometimes laced with a dash of vitriol) but his body could no longer live up to his appetite for action. His son Sebastian gave him a beautiful antique walking stick, so he could hobble around in greater style. Terence was pleased with the gift for a couple of days, but that faded quickly, and it just became a reminder of the fact that he needed a walking stick.

Part of Terence's charisma lay in his brute confidence: he radiated the sense that he could change the weather. This started to evaporate as the recession dragged on and his own eighty-year-old body refused to perform the simple tasks he asked of it with the same extraordinary energy he'd taken for granted as a forty-year-old. We all felt that loss of potency, but of course he felt it more vividly than we could imagine. It seemed to be a time of ever-lengthening shadows.

Terence was a curmudgeon: he was always grumbling about something that could have been done better or could have been designed better. But that perpetual dissatisfaction was not an unhappy characteristic. On the contrary, it seemed to have been the driver for a constant quest for improvement. Perhaps huge talent depends on constant dissatisfaction, because that is the fuel in the search for a better solution, a more imaginative answer. But as Terence aged, his curmudgeonly nature seemed to become more of an end in itself, less of a spur to find a better way.

After nearly seven years working together, I went to Barton Court to tell him that I wanted to resign.

'I suppose you're fed up with me grumbling at you the whole time,' he said.

'Of course not,' I replied. 'I just want more time to write and take photographs.'

He looked sadly into the fireplace. I don't think he believed me. I didn't really believe it myself.

Terence was right, as usual.

Twelve Things Terence Taught Me

S.B.

Terence Conran became (at least) to me a fabulously intoxicating mixture of redeemer, role model, crusader, exemplary hedonist, principled voluptuary, patron, mentor, guru, friend and avatar. Some of the complexity of his character was caught by David Hare in his 1995 play *Skylight* where the character played by Michael Gambon was widely understood to be based on Terence.

Certainly, Terence was never less than *extremely* interesting, but because he also became an antagonist, I am a little more circumspect nowadays, but some things you never forget.

I wish he was here now, as I am compiling the list. I'd offer him anchovy toast and my guess would be he did not know how to make it. Yet he would eat it heartily, but without thanking. I'd offer him a glass of something odd such as Xinomavro. He'd curl a lip in disapproval, but drink it *quand même*.

They say there were people who liked Terence . . . and people who *knew* Terence. I am the exception to that rule, since I knew him very well and retain respect and affection despite having been severely tested. It was not a love–hate relationship because there was no hate. But at the same time, Terence had no capacity for love.

Anyway, here is what Terence taught me.

1. Hire the best people and take credit for their achievements.

2. A magnum turns even rough old *vin ordinaire* into an indulgent luxury.

3. Marriage is normally very expensive. Divorce even more so. Marriages end, but divorces go on for ever. As the old Chinese sage said, the way to win a battle is not to start it.

4. Always tear basil with your fingers; never use a knife or scissors.

5. Ordinary is not the same as commonplace. The ordinary thing done extraordinarily well is at the outer limits of human potential.

6. The best way to communicate effectively is to simplify, then exaggerate. And speaking *very quietly* is a certain means to dominate others.

7. Move slowly: it impresses people.

8. Be sure to charge appropriately for everything. Always have great PR and a very good accountant.

9. It really never is too early for a glass of decent white burgundy. Chablis being a very good breakfast wine. Or, later in life, Scotch.

10. When in doubt, confuse the issue.

11. Do not wait until your eighties before opening a NetJets account.

12. Lunch is important. But so, too, is everything else: design is, most of all, an attitude, an approach to the world. You cannot escape the fact that God is in the details, but then, so too is Satan.

Appendix: The *Guardian* Obituary

S.B.

Terence Conran did more than anyone to enhance material life in Britain during the second half of the twentieth century.

He was born in Esher, 4 October, 1931. Like John Lennon and David Bowie in their rather different ways, escape from suburban norms was a continuing inspiration.

He had a brilliant eye, good taste, the zealous energy of a messiah, entrepreneurial flair, humour and great charm, the latter with a sensitive on-off switch. His was a personal life as richly textured as a tranche of *pâte de campagne*. Terence had a big appetite for life and all its sensual pleasures.

This fortunate endowment allowed the creation of a succession of influential and interesting businesses which – for an impressive while – fused design, retail, publishing, restaurants and food into an attractive belief-system that became known as 'lifestyle' (a term he disliked, perhaps because of its deadly accuracy).

In a remarkable career Terence was occasionally tempted into self-mythologising. An inspired and inspiring individual, so great was his cause that he sometimes forgot to acknowledge the sources of his own inspiration. Now and again he neglected to say 'please' or 'thank you'. But, because of his prodigal efforts, as his friend the art dealer John Kasmin once put it, everyone in Britain who needed a better salad bowl could, by circa 1975, satisfy themselves from one of Conran's Habitat shops.

Conran, who has died aged eighty-eight, had an absolutely sincere passion about the importance of ordinary things – a drinking glass, a roast chicken, a kilim, a table – and taught anyone willing to listen to share it. In conversations about design, he often used the word 'sad' to indicate the spirit in which improvements needed to be made. His passions were fixed and benevolent.

He was proud of distant ancestors imprecisely located in the Berkshire squirearchy. He even claimed descent from the author of *The Decline and Fall of the Roman Empire*. But he spoke little of his parents. His father was a city merchant, to the loss of whose business during the Blitz may be attributed Conran's own sometimes ruthless determination to make money of his own. He was much more affectionate of his mother, to whom he attributed his marked artistic temperament.

At Bryanston School in Dorset he was not bookish, but the school's art and craft traditions were a refuge. One Bryanston friend, Alexander Plunket-Greene, described him as 'surly . . . old beyond his years'. Plunket-Greene later married Mary Quant and Terence designed her second Bazaar 'boutique' in Chelsea. He left Bryanston in irregular circumstances, never fully explained, but he always said had 'something to do with girls'. At London's Central School of Art and Design he found in Dora Batty ('the sensible Ms Batty') a tutor who encouraged him. He dismissed his student colleagues as 'virgins from Surbiton'.

He left the textile design course before graduating, the Festival of Britain of 1951 becoming the stage for Terence's debut. Under Hugh Casson's cheerful direction, the festival created a sense of euphoria amongst designers. Here Terence was employed by the architect Dennis Lennon to work on exhibition stands. This was his only experience of salaried employment.

Later in 1951, he was occupying a Bethnal Green workshop with artist Eduardo Paolozzi who became a lifelong friend. A basement in Notting Hill followed. Two years on, he started making furniture at Donne Place, Chelsea, then something of a backwater. Then on to Camberwell and a workshop he called Cock-Up Yard. An early bestseller from this period was a conical basketweave flower pot in a metal stand.

In 1953 he opened what would now be called a 'bistro'. The Soup Kitchen in Charing Cross had a style that was clever, gentle modernism, making ingenious use of inexpensive materials and copyright-free illustrations. The total budget was £267. As a philosophical principle, Terence insisted on making his own stock: he revelled in such demonstrations of practicality.

In the same year, he made a gastronomic trip to France with Michael Wickham, a cultured individual and *Vogue* photographer who was Virgil to the younger man's Dante. Elizabeth David had already alerted the deprived English to the pleasures of French food, as well as to the availability of decent, chunky, vernacular French crockery in Madame Cadec's shop in Soho. Now, Escoffier's instruction *'Faites simple!'* was being passed from the kitchen to the workshop. Terence's mind was thus prepared. One way to describe his vision is to say he was the first to see the connection between wanting to make ratatouille and wanting a kitchen to make it in.

It is now difficult to disentangle the influences, but by the mid-fifties the essential elements of the 'Conran' proposition were in place. Polite, eclectic modern design, much influenced by urban Scandinavia and rural France: a fine knack with restaurants; brave business decisions; a keen sense of self-worth and a very beady eye for a good source and clever, dedicated workmates.

In 1956, when the Institute of Contemporary Arts introduced Pop Art with its exhibition 'This Is Tomorrow' and John Osborne was an angry young man at Sloane Square's Royal Court Theatre, the

Conran Design Group was founded. It was one of the very first such businesses in Britain: hitherto 'designers' had tended to be engineers in lab coats or craftsmen in smocks. Now they wore suede shoes and corduroy jackets.

By 1961, regional development grants from the London County Council had lured Terence to start his own factory at Thetford, Norfolk. But this was an ill-starred venture. Instead of manufacturing, retail became Conran's theatre.

Habitat opened on Fulham Road in 1964. It sold his own designs that had been rejected by conventional furniture stores, but lots of other stuff besides. A great many suppressed suburban longings – of both proprietor and customer – were satisfied by Habitat and its Polish enamel, Bauhaus chairs, French crocks and Braun stereos. Caroline Charles did the staff clothes. They played the Beatles.

It was an idealist adventure, perfectly conceived and brilliantly packaged for an aspiring generation of first-time buyers emerging from the new universities. To people who read Penguin Sartre, the optimistic cosmopolitanism of Habitat's merchandise was alluring. Suddenly, stuff only hitherto available on the pages of glossy foreign architecture magazines was available on Chelsea shelves.

In the psycho-social art history of Britain, Terence will always be remembered and admired for the creation of this remarkable store. Habitat catered to the sort of people who had to buy their own furniture.

Significantly, Habitat was co-eval with the new Sunday colour supplements and Conran's early collaborators – and wives – included some savvy Sunday newspaper journalists. This did no harm to the cause. The very first Habitat catalogue – a sheet of folded brown paper – was produced by Caroline Conran, whose translations of Troisgros and Guérard later introduced Britain to nouvelle cuisine and confirmed a helpful connection between the Conran name and good food.

Nearly twenty years of consistent growth, if not consistent profit, followed. Habitat Paris opened in 1973, New York in 1977 (although it had to be called Conran's for reasons of copyright). Habitat's flotation in 1981 realised the funds for expansion.

Terence detested Mrs Thatcher, but was happy to enjoy the boiling economy she created. Habitat reversed into Mothercare, a manoeuvre that displeased a City that thought he had quite enough to do already. Five years later, with the help of Mephistophelian banker, Roger Seelig, Habitat Mothercare conducted a bodged merger with the dour-but-decent British Home Stores.

Not for the first time, Terence's vanity exceeded his common sense. Although notionally – if briefly – worth billions, the new Storehouse group was a catastrophe. Terence despised the City as much as the City distrusted him: the autocratic flair that energised his own middle-sized business did not work in a huge public company. Terence could cajole young designers, blag suppliers and stroke journalists, but the money men were less amenable to style and charm.

On grounds of taste, Terence insisted some tacky British Home Stores merchandise be removed from the racks, only to be told that they were in fact the bestselling line. Terence believed that most people wanted to sleep in river-washed linen sheets. He never could accept that there might be people who actually preferred easycare nylon. In 1990, after an unhappy period with an unsympathetic chief executive, he was forced to resign as chairman.

The Storehouse misadventure cost Conran control of his beloved Habitat, ruined his reputation as a businessman and changed his personality. But with characteristic creativity and dogged determination, he reinvented himself as a restaurateur. Since 1970 his Neal Street restaurant (shared with his consigliere Oliver Gregory and Kasmin) had been a bright Covent Garden landmark. And in 1987 a masterly restoration of the Michelin Building (opposite the site of the original Habitat) had produced Bibendum, an *hommage* to all things French.

Now it was time for expansion. Eventually, there were to be more than fifty Conran restaurants, but while the early ones, including 1991's Pont de la Tour at Butler's Wharf, had true energy and style, the majority soon fell into formulaic complacency. There was tragedy here: Terence's restaurants provided exactly the sort of middle-class mediocrity he had earlier made it his purpose to eradicate. In 2007 they were bought out by management.

Still, Terence's achievement was to put middle Britain in touch with the pleasure principle. Habitat was meant to make houses cheerful. Thus, there was a sort of missionary ethos. However, the success of the mission always required a certain subjugation of other personalities involved. One man's inspiration is another man's plagiarism and many, including the distinguished furniture designer Vico Magistretti, believed Terence crossed that line.

Equally, a large measure of what we recognise as the early Conran Style (white-painted brick, quarry tiles, tongue-and-groove, bright lights) was the work of the late Oliver Gregory. Described by the press as a 'Habitat millionaire', Gregory died broke in a mysterious shooting accident in 1992. Terence had refused financial help during a crisis.

Nevertheless, Terence's accomplishment was to create an enviable personal way of life which was then commercialised in well-publicised shops and restaurants. Shop here, eat here and you can be just like me, he seemed to be saying. But people not paying full attention could get the impression that he actually invented baguettes, pâté, soup, room-dividers, the duvet.

Like all effective propaganda, these were persuasive half-truths: Terence had cleverly popularised them all. Yet of the duvet it was not sufficient to have imported it, Terence needed to claim to have changed British nocturnal sexual habits.

At this point the obituary becomes subjective. In 1980 Terence plucked me from the obscurity of a lectureship in a provincial university. I was amazed, after university life, to discover a world with

Havana cigars, fresh flowers, scent in the loo, good towels and proper coffee. And this was just the offices.

With generous funds from Habitat's flotation, we created the Boilerhouse Project in London's Victoria & Albert Museum. The twenty-six exhibitions held here in the eighties helped make design the popular subject it is today and turned the Boilerhouse Project into London's most successful gallery of the period. We then planned and created the Design Museum at Butler's Wharf, which Mrs Thatcher opened in 1989, the most turbulent year in Terence's business life. It was a world first.

What in the end made this extraordinary man? Terence Conran: puritan or sensualist? World-improver or bully?

A bohemian in *bleu de travail* who wanted to conform, he had a beautiful, big house in Berkshire. As a nod to democracy, you entered by the kitchen door. A cigar-munching tycoon who cared about the numbers, but immoderately loved art, fine food and butterflies. He was a Stakhanovite: his Covent Garden offices circa 1980 served superb coffee free to all the staff, but this was to encourage early attendance; the kitchen closed at eight thirty, not to reopen until eleven. And then for a very spare fifteen minutes.

Looking back, there was something old-world about this modern man. It is hard to decide whether he was restlessly creative, or simply incapable of concentrating. New openings of shops and restaurants gave a sense of personal direction where, perhaps, no more profound spiritual motivation existed. Concentration on his projects was like the beam of a lighthouse, brilliant for a moment, then gone. Ingvar Kamprad (whose IKEA bought Habitat in 1991) chided him, 'When shall you learn to take care of what you already have?'

Although family life was an important element of the Conran mythology, he was sometimes careless about the players in the drama. A youthful misalliance with an architect called Brenda was very rarely mentioned. His second marriage was to Shirley Pearce, a steely journalist who made her own distinctive contribution to Conran brand values: *Superwoman* (1975) was the first successful British how-to book since Samuel Smiles' *Self Help* (1859) and her pioneering bonk-buster novel *Lace* (1982) was a *roman-à-clef* containing pen portraits of many characters in the Conran universe.

This marriage produced Sebastian and Jasper, the fashion designer. Caroline Herbert became the third Mrs Conran in 1963 and Lady Conran twenty years later. This marriage produced Tom, now a successful London restaurateur, Sophie and Ned. The split from Caroline in 1996 led to Britain's largest ever divorce settlement of £10.5 million and to a fourth marriage to Vicki Davis, a Dublin socialite twenty-five years his junior. During the divorce trial, Terence had angered the judge by claiming Caroline offered only 'domestic help'.

The family extended in other directions too: Conran's sister Priscilla brought a companion on holiday who was a talented cook. This was Antonio Carluccio, who soon became her husband. Conran principles of design were directed to turn the charming and avuncular Carluccio into Britain's most popular Italian cook.

Realising from the beginning that he was not a designer of original genius, Terence instead became a unique editor of merchandise and entrepreneur of ideas (often other people's). He turned 'design' from being a description of something people do, to a commodity: something you can buy in his shops.

His great memorial is the Design Museum, which has consumed a substantial amount of his fortune. In 2016 it moved to an ambitiously, some say over-ambitiously, repurposed Commonwealth Institute in Kensington. Critical reception has been mixed. At the same time impressed by the cavernous spaces revealed by John Pawson's repurposing, its sublime emptiness hints at the essential vacuity of the subject.

Towards the end of his life, Terence's businesses were in a melancholy rallentando of decline. Prescott & Conran, his last major restaurant venture, went into receivership in 2018.

Still, the day this is published I am going to have lunch at Bibendum, although it is not what it was. The old principles of simple French food derived from Elizabeth David and Richard Olney have now given way to what Terence used to dismiss expletively as frou-frou. Anyway, I will unplug a bottle of Richebourg and drink it from a handsome glass.

I shall try to find something robust and simple on the menu. I shall very likely at some point have a cigar. It will be a Hoyo de Monterrey Epicure No. 2, because, dear Stephen, when will you ever learn that details are fucking important? And probably I shall have a glass of Marc de Bourgogne as well. There will be strong Neapolitan coffee. And I shall look across the road at the site of the first Habitat and wonder how very much poorer Britain might have been without the finger-pointing interference of this enigmatic, difficult, but fascinating man. Then I shall go home and admire my salad bowl.

Epilogue 2

Answered Prayers

S.B.

This book may resemble Truman Capote's last, unfinished and deeply flawed minor masterpiece in one respect alone. Capote's title refers to the old saw that if there's one thing worse than having your prayers ignored, it is having them acknowledged and acted upon.

1986's *Answered Prayers* is a lacerating take-down of the Manhattan society figures who nurtured the flibbertigibbet author, sparing no one's blushes and eye-wateringly indiscreet. The hands that fed Capote were not so much bitten, as chewed and spat out.

But the resemblance is not that. Or is certainly not intended to be. Instead, like *Answered Prayers*, this book has been long, long delayed.

The backstory is that since first meeting Terence in 1977, I wanted to write at length about him. Not a slavish adoration of his 'design', of which there is, frankly, not a great deal to be said, rather an account of a uniquely driven personality of quite extraordinary presence and influence.

Terence was quite unlike anybody I had ever met before or since. There are plenty of rich megalomaniacs around, but most of them are tedious people who think only of money and power. Instead, Terence, while he sometimes thought about money and power too, also had an exquisite sense of things, from butterflies to Japanese artichokes. Of these things he could talk with a persuasive force that was almost mystical.

But when I presented the idea to a publisher in the last decade of the last century, I could get no interest. At that time, Terence's reputation was stuck in a nether region between the protean young man who once revolutionised homeware shopping and the living national treasure he later became. One publisher actually said: 'Who cares?'

During this period, Terence and I became reconciled after the Design Museum rift. We lunched, contemplated books and other projects, enjoying a pleasant stasis where none of our respective grievances was aired.

Of course, I had told him my misgivings about the direction of the Design Museum, but his response was always, and I paraphrase, but the sense is accurate: 'My dear Stephen, when will you learn to let go of things?' I suspect now that, so far from being pastoral care, this was a device to separate me completely from something which I believed was, at least partially, mine. The cold steel of calculated disenfranchisement was wrapped in a comfortable velour glove.

So, with my long-time collaborator Roger Mavity agreeing to write his own account of Terence's businesses, we prepared the first version of this book, intended for publication in autumn 2016 to coincide with the opening of the new edition of the Design Museum.

The intention, then as now, was not to be hostile, but honest and accurate. Which puts me once again in mind of Arnold Bennett saying: 'I don't mind lying, but I hate inaccuracy.' Although, of course, there are often cases, and this may be one, where any disinterested and impartial factual account of events may seem damaging. Certainly, Terence was no saint. But saints are usually rather dull. Sinners make better stories.

We sent the manuscript to Barton Court saying that if there were factual inaccuracies, they would, of course, be corrected. And if there were any passages which seemed harsh or even unfair, let's please discuss. My argument to Terence was that his legacy might be best represented in an account written by people who both knew him and understood him, and who were not afraid to be frank. We heard nothing. At least not until a terrifyingly aggressive letter was received from Terence's lawyers.

The effect of this letter, not one anybody would enjoy reading, was to prevent publication of the original book, since, even to a confident publisher, the mere threat of an injunction looked very expensive indeed.

Right now, the law gives more protection to 'personal information' and one individual's concerns about 'defamation' than another individual's right to tell his story. Defamation was never the intent, we told the lawyers. Besides, it's all true. Truth is irrelevant, we were told. The fact is, any account of a living person that is not adulatory can lead to punitive legal action. So much for the craft of the memoirist.

At about this time, Vicki left Terence, making it known that she would never return to Barton Court. Over conspiratorial lunches at Palomar in Soho and Scott's in Mayfair, she offered to add her own account of life with Terence to our accounts of working with him. And then, as suddenly as she left, she returned with differences evidently resolved.

I bumped into her on King's Road and, after compulsory cheek-kissing and smiling, she said: 'You really *are* persona non grata,' a favourite expression of hers. Her own baroque pivot vis a vis the relationship was unexplained.

Thereafter, I only saw Terence a few times when we met at a charity board where we were both trustees. In late life he was visibly enfee-bled, and his once supremely sharp mind sometimes wandered in a rather diffuse style, directed, perhaps, by medication. If anything, I got only a rueful and sultry stare.

When he died people asked me, 'Are you sorry you did not make it up with each other?' I replied: 'Not at all. The conflict was of his own design. Terence knew exactly what I thought of him.' I thought he was a great and astonishing man, whose real flaw was that he loved himself much more than he loved others.

Acknowledgments, sort of

This, it will be obvious if you have got this far, is emphatically not an authorised biography with its pieties and evasions. To have been authorised would have invited interference and demanded compromise, especially from so disputatious a subject.

The task instead was to sketch a portrait. To reconcile the good and public Terence (stylish, busy, witty, charming, effective) with the sometimes less attractive private man (often grumpy, mean, self-obsessed, even cruel). In many ways, Terence as a phenomenon was a perfect example of the conflicted creative personality. This was the subject of Rudolf and Margot Wittkower's 1963 classic of art history, *Born Under Saturn*. In many ways this account of the crazed artistic temperament was an inspiration.

There is very little of Terence's private life, although that perhaps presents a truth in itself: he made domesticity, including his own, the public's concern. And besides, distinctions between home life and business life were forever blurred. Rather, this is an account of the context and culture of an extraordinary individual who deeply affected everyone who knew him and who, mostly beneficially, influenced tens of millions who did not.

What's written here is very largely based on first-hand experience and privileged access, alongside personal letters, photographs and documents, sourced both in observations made and conversations enjoyed over the past thirty or forty years.

No one who knew Terence is without an opinion about him, and packaging these opinions, almost all of which combine admiration with dismay, affection with anger, has been one of the pleasures and challenges of the writing.

Many of Terence's closest contemporaries and collaborators whose ideas and opinions are included here are, alas, now dead. These include Justin de Blank, Rodney Fitch, Alan Fletcher, Max Gordon, Oliver Gregory, Brian Henderson, Keith Hobbs, Min Hogg, Antonio Carluccio, Fiona MacCarthy and John Stephenson. Of these, Oliver Gregory was the very closest and Rodney Fitch the most bitterly resentful.

Other important or interesting sources are, happily, very much alive. Over the years, conversations with the following have added colour and context to our own experience, although that is not to say they endorse this account. These include Celia Brayfield, Caroline Conran, Vicki Conran, Loyd Grossman, Nicky Haslam, Simon Hopkinson, John Kasmin, Robert Kime, Joel Kissin, Jonathan Meades, Stuart Mosscrop, Suzy Slesin and Peter York.

Ultimately, *Terence* is meant to be honest, interesting and true. If that's the case, everyone mentioned above deserves a big thank-you. But most of all thanks to Terence himself, a difficult, but fascinating man, who, by being absolutely impossible most of the time, made a lot of very good things possible for some of the time.

S.B. & R.M.

Index